CAMBODIA
REBORN?

CAMBODIA REBORN?

The Transition to Democracy and Development

GRANT CURTIS

BROOKINGS INSTITUTION PRESS *Washington, D.C.*
and
THE UNITED NATIONS RESEARCH INSTITUTE FOR
SOCIAL DEVELOPMENT *Geneva*

Cambodia Reborn? may be ordered from:
Brookings Institution Press
1775 Massachusetts Avenue NW
Washington, D.C. 20036
Tel.: 1-800-275-1447/(202) 797-6258
Fax: (202) 797-6004
www.brook.edu

Library of Congress Cataloging-in-Publication data

Curtis, Grant.
Cambodia reborn? : the transition to democracy and development
/ Grant Curtis.
p. cm.
Includes bibliographical references and index.
ISBN 0-8157-1646-X (cloth: alk. paper) — ISBN 0-8157-1645-1 (pbk.: alk. paper)
1. Cambodia—Politics and government—1975- 2. Cambodia—Economic
conditions. 3. Cambodia—Social conditions. I. Title.
DS554.8.C87 1998
959.604'2—ddc21   98-25364
                                                                       CIP

9 8 7 6 5 4 3 2 1

The paper used in this publication meets minimum requirements of the American
National Standard for Information Sciences—Permanence of Paper for Printed Library
Materials: ANSI Z39.48-1984.

Typeset in Palatino

Composition by Northeastern Graphic Services, Inc.
Hackensack, New Jersey

Printed by R. R. Donnelley & Sons
Harrisonburg, Virginia

THE BROOKINGS INSTITUTION

The Brookings Institution is a private nonprofit organization devoted to research, education, and publication on important issues of domestic and foreign policy. Its principal purpose is to bring knowledge to bear on current and emerging policy problems. The Institution was founded on December 8, 1927, to merge the activities of the Institute for Government Research, founded in 1916, the Institute of Economics, founded in 1922, and the Robert Brookings Graduate School of Economics and Government, founded in 1924.

The Institution maintains a position of neutrality on issues of public policy. Interpretations or conclusions in Brookings publications should be understood to be solely those of the authors.

THE UNITED NATIONS RESEARCH INSTITUTE FOR SOCIAL DEVELOPMENT (UNRISD)

The United Nations Research Institute for Social Development (UNRISD) is an autonomous agency engaging in multidisciplinary research on the social dimensions of contemporary problems affecting development. Its work is guided by the conviction that, for effective development policies to be formulated, an understanding of the social and political context is crucial. The Institute attempts to provide governments, development agencies, grassroots organizations, and scholars with a better understanding of how development policies and processes of economic, social and environmental change affect different social groups. Working through an extensive network of national research centers, UNRISD aims to promote original research and strengthen research capacity in developing countries.

Current research programs include Business Responsibility for Sustainable Development; Crisis, Adjustment and Social Change; Culture and Development; Emerging Mass Tourism in the South; Gender, Poverty and Well-Being; Globalization and Citizenship; Grassroots Initiatives and Knowledge Networks for Land Reform in Developing Countries; New Information and Communication Technologies; Public Sector Reform and Crisis-Ridden States; Social Policy, Institutional Reform and Globalization; Technical Co-operation and Women's Lives: Integrating Gender into Development Policy; Volunteer Action and Local Democracy: A Partnership for a Better Urban Future; and the War-torn Societies Project. Recent research programs have included Environment, Sustainable Development, and Social Change; Ethnic Conflict and Development; Participation and Changes in Property Relations in Communist and Post-Communist Societies; Political Violence and Social Movements; and Socio-Economic and Political Consequences of the International Trade in Illicit Drugs. UNRISD research projects focused on the 1995 World Summit for Social Development included Economic Restructuring and Social Policy; Ethnic Diversity and Public Policies; Rethinking Social Development in the 1990s; and Social Integration at the Grassroots: The Urban Dimension.

A list of the Institute's free and priced publications can be obtained by contacting the Reference Centre at the United Nations Research Institute for Social Development, Palais des Nations, CH 1211 Geneva 10, Switzerland; Tel (41 22) 798 84 00/798 58 50; Fax (41 22) 740 07 91; Telex 41.29.62 UNO CH; e-mail: info@unrisd.org; World Wide Web Site: http://www.unrisd.org

*To Susanne, who made it all possible,
and to Sarom and Sovann,
who make everything worthwhile*

Contents

Preface

This book was commissioned by the United Nations Research Institute for Social Development (UNRISD) as part of a series of studies examining developments in post-UNTAC Cambodia.[1] It complements a cycle of action-research on "rebuilding war-torn societies" undertaken jointly by UNRISD and the Program for Strategic and International Security Studies, Graduate Institute of International Studies (Geneva).[2]

A Canadian, I lived in Cambodia from 1987 through 1993. In 1990–92 I served as assistant resident representative, United Nations Development Program (UNDP), and during the UNTAC period I was a senior program officer with UNTAC's Rehabilitation and Economic Affairs Component. My article, "Transition to What? Cambodia, UNTAC and the Peace Process," was included in a 1994 UNRISD-published monograph, *Between Hope and Insecurity: The Social Consequences of the Cambodian Peace Process*.[3]

This book is based on research conducted during four field visits to Cambodia between October 1994 and March 1996, including interviews with Royal Government of Cambodia officials, members of the diplomatic and aid communities, staff of international and local nongovernmental organizations, and Cambodian friends and former colleagues. Besides official documents prepared by or for the Royal Government and other analyses prepared for international donor forums, this book draws on information from an ever-growing amount of research and other material dealing with contemporary Cambodia, including reports commissioned by the Swedish International Development Authority (SIDA).[4]

This book was drafted in late 1996. Because of the ever-changing nature of Cambodian politics, and especially in view of the July 1997 coup de force that ousted Prince Norodom Ranariddh, the country's elected first prime minister, I made a follow-up visit to Phnom Penh in September 1997 and then updated the manuscript.

I am grateful to UNRISD for giving me the opportunity to return to Cambodia to examine the country's post-UNTAC development path. In particular, I thank UNRISD's Peter Utting for his guidance and insight—as well as his considerable patience.

At Brookings, Theresa Walker edited the manuscript, Carlotta Ribar proofread it, and Susan Fels prepared the index.

I also thank all those who agreed to share their experience, views, fears, and hopes for Cambodia's future. Unless otherwise credited, however, the opinions and interpretations expressed here are mine alone.

Abbreviations

AsDB	Asian Development Bank
ASEAN	Association of South-East Asian Nations
BLDP	Buddhist Liberal Democratic Party
CARERE1	Cambodia Resettlement and Reintegration Project
CARERE2	Cambodia Resettlement and Regeneration Project
CCC	Cooperation Committee for Cambodia
CCCR	Cambodia Centre for Conflict Resolution
CDC	Council for the Development of Cambodia
CDRI	Cambodia Development Resource Institute
CGDK	Coalition Government of Democratic Kampuchea
CIB	Cambodian Investment Board
CICP	Cambodian Institute for Cooperation and Peace
CPP	Cambodian People's Party
DDC	District Development Committee
DK	Democratic Kampuchea
DNUM	Democratic National United Movement
EU	European Union
FAO	Food and Agriculture Organization
FUNCINPEC	National United Front for an Independent, Neutral, Peaceful, and Cooperative Cambodia
GDP	Gross Domestic Product
ICORC	International Committee for the Reconstruction of Cambodia
IDP	Internally Displaced Person

IDTA	Institutional Development Technical Assistance
IMF	International Monetary Fund
KNP	Khmer Nation Party
KPNLF	Khmer People's National Liberation Front
LDF	Local Development Fund
MIME	Ministry of Industry, Mines, and Energy
MSA	mission subsistence allowance
NADK	National Army of Democratic Kampuchea
NGO	nongovernmental organization
NSP	National Solidarity Party
NUF	National United Front
NUP	National Unity Party
ODA	Overseas Development Administration (United Kingdom)
OECD	Organization for Economic Cooperation and Development
PDK	Party of Democratic Kampuchea (the Khmer Rouge)
PERC	European Rehabilitation Program for Cambodia (European Union)
PGNUNS	Provisional Government of National Unity and National Solidarity
PIP	Public Investment Program
PIU	Project Implementation Unit
PRASAC	Rehabilitation and Support Program for the Cambodian Agricultural Sector (European Union)
PRDC	Provincial Rural Development Committee
PRK	People's Republic of Kampuchea
RCAF	Royal Cambodian Armed Forces
SAP	Structural Adjustment Program
SFKC	Social Fund of the Kingdom of Cambodia (World Bank supported)
SIDA	Swedish International Development Authority
SNC	Supreme National Council
SOC	State of Cambodia
UCNP	Uphold the Cambodian Nation Party
UN	United Nations
UNAMIC	United Nations Advance Mission in Cambodia
UNBRO	United Nations Border Relief Operation
UNCDF	United Nations Capital Development Fund

UNCHR	United Nations Center for Human Rights
UNDP	United Nations Development Program
UNHCR	United Nations High Commissioner for Refugees
UNICEF	United Nations Children's Fund
UNOPS	United Nations Office for Project Services
UNRISD	United Nations Research Institute for Social Development
UNTAC	United Nations Transitional Authority in Cambodia
VDC	Village Development Committee

Cambodia

Chapter 1

Introduction

Changes in circumstances associated with the end of the cold war forced a number of countries to radically alter their policies and strategies, thus launching them on some transitional path. Several countries abandoned command economies and thus had to adjust to market liberalization and the dictates of the global economy. Others experimented with new political forms, including the introduction of such democratic practices as pluralist politics and "free and fair" elections. Yet others have begun to rebuild after war or other "complex emergencies," steering a course along the so-called relief-to-development continuum.[1]

The varied experience of these several transitional paths has brought increased attention to the problems faced by societies attempting to adjust to some form of radical transformation. Besides describing the process of transition, effort is being made to better understand the essential elements of successful transition as well as the various influences that shape or otherwise determine economic, political, social, and developmental transformation. Particular attention is given to development as an essential precondition of any transitional process, as well as being the end product of such transformation.

Many countries are undergoing some form of transition. Cambodia is one of only a few that, in a very short time, have been faced with a complete economic, political, and social transformation. Furthermore, the international community, including the United Nations, has been involved to an extraordinary degree in Cambodia's several transitions.

Cambodia's unique experience as a "transitional society" makes it an excellent case study of the transition process.

The events of Cambodia's recent past are relatively well known, as are the tragic consequences of the misfortunes, injustices, errors, and crimes that have befallen the country and its people. If the magnificence of the Angkor temple complex speaks to Cambodia's glorious history, Cambodia today is equally well known for the "Killing Fields" of the Pol Pot era.

Cambodia, of course, is more than either Angkor Wat or the Toul Sleng Genocide Museum. The October 23, 1991, *Agreements on a Comprehensive Political Settlement of the Cambodia Conflict* (hereafter Paris Agreements or simply the Agreements) launched a new period in Cambodian history.[2] Although the Agreements and the United Nations Transitional Authority in Cambodia (UNTAC), the resulting UN "peacekeeping" operation, did not bring immediate peace to Cambodia, they did signal a dramatic change in Cambodia's circumstances and offered hope for a new future for the country and its long-suffering people.

The mandate of UNTAC in Cambodia ended with the establishment of a duly elected government and the promulgation of a new Constitution. Although the UNTAC operation ended in late 1993, Cambodia's transition has continued beyond the end of the UNTAC period: a transition toward some form of democracy, the further transition to a market economy, a transition from rehabilitation toward development, and, it is hoped, a transition from war to peace. Cambodia's several transitions are the subject of this book.

The challenge of "rebuilding Cambodia" has at least three components: forging a new political culture; reconstructing and developing the country's economy, infrastructure, and human capital, with particular attention to rural development; and giving rebirth to Cambodian society—creating new ways of behavior appropriate to a modern, developing state that avoid, in particular, "the practices of the recent past."

More than four years after the UN-sponsored election and the establishment of the new Royal Cambodian government, it is possible to begin to assess the success of efforts to rebuild Cambodia. This book considers Cambodia's uneasy renaissance by focusing on the creation of new political structures and by scrutinizing efforts under way to rehabilitate, reconstruct, and develop Cambodia. The book especially analyzes the contribution of the international community to Cambodia's rebirth. The book also addresses the difficulties faced by the new government in reestablishing, or creating anew, Cambodian society and explores the following questions:

—What is the nature of the Cambodian state in the post-UNTAC period, and what are the prospects for Cambodia's further evolution toward the kind of pluralist, liberal democratic, and market-based society envisaged by the Paris Agreements?

—What is the impact of internal politics, particularly the postelection phenomenon of "power sharing," on the process of rehabilitation, reconstruction, and development?

—What is the relationship between the Royal Government and international agencies in the post-UNTAC era?

—To what extent has the Royal Government been able to determine or otherwise assert control over the country's development path or, conversely, the extent to which the priorities, agendas, and practices of international agencies have continued to determine the direction of the country's development in the post-UNTAC period?

—What are the roles of local interest groups and other "actors" in the country's reconstruction and development?

—To what extent are the Cambodian state and international agencies responsive to popular needs and demands, particularly the needs of 85 percent of the Cambodian population living in rural areas?

—To what extent can disadvantaged groups, people's organizations, or other elements of "civil society" influence or otherwise exert pressure on the policy process and on Cambodia's further reconstruction and development?

—Five years beyond UNTAC, what might lie in store for the country and its people?

Chapter 2

Toward Settlement
of the Cambodian Conflict

In 1970 Prince Norodom Sihanouk (the once and, since 1993, again king) was deposed by an American-backed republican coup d'etat. The coup launched a bitter and bloody civil war at a time when Cambodia increasingly was being drawn into the war in Viet Nam. The escalation of the civil war, together with the bombing of eastern and central Cambodia as part of the American "Secret War," killed more than 700,000 persons and drove millions of peasant refugees to the country's few urban areas.

Holocaust, Isolation—and War

On April 17, 1975, radical Khmer Rouge forces "liberated" the country, establishing "Democratic Kampuchea." Rather than ending the horror of the preceding years of war, a new kind of terror descended on Cambodia as the Khmer Rouge embarked on a grotesque social experiment of agrarian communism. Within days of assuming power, the Khmer Rouge evacuated all of Cambodia's cities and towns, forcing virtually the entire Cambodian population into the countryside to live and work on a communal basis. Sheer human labor was harnessed to establish a new agricultural base as the foundation for economic self-sufficiency, if not autarky. More than 1 million Cambodians died under the Maoist-inspired rule of the Khmer Rouge as the result of forced labor, starvation, lack of medical care, and wholesale execution. No

4

Khmer family was spared. Much of the country's physical infrastructure was dismantled or destroyed. In its efforts to create a new society, the Khmer Rouge all but destroyed the Cambodian nation and people, including the country's very social fabric.

Vietnamese troops invaded Cambodia in late 1978 in response to repeated and bloody border provocations. Meeting little resistance as they swept westward, the Vietnamese forced the Khmer Rouge across the border to Thailand. In place of the Khmer Rouge, the Vietnamese installed a new communist government composed largely of disaffected Khmer Rouge cadre.

The gruesome discovery of Cambodia's "Killing Fields" and the desperate plight of the country's surviving population, including the threat of widespread famine and the associated exodus from the country of more than 500,000 traumatized refugees, briefly brought Cambodia international attention as well as significant humanitarian assistance. As the threat of famine passed, however, the realities of cold war politics were reasserted, and Cambodia and its people were again isolated by an American-led political and economic embargo based on Viet Nam's continued military involvement in the country as well as the Soviet Union's economic and ideological support to the Vietnamese-backed and communist-inspired People's Republic of Kampuchea (PRK).

The embargo effectively isolated Kampuchea from the nonsocialist world and deprived the Cambodian people of all but minimal levels of international humanitarian and development assistance. Worse, in spite of the "auto-genocide" wrought by the Khmer Rouge, the Western world from 1982 chose to bestow diplomatic legitimacy on the Coalition Government of Democratic Kampuchea (CGDK), an uneasy but politically expedient alliance of the ousted Khmer Rouge and two smaller "noncommunist resistance forces," the monarchist National United Front for an Independent, Neutral, Peaceful, and Cooperative Cambodia (known by its French acronym, FUNCINPEC) led by Prince Norodom Sihanouk and the republican Khmer People's National Liberation Front (KPNLF).

During the 1980s the CGDK, with support from China, the United States, and other Western and ASEAN countries, waged guerrilla war against the Phnom Penh government. The PRK, meanwhile, received continued military support from Vietnamese regular forces and economic and technical assistance from the Soviet Union and other members of the socialist bloc. A conflict born at least partly as the result of external involvement in the countries of Indochina became a lopsided cold war battle involving the superpowers as well as their allies and regional proxies.

Launched and sustained as part of the cold war, the Cambodian conflict continued until the breakup of the former Soviet Union resulted in the termination of vital economic assistance to its former client states. The end of the cold war was accompanied by other major geopolitical changes. The dismantling of the Berlin Wall reunified East and West Germany. The massacre of prodemocracy demonstrators in Beijing's Tiananmen Square focused international attention on human rights in China. The expanding economies of East Asia began to look with interest on new market prospects in the battlefields of Indochina. Given the great changes in global power politics, the international community saw an opportunity to end the long-festering Cambodian conflict.

Diplomatic efforts spearheaded by the United Nations, France, and Indonesia led to bilateral meetings between Prince Sihanouk and Hun Sen, the prime minister of the PRK, beginning in 1988. Informal meetings subsequently were held in Indonesia involving all four Cambodian factions. Although inconclusive in themselves, these "cocktail parties" (the Jakarta Informal Meetings, or JIM-1 and JIM-2) served as an "essential preamble to a broader internationalization of the problem that would feature the direct participation of the ultimate power brokers of the Cambodia stalemate: China, the Soviet Union, and the United States."[1] The International Conference on Cambodia held in Paris in July-August 1989 brought together the four Cambodian factions, the Permanent Members of the Security Council, as well as thirteen other countries.[2] Although the 1989 session of the International Conference on Cambodia ended without agreement, progress was made in developing a framework for a comprehensive settlement of the Cambodian conflict, including the establishment of a UN-led peacekeeping operation.

On August 28, 1990, the five permanent members of the UN Security Council announced their agreement on an Australian-drafted plan for UN supervision and monitoring in Cambodia during a period of transition between the establishment of a cease-fire and the holding of elections. On September 9, 1990, the four Cambodian factions, meeting in Jakarta, issued a statement agreeing to the process outlined in the Perm-5 document and agreed to the creation of a Supreme National

Council (SNC) to represent Cambodian sovereignty during the transitional period.

An August 30, 1990, letter from China, France, the USSR, the United Kingdom, and the United States transmitting the statement and framework document adopted by their representatives at a late August meeting in New York suggested that Cambodia's Supreme National Council should be composed of "representative individuals with authority among the Cambodian people. They should be acceptable to each other. They may include representative individuals of all shades of opinion among the people of Cambodia. The members of the SNC should be committed to the holding of free and fair elections as the basis for forming a new and legitimate government."[3]

When Cambodia's Supreme National Council finally was established a year later, it was composed of twelve members representing FUNCINPEC, the KPNLF, the Party of Democratic Kampuchea, and the State of Cambodia, with Prince Norodom Sihanouk, the council's chairman, serving as the "thirteenth member." It was significant that all of the SNC's members were first and foremost politicians, with no "members at large" drawn from Cambodian "civil society," for example, the country's religious leaders. Nor did the SNC have any women members.

With the creation of the SNC, the International Conference on Cambodia was reconvened, and on October 23, 1991, the *Agreements on a Comprehensive Political Settlement of the Cambodia Conflict* were signed by the Cambodian factions (and other countries participating in the conference) in the presence of the UN secretary general.

The United Nations Transitional Authority in Cambodia (UNTAC)

As outlined by long-term Cambodia-watcher William Shawcross:

The Paris Agreement had many purposes, several of them unspoken—and certainly unwritten. One was to remove an impediment to US-Soviet-Chinese détente. Another was to get the international community off the hook of recognizing the Khmer Rouge and their allies as the legitimate government of Cambodia. Many people involved in the peace process expected that the elections to be held by the UN would allow the legitimization of the Hun Sen regime, perhaps in coalition with other parties. At the same time the agreement distanced the Khmer Rouge from their principal sponsor, China. In return for allowing their Khmer Rouge clients into the political process, the Chinese agreed to stop supplying them with weapons. They apparently abided by their commitment. The Chinese saw the agreement as a means of ending Vietnamese hegemony over Indo-China, restoring Prince Sihanouk to Phnom Penh, and allowing Beijing to resume a position in Cambodia.[4]

The Paris Agreements invited the Security Council to establish the United Nations Transitional Authority in Cambodia, or UNTAC, and to provide it with a mandate to restore peace in Cambodia, establish national reconciliation, and achieve liberal democracy through a free and fair election. The Agreements determined that the transitional period would begin with the entry into force of the Agreements and would terminate when the Constituent Assembly, elected in conformity with the Agreements, approved a new Cambodian Constitution and transformed itself into a legislative assembly, thus creating a new Cambodian government. The Agreements also called for an internationally supported program of rehabilitation, focusing on infrastructural development, institutional development, and human resources capacity building as a foundation for the longer-term reconstruction and development of the country.

The Paris Agreements recognized the Supreme National Council as "the unique legitimate body and source of authority in which, throughout the transitional period, the sovereignty, independence, and unity of Cambodia are enshrined."[5] Although the SNC was invested with Cambodian sovereignty and was charged with representing the country externally during the transitional period (for example, in the UN General Assembly), UNTAC was delegated "all powers necessary to ensure the implementation" of the Agreements. Such wide-ranging powers gave UNTAC authority to place under its "direct control" all administrative agencies, bodies, and offices in the fields of foreign affairs, national defense, finance, public security, and information so as to ensure neutrality and nondiscrimination in the run-up to the election. The Agreements further stipulated that UN personnel were to have unrestricted access to all administrative operations and information in the "four administrative structures," that is, the areas under the control of the respective factions. UNTAC also was provided with the authority to require the reassignment or removal of any personnel within any of the four factions' administrative agencies.

In order to assist the Cambodian parties to maintain the cease-fire and to prepare for the establishment and deployment of the full UNTAC operation, the secretary general recommended that the United Nations field a small preparatory mission in Cambodia. The Security Council subsequently authorized the establishment of UNAMIC, the United Nations Advance Mission in Cambodia. UNAMIC became operational on November 9, 1991, and consisted of civilian and military liaison staff, logistics and support personnel, and a military mine awareness unit. On January 8, 1992, the Security Council expanded the mandate of UNAMIC to include the training of Cambodian personnel in the clearance of land mines as well as initiation of a mines clearance program.

On February 19, 1992, the secretary general submitted to the Security Council a report detailing the proposed implementation plan for UNTAC. With a firm commitment of an initial $U.S.200 million against a budgeted cost of more than $U.S.2.1 billion, the Security Council on February 28, 1992, established UNTAC under its authority for a period not to exceed eighteen months. Upon becoming operational in Cambodia on March 15, 1992, UNTAC absorbed UNAMIC.

Headed by Yasushi Akashi (Japan), the special representative of the secretary general for Cambodia, UNTAC in Cambodia had seven distinct components: Military, Civilian Police, Electoral, Civil Administration, Repatriation, Human Rights, and Rehabilitation and Economic Affairs. The UNTAC operation also included an Information and Education Service, a coordination and liaison team, political and legal advisers, and executive management staff. At peak strength, UNTAC had more than 20,000 international personnel, including some 16,000 military and 3,500 civilian police. The UNTAC operation was supplemented further by some 60,000 locally recruited Khmer staff, most of whom were involved in election-related activities. Although UNTAC's Khmer staff received monthly salaries lower than the daily mission subsistence allowance (MSA) paid to international staff, thousands of Cambodian civil servants and teachers left their offices and classrooms to work for UNTAC, resulting in a serious curtailment of basic services.

It is beyond the scope of this book to analyze the successes or the failures of the UNTAC operation.[6] For many reasons, not the least of which was the failure of the Party of Democratic Kampuchea to comply with the Agreements it had signed, UNTAC in Cambodia was unable to fully prosecute its mandate. Most important, UNTAC failed to bring effective peace to Cambodia. The UNTAC operation, however, did successfully repatriate 370,000 Cambodians from border camps in Thailand; introduced the concepts of multiparty democracy, human rights, and a free press; helped to promote the reemergence of "civil society"; and initiated a process of rehabilitation and reconstruction. UNTAC's most noticeable achievement, of course, was the conduct of a "free and fair election," which resulted in an internationally recognized Cambodian government.

The UNTAC-sponsored election was held from May 23 to 28, 1993, with a turnout of some 90 percent of registered voters. Despite some preelection violence, and without the participation of the PDK, the election was declared by UNTAC and other international observers to have been free and fair. The election gave no party an absolute majority in the 120-seat Constituent Assembly, with FUNCINPEC winning fifty-eight seats (with 41 percent of the popular vote) and the Cambodian People's Party (CPP) taking fifty-one seats (with 38 percent of the vote). The Buddhist Liberal Democratic Party (BLDP) somewhat surprisingly received only 3.8 percent of the vote, winning ten seats, with a fourth party, Moulinaka (an offshoot of the BLDP) winning a single seat. None of the seventeen other parties that stood for election received a seat, with the country's voters clearly choosing between FUNCINPEC's promise of peace (under the quasi-leadership of the party's founder, Norodom Sihanouk) and the incumbent—and entrenched—Cambodian People's Party. As noted by Shawcross: "Over most of the country, people had voted for peace, for reconciliation, for Sihanouk, and, perhaps above all, for change. It was a lot to hope for."[7]

After a sometimes bitter election campaign marked by intimidation and occasional violence—although not ultimately by any serious attempt by the Party of Democratic Kampuchea to disrupt the election itself—the Cambodian People's Party was not prepared for its narrow defeat at the polls. As UNTAC announced rolling tallies from provincial counting centers, the CPP called for new elections in several key provinces owing to "voting irregularities." On June 3, as UNTAC personnel slowly continued to count the ballots, the CPP's Chea Sim and Hun Sen went to the Royal Palace and asked Prince Sihanouk to assume absolute power so as to avoid post-election violence. Having earlier flirted with ideas of a presidential election or a quadripartite "Government of National Reconciliation," Sihanouk immediately announced the formation of the "National Government of Cambodia" with himself as head of state, prime minister, and supreme commander of the armed forces and police and with FUNCINPEC's Prince Norodom Ranariddh and CPP's Hun Sen as deputy premiers.

This "constitutional coup," launched even before UNTAC had completed the counting of ballots, was rejected by Prince Norodom Ranariddh (Sihanouk's son), by UNTAC, as well as by the United States and other members of the "Expanded Perm-5" (in a surprising lack of diplomatic solidarity, France backed Sihanouk's initiative).

One day later, spurned by the negative international response, Prince Sihanouk withdrew his nation-saving plan. The prince did not recant, however, saying that FUNCINPEC and the CPP bore responsibility "for whatever bloody and tragic events that could happen to our hapless country and unfortunate people."[8] He also again proposed to head a "transitional government, to bring Cambodia from insecurity to a bright future of peace," although he offered no details about the structure or duration of such a government or its relation to the results of the UNTAC-sponsored election. In fact, the attempt by Sihanouk to assume direct power presaged the future structure of the Royal Government of Cambodia—although with one important distinction—Sihanouk's power ultimately was limited to that of a constitutional monarch.

The immediate postelection period, however, had one final dramatic act: the establishment of an "autonomous zone" in the eastern provinces of Prey Veng, Svay Rieng, and Kompong Cham by another of Sihanouk's sons, Prince Norodom Chakrapong (a former guerrilla fighter-warlord, and from 1992 a CPP deputy prime minister and, not incidentally, sworn enemy of his half brother, Prince Ranariddh) and General Sin Song, the CPP's minister of interior. The secession attempt two days later was extended to include Kratie, Stung Treng, Ratanakiri, and Mondulkiri provinces—or most Cambodian territory east of the Mekong River.

It is unlikely that the CPP (or at least the hard-line faction of the CPP normally identified with the group led by Chea Sim, as opposed to the supposedly more moderate Hun Sen faction) really intended to establish an autonomous zone. The demonstration of the CPP's province-based power, however, was sufficient to force Prince Ranariddh's FUNCINPEC to accept a political accommodation that awarded the CPP more real power in the new government than it had actually won (or been given by the Cambodian people) in the UNTAC-sponsored election. The threat of secession also underscored the fact that FUNCINPEC lacked the personnel, resources, or experience to effectively assume full administrative control of the country as the election's winning party.

The newly elected Constituent Assembly held its first meeting on June 14, 1993, and, following a "family meeting" a day later at the Royal Palace, the secession ended with Prince Sihanouk's announcement of the formation of the Provisional National Government of Cambodia. Two weeks later, the Constituent Assembly endorsed the provisional administration. Rather than observing the actual election results, the Provisional Government, headed by co-prime ministers Prince Ranariddh and Hun Sen, gave 45 percent of ministerial portfolios to FUNCINPEC, an equal 45 percent to the CPP, and 10 percent to the BLDP.

According to many observers, Prince Sihanouk was not happy with the provisional arrangements, including the agreement whereby all votes in the new Constituent Assembly required passage by a two-thirds majority, thus granting the CPP effective control of the new body. Prince Sihanouk claimed that in the face of the CPP's threat of secession and civil war he—or more accurately, FUNCINPEC—had no choice but to accept an equal coalition, despite FUNCINPEC's plurality in the election and its slight majority of seats in the Constituent Assembly.[9]

Under the terms of the Paris Agreements the transitional period was to end with the adoption of a new constitution and the formation of a new government by the Constituent Assembly. The Agreements gave no particular guidance to the process through which a new government would be established, other than that within three months of the election the Constituent Assembly should adopt a new constitution "and transform itself into a legislative Assembly which will form a new Cambodian Government."[10] With the election over, and only a few months until the end of its mandate, UNTAC allowed the Cambodian parties relatively free rein in the creation of the new government. UNTAC had little role in the drafting of the new constitution and provided virtually no support.[11] Indeed, UNTAC barely was consulted as Prince Sihanouk and later Prince Ranariddh met with Khieu Samphan, the nominal head of the Party of Democratic Kampuchea, to discuss Khmer Rouge participation in the new government.

Despite its rocky beginnings, however, the Provisional Government "functioned surprisingly well, at least on the surface and at the upper level. The [Cambodian] People's Party retained control of all the provinces, even those it had lost in the election, the police remained firmly in the hands of the hardliners, and in many ministries personnel and policies remained unchanged."[12]

Responsibility for drafting the new national constitution was assigned to a thirteen-member committee of the Constituent Assembly, which based its work on drafts prepared by UNTAC and other parties. Because of pressure of time, as well as the inherently political nature of the task—a major test for the Provisional Government—the committee's work was conducted *in camera*. The committee's closed door meetings and the lack of public debate over the contents of the draft constitution caused considerable concern to UNTAC and the international sponsors of the peace process, who found that they suddenly had little direct influence on what was the most important outcome of the entire UNTAC-led effort. The lack of public consultation also concerned a number of indigenous human rights and other local groups who banded together under the umbrella of *Ponleu Khmer*, a Citizens' Coalition for the Constitution. Given the fact that public debate on substantive issues was absent during the entire electoral process, the interest shown in the provisions of the draft constitution was an indication that some notion of democratic practices had, indeed, taken root in Cambodia. Such interest, however, also indicated limited faith in the country's elected representatives, who ultimately bore responsibility for reviewing, revising, and approving the draft constitution prepared by the Constitutional Committee.

If the international community had limited input into the deliberations of the Constitutional Committee, it is to be noted that the broad outlines of the new constitution already had been determined by the Agreements and had been agreed to by the four Cambodian factions in October 1991. A free and fair election was but the vehicle by which Cambodia would become an "independent, neutral and non-aligned state and a liberal democracy." One issue that had not been determined, however, was the nature or structure of government, and in this respect Cambodia had had experience as both a monarchy and a republic (as well as a one-party state). Whatever the form, it was a foregone conclusion that Norodom Sihanouk, prince, king, again prince, prime minister and head of state, rebel leader, hostage and nominal ruler, faction leader, neutral SNC chairman, and father of the nation would once again become Cambodia's head of state.

When the (oxymoronic) first and second prime ministers of the Provisional Government traveled to Pyongyang in early September 1993 to discuss the new constitution with Prince Sihanouk, they reportedly carried with them two alternative drafts, one for a constitutional monarchy and one for a republic. Given that one of the first acts of the newly elected Constituent Assembly had been to declare null and void the March 1970 republican coup that had ousted Prince Sihanouk from power, it is no surprise that Sihanouk chose the monarchical model and the Cambodian crown.

The Constituent Assembly publicly debated the draft constitution over a five-day period, and ultimately agreed to restore the monarchy, retain a two-thirds majority vote to pass all legislation, and keep the system of two prime ministers. While the debate sanctioned power sharing through a coalition between FUNCINPEC and the CPP (with the BLDP included for good measure), there was no discussion as to how power might actually be exercised or how loyal opposition might be voiced as part of the country's new—and internationally sanctioned—political arrangements.

On September 21, 1993, the Constituent Assembly adopted the new Constitution by a vote of 113 to 5, with two abstentions. Three days later, Norodom Sihanouk signed the Constitution and was reinstated to the Cambodian throne as a constitutional monarch who "reigns, but does not wield power." The country again became the Kingdom of Cambodia and the Constituent Assembly transformed itself into a National Assembly, with the CPP's Chea Sim as its president.

With the creation of a new, popularly elected, and—in the eyes of the world—legitimate government, the special representative of the secretary general for Cambodia, Yasushi Akashi, and the UNTAC military chief, General John Sanderson, left the country. The withdrawal of what remained of the UNTAC operation was effected in the final weeks of 1993.

The promulgation of the Constitution of the Kingdom of Cambodia brought a formal end to the mandate of UNTAC in Cambodia. The end of the "transitional period," however, signified more than the completion and withdrawal of the UNTAC operation. The formal establishment of the Royal Government of Cambodia launched a new period in Cambodia's political history.

Chapter 3

Creating a State:
The (Second) Kingdom
of Cambodia

The Paris Agreements determined that a new Cambodian government would be established through an electoral process supervised by the United Nations Transitional Authority in Cambodia. To those people steeped in democratic tradition (such as the architects of the Agreements and UNTAC's sponsors) it was understood that the party that won a majority of seats in the May 1993 election would form the new, duly elected government. Although the Cambodian factions also seemingly agreed to this basic democratic principle, little thought was given to the possible outcomes of the election, including various possibilities or contingencies for either the division or sharing of political power. It was not questioned whether the Cambodian People's Party's (CPP) would be prepared to relinquish its administrative control of the country, or whether the National United Front for an Independent, Neutral, Peaceful, and Cooperative Cambodia (FUNCINPEC) (or any other party) had the ability or capacity to assume the reins of government. Similarly, no real efforts were made during the UNTAC period to discuss or otherwise delineate the role of a loyal opposition in the future Cambodian government. Nor was consideration given to the potential importance of smaller parties in terms of their possibly holding the balance of power as a result of the electoral process. Rather, the "winner takes all" formulation assumed that the May 1993 balloting would result in a clear or decisive electoral victory.

The election, of course, did not result in any party winning an absolute majority. The CPP's refusal to cede control (including its half-hearted postelection effort toward the establishment of an "autonomous zone" in the eastern half of the country) and the patent inability of the monarchist FUNCINPEC to establish a functioning administration resulted in what in hindsight should have been a predictable political accommodation: power sharing. Besides reflecting the realities of Cambodian politics, such a formulation also presented an acceptable (to the outside world) means by which to create a new and legitimate Cambodian government. A coalition government, again by a Western definition, might provide Cambodia with a true "Government of National Reconciliation."

Power Sharing

The Royal Government of Cambodia was formally established in November 1993 with FUNCINPEC's Prince Norodom Ranariddh as first prime minister, CPP's Hun Sen as the second prime minister, and cominister from both parties heading the Ministries of Defence and Interior/National Security. Other ministerial portfolios were divided between FUNCINPEC and the CPP, with one ministry (Information and Culture) allocated to the Buddhist Liberal Democratic Party (BLDP).

In a uniquely Cambodian fashion, such power sharing was extended to the senior levels of each ministry, with the appointment of a vice minister from the party other than that represented by the minister (the ministries of Defence and Interior had *two* vice ministers, one from each party). Although there was a certain political logic to this division of power, biparty power sharing was extended even further through the appointment of two "undersecretaries of state" for each ministry, one each from the two "winning" parties, so as to effect—in theory—a kind of parity. The power-sharing formula was used for senior appointments in the Council of Ministers and also was extended to the provincial level with the appointment of a governor, a first vice governor from the competing party, and two additional vice governors (one from each of the winning parties) to form a provincial management "team." Instituted as a means of sharing power and promoting political reconciliation, the division of power in the wake of the UNTAC-sponsored election actually resulted in a disquieting duality in the ranks of the country's bureaucracy.

The homegrown solution to the problem of sharing political power should have been anticipated by the architects of the Paris Agreements, as well as by UNTAC. Rather, the utopian focus on "liberal, multi-party democracy" and a "free and fair election" blinded everyone to the possibility of less than peaceful consequences—in Cambodia as well as other politically fractured states—of any winner-takes-all electoral contest. Yet the fact that the Cambodian electorate divided its support largely between the CPP, with which it was familiar, and FUNCINPEC, which promised peace and a return to Cambodia's Golden Age, necessitated some sharing of power, as well as the benefits accruing from such power.

Rather than reinforcing zero-sum politics throughout the UNTAC period with an election campaign fought among twenty-one parties in the total absence of what could be called a debate involving public policy, UNTAC should have devoted much more effort to helping the Cambodians develop a new and distinctly "Khmer" form of consensual politics through efforts directed toward the art of compromise, including improved negotiation techniques for "national reconciliation."[1]

It is less what UNTAC might have done than the manner in which things could have been done. Both the election process and UNTAC's dealings with the Cambodian factions, specifically through the Supreme National Council (SNC), were based on confrontational politics and zero-sum games, rather than encouraging or forcing supposed statesmen to act in the best interests of the country and the Cambodian people as a whole. The UNTAC-led process rarely, if ever, rose above politics to contribute toward nation building. Although the SNC was invested with Cambodian sovereignty, UNTAC could and should have demanded much more in the way of constructive statesmanship. After more than two decades of internecine battles, as well as very complicated patterns of self-interested alliances, it was naive to think that the UNTAC process, including a "free and fair" election, would promote "national reconciliation." The UN-sponsored process was too much confined to political actors, excluding other forms of Cambodian leadership, such as the Buddhist *sangkha* or other elements with some social legitimacy.

In addition, it was a serious mistake for UNTAC to take over the former (French) governor's palace at Wat Phnom as its headquarters, thus displacing the Supreme National Council. Although a convenient and somewhat prestigious venue for UNTAC, the move deprived the

SNC of a real as well as symbolic base in Phnom Penh, further under-mining the SNC's already somewhat fictitious claim to be "the unique legitimate body and source of authority in which, throughout the transitional period, the independence, sovereignty and unity of Cambodia is embodied."[2] Rather than having the SNC meet only occasionally in formal session, UNTAC should have required the SNC representatives to meet on a regular and sustained basis to facilitate their working together (something which did happen within the SNC Secretariat, housed on the grounds of the Royal Palace).

Furthermore, as noted by Cambodia analyst Raoul Jennar, the Paris Agreements had proposed a political system based on proportional representation of voters.[3] Had such a system in fact been adopted, it necessarily would have resulted in greater sharing of influence and probably would have been more conducive to post-UNTAC political stability than the "first past the post" system ultimately agreed to by the SNC. Cambodian political reality, including both the CPP's entrenched position and Western support of the erstwhile opposition forces, neces-sitated some accommodation of power and influence

Surprisingly, however, the need for some kind of coalition govern-ment came as a surprise to the international community, including UNTAC, who unwittingly had fallen prey to the notion that a "compre-hensive settlement" featuring a "free and fair election" would indeed solve the long-standing Cambodian imbroglio. Cambodians probably were less surprised. Although the electorate clearly voted for change, particularly a change toward peace and stability, the Cambodian peo-ple could have had no illusion about the nature of the country's politics or Cambodian politicians. Similarly, the Cambodian people were not unfamiliar with the complicated web of factional interests and alliances, including personality-based factions and ever-shifting patron-client re-lationships. Nor are Cambodians naive to the clear linkages between political power and economic interests. Thus, while Cambodians placed their faith in the UNTAC-sponsored election as a way toward positive change, they were not convinced that the electoral process would re-solve Cambodia's political problems—or that a mere election would fundamentally alter or restructure the country's political culture.

The coalition between FUNCINPEC and the CPP, then, represented a necessary compromise that should have been foreseen as the logical result of the internationally sponsored peace process. Some form of political compromise was predetermined by several factors. First, although multiparty democracy through a free and fair election might be a laudable goal, an actual, healthy democracy cannot be created by fiat or by a single election, particularly in a political environment as complex as Cambodia's. Although the efforts of UNTAC's Information/Education and Human Rights components were impressive, it was widely understood that the UN-sponsored process could, at best, only plant the seeds of democracy in a country without any real tradition or experience of democracy, much less multiparty democracy.

Second, the election campaign, such as it was, was fought among parties with dubious claim to leadership of Cambodia. Few of the parties had a political track record of any kind and certainly no experience in good governance. FUNCINPEC used the name and image of Sihanouk the god-king to invoke a past and largely mythical Golden Age of peace, democracy, and prosperity. The Party of Democratic Kampuchea, which ultimately did not stand for election, never addressed its nearly four years of genocidal rule. The CPP tried to take credit for achievements both real and imagined but, in what certainly was a tactical campaign error, promised further war rather than the peace so desperately sought by the Cambodian people. Although election campaigns the world over often feature little real debate, Cambodia's signal UN-sponsored election campaign was devoid of substance, including any real vision for the future of the country. Cambodian voters were asked to choose among parties with no apparent ideological differences. All parties that stood for election voiced support for liberal democracy, free enterprise, and human rights (although "human rights" certainly was an abused and ill-understood concept that implied personal liberty at least as much as the protection of basic human rights). Faced with a choice between a continuation of the country's recent unhappy circumstances and "The Future is the (Golden) Past," between more war and at least the promise of peace, the majority of Cambodian voters exercised their franchise for what they thought would provide maximum stability.

Similarly, when it came to forming a new government, a fragile and possibly unhappy coalition promised greater stability than any winner-takes-all formulation, especially in light of the postelection attempt by elements of the CPP to establish an "autonomous zone" in eastern Cambodia. By entering into a marriage less of convenience than of necessity, both FUNCINPEC and the CPP bought themselves time to prepare for future political and electoral battles.[4]

Coalition governments everywhere are fragile constructs. In Cambodia, with no history whatsoever of any form of multipartyism, and with the entrenched interests of the CPP, which clearly was dominant in every way except for a majority mandate from the country's electorate, a coalition could be nothing but a construct based on compromise—in this case FUNCINPEC's accommodation to the (entrenched) position and interests of the dominant CPP.

While FUNCINPEC and the CPP—together with the BLDP—forged a coalition government, "coalition" is less accurate a term than "accommodation." For, as much as a "coalition government of national reconciliation" was the logical outcome of the internationally designed and supported peace process, the government that emerged was both less and more than a "temporary combination between parties that retain distinctive principles."[5] The post-UNTAC Royal Government of Cambodia clearly was less than a coalition owing to the lack of distinguishing, much less distinctive, principles on the part of its constituent parties, at least in terms of any unique vision of Cambodia's future. Although all three parties advocated peace and prosperity and professed their commitment to liberal democracy and free market policies, all remained rooted in the power divisions of the past. Any difference among the three coalition parties stemmed from their historical "track records" from which the electorate was asked to choose. Given the severe disruption of the Khmer Rouge period, followed by more than a decade of international isolation and then the internationally sanctioned peace process, the fixation with the past was at best irrelevant and at worst dysfunctional given the enormous challenges confronting any new government in rebuilding both the country and Cambodian society.

The postelection Royal Government of Cambodia was something more than a coalition in that the supposedly temporary merging of interests resulted in the establishment of a relatively monolithic government that left little scope for any real opposition voice. As a consequence, the Royal (coalition) Government of Cambodia provided the country and its people with much less than was promised through the exercise of a free and fair election, and presumably less than the Perm Five had envisaged.

Within the coalition, FUNCINPEC and the CPP remained the dominant and, for all intents and purposes, equal partners. Although the BLDP's inclusion in the government was a concession to its performance at the polls, it soon was rendered somewhat irrelevant as a result of factional divisions within its ranks and the emergence of other more credible, if no more powerful, opposition forces. Given that FUNCINPEC and the CPP had been both battlefield and electoral adversaries, what was the nature of their postelection accommodation?

At its most basic, the accommodation allowed FUNCINPEC, the electoral "winner," to form at least half the Royal Government, and to assume at least some of the trappings—and benefits—of political power. For FUNCINPEC, in the face of the CPP's well-entrenched administrative structure and experience in governance, a coalition was perhaps the only way it realistically could exercise any measure of political power and influence. Although FUNCINPEC clearly underestimated the control the CPP retained over the country's bureaucracy, particularly at the provincial and district levels, the FUNCINPEC leadership clearly saw that there was no hope of supplanting the CPP and that only over time could it hope to control or otherwise co-opt the Cambodian bureaucracy to its own political ends.

For the CPP, still smarting from its narrow but unexpected defeat at the polls, the coalition with FUNCINPEC allowed it to retain its control of a number of key ministries and provinces if not the administration as a whole. Although appearing to concede at least some measure of power to its former adversary, the CPP in fact kept a firm grip on the reins of government.

Given the CPP's almost complete control of the Cambodian bureaucracy, as well as a major share of the country's military and police, and given FUNCINPEC's lack of manpower and experience, the strategic alliance thus served the interests of both parties. Furthermore, both entered the relationship under the convenient umbrella of "national reconciliation," a politically expedient means by which they could share power. In addition, both parties were more than aware that the international community, having just spent some two billion dollars on the UNTAC operation, expected a "legitimate" and functioning government, even if such a government was based on a somewhat unclear political accommodation between the erstwhile battlefield foes.

The political compromise of a coalition government, however, resulted in little effective sharing of power. Rather, power was divided, with FUNCINPEC claiming only as much power and influence as the CPP was prepared to relinquish. The division of ministerial posts be-

tween FUNCINPEC and the CPP (with the BLDP holding one ministerial portfolio) represented only the veneer of power and control:

> The traditions of real power in Cambodia are rooted in control of the
> armed forces, security apparatus, state bureaucracy and, importantly, the
> provincial political structures which control police, armed forces, tax col-
> lection, and civil service. These areas remain under the control of the CPP
> and respond to political loyalties before central authority.[6]

At the time of the formation of the Royal Government a source close
to King Sihanouk was reported to have said: "The official titles are just
theatre—a cinema. Inside, the roots of the CPP are too deep. . . . The
administrative structure has been maintained, the military status quo
and the administrative status quo. Not 100 percent but 90 percent. Only
10 percent will be fulfilled by FUNCINPEC."[7] Another official close to
the king claimed, "They [FUNCINPEC] control their offices, their cars,
but they do not control the bureaucracy."[8]

Although the apportionment of power was intended to provide
FUNCINPEC with status commensurate with its victory at the polls,
including some "checks and balances" in the senior reaches of each
ministry, in fact the postelection sharing of power further politicized the
country's senior bureaucracy and also encouraged a wholesale politicization of the entire civil service, with a new set of patron-client relationships and even more divided loyalties between party and state. The
more or less equal division of senior political positions along party lines
also complicated normal bureaucratic procedures, with even routine
matters subject to partisan scrutiny and approval. At the ministry level,
power sharing promoted more discord than harmony and further complicated decisionmaking in the bloated and already hopelessly consti-
pated Cambodian bureaucracy.

In most cases the actual division of power or responsibility was
somewhat ambiguous, based less on clear terms of reference or division
of responsibility than on the personalities of the individuals involved.
The relationship between minister and vice minister and the two undersecretaries of state was inherently political and thus served to preserve
a party-based structure, rather than a true coalition or "government of
national reconciliation."

Apart from a few, rare instances where a minister and vice minister
managed to forge a good or at least professional working relationship,
the "two-headed" structure worked to the considerable disadvantage of

FUNCINPEC. Despite having being transformed into the kingdom of Cambodia, the administrative and technical structure of the former State of Cambodia remained largely intact. All of the CPP's ministers and vice ministers had long experience with the Cambodian bureaucracy, and through the coalition mechanism were able to retain a well-developed system of information, influence, and control, as well as to continue cultivating traditional Khmer-style patron-client relationships. To a very great extent, although not necessarily to the advantage of the Cambodian people, CPP politicians and bureaucrats were more rooted in the realities of Cambodia, all having been part of or surviving the Pol Pot period and with experience in the PRK/SOC administration. At best, such experience meant that elected CPP officials and civil servants had a long-standing and intimate knowledge of the development and other challenges that faced the country. At worst, such officials were able to use their positions of influence and control for the CPP's and their own political and economic benefit.

Senior FUNCINPEC and BLDP officials, however, lacked such experience, with most having been outside of Cambodia for as long as twenty-five years. Although presumably deeply committed to Cambodia, many were educated outside the country, most had virtually all their working experience abroad, and all retained foreign citizenship.[9] Some initially refused to talk with senior and midlevel technical staff, viewing those who had worked with the previous PRK/SOC administration with suspicion and often treating them with disdain as inept and undereducated. Although much better educated than their CPP counterparts, and supposedly more familiar with the concepts of liberal democracy and free market principles, only a few FUNCINPEC and BLDP officials had, at least initially, any real understanding of the country, and particularly rural Cambodia. Instead, they dreamed of a future Cambodian utopia or fell back on idyllic remembrance of a Cambodian past that never really existed. In addition, they had no experience or understanding of the Cambodian bureaucracy, including vital networks of information or established patron-client relationships. Many FUNCINPEC ministers, as well as FUNCINPEC governors, complained that they were unable to exercise due control over their portfolios. At worst, information was withheld and directives were conveniently ignored or countermanded; at best, the CPP-dominated administration simply excluded them from effective decisionmaking processes. Some ultimately were able to effect an accommodation with their CPP colleagues, at least on a technical or working level. Others capitulated, merely rubber-stamping that which was put before them by CPP functionaries, while some did battle, mostly losing in the face of the CPP's overwhelming and entrenched administrative control.

In addition to retaining significant, and certainly majority control over the central government, the Cambodian People's Party in the post-UNTAC period also retained an effective stranglehold over most provincial administrations. Cambodia's provinces are controlled by governors who, in the pre-UNTAC period, also headed the provincial party apparatus, controlled the military, police, and security forces at the provincial level, and were responsible for the collection of taxes. In the post-UNTAC period, the CPP party structure, including control over most facets of provincial governance, remained intact.

In February 1995 the *Phnom Penh Post* quoted FUNCINPEC governor of Kompong Som province, Thoam Bun Sron, as saying he could not even get a letter signed without CPP approval. The governor also claimed that local CPP civil servants actively ignored his orders, preferring to defer to their former CPP leaders who, in practice, retained all power.[10] In the case of Kompong Som, the *Phnom Penh Post* article indicated that all of the governor's decisions required the agreement of the CPP-appointed first vice governor, Kim Bo, who was the province's former (State of Cambodia) governor. The FUNCINPEC governor complained that all of his decisions were vetoed "and so if we can't agree on anything, nothing is done." The governor further complained that "the whole administration belongs to them [the CPP], it is their people and their system . . . the structure has not been changed." According to the governor, most provincial civil servants remained under the "patronage" of their former CPP leaders and thus refused to implement any FUNCINPEC decisions or policies, a situation described by the governor as "passive sabotage." It is to be noted, however, that in provinces headed by the CPP, FUNCINPEC vice governors enjoyed no similar power of veto. Again according to Bun Sron, "If it pleases [the CPP governors] to let their FUNCINPEC deputies know something, it's good, but it is luck."[11] It also is to be noted that in four provinces where FUNCINPEC topped the polls, the governor remained a member of the CPP. In five provinces that voted CPP, the post of governor was awarded to a FUNCINPEC candidate. As detailed by Shawcross, "Three of the four provinces where the election results were not respected, to the detriment of FUNCINPEC, are among the five most important provinces in the country, while of the five provinces lost by the CPP to FUNCINPEC although the CPP won, three are among the four least important in the country."[12] Rather than power sharing, then, the reality at the provincial level left ultimate power and control either to a CPP governor or, if the province was nominally headed by a FUNCINPEC governor, to the CPP first vice governor.

Although the Royal Government, at the behest of the World Bank and other donors, committed itself to reducing the size of the country's public administration by 20 percent, in the post-UNTAC period both FUNCINPEC and the BLDP arranged civil service positions for hundreds, if not thousands, of their supporters. Despite an end to the automatic recruitment of tertiary-level graduates to government service and restrictions on additional civil service hiring, in 1996 both Prince Ranariddh and Hun Sen promised government positions to a new generation of graduating students.

Although understandable as an effort to reward party faithful and establish a base of power and support within the Cambodian bureaucracy, the appointment of party loyalists to government positions further politicized what had been hoped would become a professional and neutral civil service. Furthermore, not all of the new placements were on the basis of merit or, indeed, of need. For example, the Secretariat of State for Women's Affairs, headed by a BLDP member, hired scores of BLDP supporters without regard to qualifications. Many of the new recruits performed no real function other than filling a party-based position, a sinecure that, while not paying very much, at least provided a regular income, ample opportunity for outside employment, and a claim to status, important in Khmer culture. As a result, the Women's Secretariat was considerably overstaffed, with only a limited number of experienced individuals performing the bulk of its work.

As of 1997 it was somewhat unclear whether FUNCINPEC had made any inroads into the Cambodian bureaucracy. With the CPP having retained firm control of most of the country's bureaucracy, it was a matter of speculation whether there had been any shift in party loyalties. There were two conflicting analyses. One, propagated by FUNCINPEC officials, suggested that FUNCINPEC had quietly burrowed into the power and strongholds of the CPP. The other, more commonly held, view was that FUNCINPEC's claim to power really was restricted only to the upper reaches of the bureaucracy and that real structural power remained in the hands of the CPP. Significantly, despite considerable efforts to incorporate non-CPP elements into the country's military and police forces, both remained dominated by the CPP.[13] FUNCINPEC also appeared to have been unsuccessful in expanding its base of support beyond Phnom Penh, Battambang, and other urban centers. During late 1997, many of FUNCINPEC's provincial and district party offices seemed inactive, although such inactivity could well have been the result of the negative political climate following the July 1997 coup de force.

By the end of 1997 it also remained unclear when the next national election might be held—if at all—as well as on what basis such an election might be contested. Given the experience of the post-UNTAC period, and the country's confused political circumstances, it was hard to imagine that either FUNCINPEC or the CPP might win an absolute majority, thus necessitating a continued coalition or other form of power sharing. At the same time, it was difficult to foresee the same kind of multiparty election as was held under UNTAC auspices. The reasons for this were twofold. First, sixteen of the twenty parties registered in the May 1993 election were without seats in the National Assembly and thus appeared to have no power base upon which to build. Without significant financial support, particularly external support, few of the smaller parties—if they still existed—would be able to mount a credible national campaign. Indeed, four years after the UNTAC election most of the small parties that contested the election were assumed to be defunct. Second, and possibly more important, small parties, including any new parties that might be established in advance of the 1998 polls, would be without the kind of protection afforded by UNTAC during the 1993 election. It thus was a considerable irony that whereas the 1993 UN-sponsored electoral process encouraged multiparty democracy, the legacy of that process focused power on the two largest parties who, for most of the post-UNTAC period, had been locked in an uneasy if somewhat mutually advantageous coalition. In addition, at least in the immediate post-UNTAC period, the Royal Government had some of the characteristics of a monolithic, one-party state, particularly in its lack of tolerance for any kind of opposition or dissent.

By the end of 1996, however, it was clear that the increasingly strained relationship between Prince Ranariddh, the first prime minister, and Hun Sen, the second prime minister, imperiled continuation of the coalition, as well as any mutual accommodation. Their relationship continued to deteriorate in the first six months of 1997, leading to Prince Ranariddh's negotiations with the hard-line Khmer Rouge, charges against FUNCINPEC of illegal importation of heavy weaponry and unauthorized troop movements, and, ultimately, the July coup de force that saw Prince Ranariddh flee the country and, from self-imposed exile, try to mount a military campaign against the Phnom Penh government.

Although intraparty dynamics in the post-UNTAC period continued to fascinate and preoccupy observers of the Cambodian political scene, no outsider could begin to fathom the complex web of relationships among key individuals within the respective parties, much less relationships between and across party lines. Much attention was devoted to supposed schisms within the Cambodian People's Party, particularly between the party's "hard-line" element (chiefly associated with the party's president, Chea Sim, and his interior minister protégé, Sar Kheng) and the Hun Sen "faction."[14]

Although intrigue and power struggles within the CPP were widely speculated upon—again mostly by foreign observers, in the four years following the UNTAC-sponsored election, serious schisms also emerged within FUNCINPEC and the BLDP. In October 1994 Sam Rainsy, the outspoken (FUNCINPEC) minister of finance, was relieved of his post. In protest, Prince Norodom Sirivudh (King Sihanouk's half-brother and hence Prince Ranariddh's uncle) resigned his post as minister of foreign affairs, though maintained his position as FUNCINPEC secretary general. Sam Rainsy's FUNCINPEC party membership was revoked several months later as a direct result of his continued criticism of both the Royal Government and FUNCINPEC. In June 1995 the National Assembly voted to remove him from the assembly on the grounds that without party membership, he could no longer hold the seat to which he had been elected. In December 1995, Prince Sirivudh was arrested after supposedly uttering a threat to assassinate Hun Sen; he subsequently accepted exile in France based on his promise to have no further involvement in Cambodian politics. In late 1996, however, the prince announced his intention to return to Phnom Penh—quite possibly to establish a new opposition party, possibly together with Sam Rainsy.[15]

Factionalism, of course, long has been a feature of Cambodian political life. Given the country's modern political history and the highly personalized nature of Cambodian politics, it came as no surprise that all the Cambodian political parties, to lesser or greater extent, came to be riven by internal schisms in the post-UNTAC period. What was surprising, however, was the relative durability of the coalition government in the first three years following the UNTAC-sponsored election. Although FUNCINPEC did threaten to withdraw from the coalition in early 1996 over the issue of increased power sharing at the district level, both FUNCINPEC and the CPP seemed to accept the coalition—and power sharing—as a political necessity.

The "success" of the coalition government in the immediate post-UNTAC period was tied to four closely related conditions. First was an effective, if never close, working relationship between the first and second prime ministers. Although very much a marriage of convenience, it was clear that should either depart or be replaced, for whatever reason, it would be unlikely that the accommodationist government could survive, at least in its current form or with the same *modus operandi*. Second (and not unconnected with the first condition), it was clear that the death (or abdication) of King Sihanouk and the selection of his successor would significantly, or even completely, alter the coalition, forcing, for example, an early general election. Third, there remained the possibility of a coup, particularly one engineered from within the Cambodian People's Party. And finally, the unlikely inclusion of the Party of Democratic Kampuchea (the Khmer Rouge) as part of the ruling coalition would necessitate a new government structure as well as a new balance of power (or power sharing).[16]

In a May 1995 interview with *Le Mekong*, Second Prime Minister Hun Sen noted that a coalition-type government was essential to ensure political stability: "Political stability in Cambodia is the product of an alliance made between the two political parties under the direction of His Majesty the King. This stability would be immediately called into question if there were a division within the coalition government."[17] The second prime minister further speculated that Cambodia would continue to need a coalition form of government for as much as ten or fifteen years:

Personally, I am very optimistic about cooperation between the two largest parties as well as with other parties represented in the National Assembly and those which are not. Such cooperation is a basis for stability. From now until 1998, this alliance will continue to exist. If I had to predict the future, I would say that Cambodia will need a coalition government for at least 10 to 15 years. . . . I believe that even if the People's Party were able to obtain a majority of the votes in the next election, I would again form a coalition government. This is the only way of guaranteeing stability in Cambodia and to mobilize resources for the country's reconstruction.[18]

As proven elsewhere in the world, political reality can be accommodated through a coalition-form of government. What appeared potentially dangerous in the Cambodian context, however, was the failure to create a coalition that encouraged (or at least tolerated) any real debate, much less engendered a real government of national reconciliation. Cambodia's post-UNTAC coalition government demonstrated considerable intolerance of any opposition, including from members of the National Assembly, new or reconstituted political groupings, from the press, or from other elements of the country's emerging civil society. The CPP's firm control of the reins of government, together with FUNCINPEC's limited administrative capabilities and the weakness of the elected National Assembly, resulted in a somewhat monolithic Royal (coalition) Government of Cambodia. Thus, rather than a liberal, multiparty democracy, Cambodia's postelection government demonstrated some of the elements of a one-party state.

Given the political accommodation or marriage of convenience between the dominant CPP and its coalition partners (that is, FUNCINPEC and the BLDP—or, with the exception of the BLDP-aligned Moulinaka party, *all* the parties winning seats in the 1993 election), what was the role and function of the National Assembly? Concern over the relative powerlessness of the legislature, and how it was used to ratify decisions made by the leadership of the two dominant parties in the Coalition Government began with the *in camera* drafting of the country's constitution by a committee of the newly elected Constituent Assembly. Though expedient, given the three-month time frame imposed by the Paris Agreements, the closed-door determination of the country's new constitution reestablished the practice of political exclusivity in Cambodia whereby governance was the preserve of the few. As the Constituent Assembly's first, and most important act, it was significant that the Cambodian people were neither consulted nor informed about the work of the Constitutional Committee. Although it was true that prolonged or divisive debate over the new Constitution might have been damaging, including to the initial establishment of the coalition, the lack of open debate on the country's new constitutional provisions established a decidedly antidemocratic precedent.

In its first three years, the country's National Assembly proved a disappointment as the centerpoint of Cambodia's new liberal democracy. The National Assembly undertook little real debate on any of the major issues and challenges facing the country and proved unable to wield any effective power or influence. The subservience of the legislature to the executive and the lack of any real political opposition was not anticipated by the Agreements. However, considering recent Cambodian history, it was not surprising that the National Assembly became little more than a rubber stamp for decisions made by the two-headed Coalition Government.

An example of the powerlessness of the National Assembly can be seen in the assembly's very limited role in the initiation of legislation. Under the 1993 Constitution, legislation could be initiated by any of nine parliamentary commissions. However, virtually all of the legislation presented to the National Assembly was drafted at the ministry or Council of Ministers level. As noted by Shawcross, this was not surprising, given the assembly's lack of collective experience, research services, a library, and legal expertise.[19] More serious, however, was the fact that the National Assembly appeared unable to develop any kind of independent stance, much less to assert itself as the paramount source of power in the country. Voting in the National Assembly typically was unanimous and public, "just like under communism" as one member of the assembly trenchantly noted.[20] Similarly, one political commentator suggested that "Democracy will emerge in Cambodia from the *practice* of government, but only if that practice is participatory."[21]

In the post-UNTAC period, then, the National Assembly lacked authority to exercise the kind of influence that might be expected of an elected assembly. In addition, "under the policy of 'national reconciliation,' no real opposition had emerged in the assembly. Indeed, the concept of a 'loyal Opposition' was, understandably, still remote to most Cambodians. Instead, reconciliation became the rationalization for all compromise."[22]

Although such "rationalization" clearly was rooted in the country's political realities, the use of compromise to promote national reconciliation need not have precluded either debate or principled opposition, especially as part of any process preceding decisionmaking or leading to political compromise. In the National Assembly, however, both

FUNCINPEC and the CPP enforced loyalty to government policy as determined by the executive. As a result, the process of government in Cambodia assumed a form not envisaged by the Paris Agreements. In post-UNTAC Cambodia, the role of ordinary members of the National Assembly was devalued if not subverted. The CPP went so far as to have its elected members sign an oath of loyalty to the government. Efforts also were made to silence those individuals who became too outspoken in their criticism of the government, as evidenced in the case of Sam Rainsy, who was expelled from the assembly. Such treatment hardly was conducive to the expression of any kind of opposition, much less real dissent.[23]

As just noted, the establishment of the coalition government was the logical result of an externally imposed solution to the "Cambodian problem." If such power sharing as existed in the post-UNTAC period was a uniquely Cambodian adaptation to the country's political realities, the international community was quick to criticize the coalition government's deficiencies. In a diplomatic cable subsequently leaked to the press, Australian Ambassador John Holloway provided "an unvarnished account of the political and military shortcomings in Cambodia." Holloway's June 1994 cable reported that "drift in government, stagnation in the countryside, the army in disarray, the marginalization of FUNCINPEC, and corruption everywhere favour the growth of an insurgency in Cambodia."[24] An April 1995 *Globe and Mail* report similarly criticized the early performance of the Coalition Government: "A year after the withdrawal of the biggest and costliest United Nations operation ever, Cambodia's dawn of democracy has turned into a morning storm of corruption and intolerance, raising concern among Khmers and foreigners alike that the impoverished country may slide back to its former authoritarian state."[25] Or, as suggested by another commentator, "The successor government may not have a firm hold on power. It would not be surprising if it fell apart from personal and factional division, or if the Khmer Rouge launched a major destabilizing effort, or if the political rivals fell back on the traditional practices of eliminating opponents rather than respecting them as 'loyal opposition'."[26]

Such criticism, though to some extent valid, demonstrated the unrealistic expectations placed on the Royal Government by the outside world. Yet Cambodia's recent history provided little precedent and limited foundation for a stable form of parliamentary governance. No one, therefore, should have expected that a single and somewhat inconclusive election would launch Cambodia into the liberal, pluralistic, democratic future envisaged by the Paris Agreements.

As noted by Steven Heder in a review of William Shawcross's *Cambodia's New Deal*,

> The contradiction between UNTAC-era hopes and post-UNTAC blues points toward a clearer characterization of what UNTAC made possible, which Shawcross himself suggests when he writes about the "startling resemblance" that Cambodia in 1994 bears to Lon Nol's Khmer Republic of the early 1970s. What UNTAC allowed was not so much a social revolution as a social restoration. Finally, after years of suppression and involution in neo-traditional forms under the CPP, old patterns of patron-client neo-patrimonialism have re-emerged in more readily recognizable forms under the FUNCINPEC-CPP coalition and Sihanouk's kingship. This is not the fault of the current political leadership, nor of UNTAC, but has deeper historical roots.
>
> In fact, the Paris Agreements did not place a high priority on the consolidation of liberal democracy in Cambodia. All they insisted on was the achievement of a new political arrangement via a free and fair electoral process, and thus as the result of a democratic transition. However, the Agreements indeed committed Cambodian politicians to constitutional provisions enshrining liberal democracy and pluralism and left it to them to integrate this commitment with the political, military, social, economic, cultural, and diplomatic realities facing the country once UNTAC was gone. The challenges for Cambodians in doing so are enormous, much greater than those that were bestowed on UNTAC in effecting a democratic transition. This is because most of the preconditions normally associated with consolidation of democracy are lacking in Cambodia.[27]

According to Heder, the absence of socioeconomic preconditions favoring liberalization and democratization perfectly reflected a political culture antithetical to any such transition. Thus, Heder (quoting political scientist O'Donnell) suggested that the prospects for a democratic consolidation in Cambodia would almost certainly be profoundly threatened by a "high degree of continuity of . . . bureaucratic authoritarian politics" and that further liberalization and democratization likely would be obstructed by the ongoing "influence and institutional presence" of the security forces, of the "notables of the authoritarian regime" and of a "patrimonial political style" including "clientism

[and] personalism . . . not only in the style of doing politics, but also in the style of governing."[28]

In addition to explicating how the UNTAC experience helped to shape, but not determine, the nature of the Royal Government, Heder's analysis provided some insight into Cambodia's likely political future.

The Kingdom of Cambodia and the Khmer Rouge

The phenomenon of the Khmer Rouge remains one of the least understood aspects of Cambodian life. The auto-genocide perpetrated by the Khmer Rouge during its "three years, eight months, and twenty days" in power stands among the bloodiest of modern times. How the Khmer Rouge was able to use cold war politics to consolidate its position, how the Khmer Rouge became legitimized as an equal actor in the internationally sponsored peace process, how the Party of Democratic Kampuchea successfully defied the United Nations Transitional Authority in Cambodia, and how the guerrilla movement continued to dominate the Cambodian political agenda will long remain subjects of academic debate.[29] Of more insistent concern, however, was how the Royal Cambodian government might deal with the continuing challenge posed by the Khmer Rouge and how the international community might help the government both to rid the country of the Khmer Rouge threat and ensure that a movement like the Khmer Rouge could never again come to power in Cambodia.

Although the demise of the Khmer Rouge was predicted for some years, the continued existence of the guerrilla movement into the post-UNTAC period represented perhaps the most serious problem faced by the Royal Government. The often repeated connection between peace and security and development became accepted as a truism: "No peace without development; no development without peace." And, indeed, widespread insecurity throughout much of Cambodia—whether directly attributed to the Khmer Rouge or to other rogue elements, including the undisciplined military—prevented the establishment of an environment conducive to the country's reconstruction and development, including its further political development. Ongoing hostilities, including the continued ebb and flow of fighting according to the country's seasons, continued to divert human, material, and financial resources badly needed for the country's reconstruction. Continued

Khmer Rouge control of gem and timber-rich areas along the Thai border also denied the government important sources of revenue.

In addition, it should have been more clearly understood that the context of ongoing war or insecurity does not lend itself to the consolidation of democratic liberalism. Rather, hostilities or other threats to weak government structures promotes authoritarian rule as well as the strong influence of the military. Differences of opinion as to how best to deal with the Khmer Rouge and efforts to court Khmer Rouge defectors and other dissident elements also served to split the coalition government. In particular, Prince Norodom Ranariddh's 1997 efforts to court the remnants of the "hard line" Khmer Rouge in Anlong Veng precipitated the July 1997 coup de force that resulted in his ouster.

To some observers, the failure of the Khmer Rouge to participate in the May 1993 election signaled the end of the Khmer Rouge, at least as a political force. Such observers proposed that to vanquish the Khmer Rouge, the Royal Government first would have to contain the Khmer Rouge, including by military means, and then gradually eliminate any residual support the movement might have in the countryside by promoting rural development. According to this theory, as the benefits of development—roads, schools, health posts, agricultural services—were extended throughout the country, the Khmer Rouge would simply wither away. This "leopard spots" theory had the weight of logic; it also had historical precedent in both Thailand and Malaysia, where communist insurgencies were eliminated through effective rural development.

One of the major themes of the first meeting of the International Committee for the Reconstruction of Cambodia (ICORC) was the importance of sustained international support to development activities as the best, if not the only, means to effectively eliminate the threat of the Khmer Rouge. In April 1995 Nate Thayer, the *Phnom Penh Post's* senior political reporter indicated that "cautious military pressure" as well as the offer of amnesty to Khmer Rouge troops had "turned Siem Reap province into a model of national reconciliation that has brought a level of peace and development unseen in decades. In many areas long under guerrilla control, the Khmer Rouge defectors have rallied to the government and continue to administer the same zones they did as guerrilla cadre."[30] According to Thayer, wholesale Khmer Rouge defection in Siem Reap produced unprecedented levels of security in many areas of the province. The improved security, in turn, permitted "an array of development projects such as road construction, dam repair, demining around former front-line villages, and agricultural infrastructure improvements. These efforts have increased levels of local support for the government, further eroding the rebels' ability to appeal to the sympathies of long neglected villagers."[31] If the experience in Siem Reap demonstrated that increased security and development would ultimately eliminate the Khmer Rouge, Thayer's report also noted that the government's clear-cut success in marginalizing the Khmer Rouge in Siem Reap was in stark contrast to the situation in Battambang province, where the Khmer Rouge continued to pose a potent threat.

Following years of strife and isolation, however, the entire country was in need of rehabilitation and development. Effective rural development clearly would take years and far greater financial and human resources than realistically could be mobilized for the task. Furthermore, a strong military served as a unifying force in both Malaysia and Thailand. In post-UNTAC Cambodia, the Royal Cambodian Armed Forces (RCAF), an amalgam of officers and troops from the various Khmer factions, remained weak, factionalized, and undisciplined. Thus, it appeared that elimination of remaining pockets of Khmer Rouge influence through rural development could take considerable time.

Others, including King Sihanouk, held the conviction that the Party of Democratic Kampuchea could only be annihilated as a political force through its inclusion in a "government of national reconciliation." The king's repeated efforts to co-opt the Khmer Rouge, however, were rejected by the coalition government—particularly the CPP—as well as by the Khmer Rouge, who continued to make unrealistic demands regarding their representation and influence within any reconciliation government.[32]

In July 1994 the National Assembly passed legislation that outlawed the Khmer Rouge. The legislation also provided a six-month amnesty to encourage Khmer Rouge rank and file to defect to the government without reprisal. In response, the Khmer Rouge announced the formation of the Provisional Government of National Union and National Salvation (PGNUNS), based in Preah Vihear province. By the end of 1994, the Royal Government announced that some 6,600 Khmer Rouge soldiers and militia had defected in response to the amnesty program. The amnesty subsequently was extended to encourage further defections.

In the post-UNTAC period, reports concerning the strength and continuing influence of the Khmer Rouge remained confusing and contradictory. Immediately after the formation of the new government in late 1993, the *Phnom Penh Post* quoted Khmer Rouge sources as saying "that despite the widely-held belief that they are terminally ill as political force in Cambodia, they remain confident that the new government will collapse under the pressure of internal conflicts. They predict an increase in corruption and say a declining economic state in the rural areas will undermine popular support for the new government after an initial political 'honeymoon' of several months."[33] One year later, however, Thayer reported that "the remnants of one of the world's last communist guerrilla movement wages what now seems a war without issue. Despite the depressing scenario of ongoing warfare . . . the Khmer Rouge appear, ultimately, to be doomed."[34] His April 1995 account was based on the military reversals suffered by the Khmer Rouge in northern Cambodia, as well as the defection of nearly one-half of Khmer Rouge forces in the once-key stronghold of Siem Reap. As reported by Thayer, "While it may be a few years away, analysts agree that the group is dying a slow death, with little chance of recovering as a potent political force."[35]

Thus, from the end of the UNTAC operation, assessments of the Khmer Rouge's remaining military and ideological strength changed from month to month, often completely contradicting earlier reports. One month, a spate of defections from the Khmer Rouge was seen to signal the end of the Khmer Rouge as an organized force. The next month, the kidnapping or murder of a foreigner or the massacre of ethnic Vietnamese villagers or forest workers was taken as evidence of the movement's continued lethal vitality. Reports in May 1996 that Pol Pot had died from malaria promoted further speculation about the end of the Khmer Rouge; at the same time, the movement's vigorous defense of Pailin and other strongholds continued to provide ample evidence that the guerrilla faction was not yet a spent force in Cambodia's political life.

In March 1994, for example, the Royal Cambodian Armed Forces launched a dry season offensive and actually took control of Pailin, the Khmer Rouge's nominal capital. Twenty thousand rebel fighters and civilians fled to Thailand, as some 5,000 government soldiers, with tanks and artillery support occupied—and looted—Pailin. The victory, an apparent beginning of the end for the Khmer Rouge, was short-lived, with the Khmer Rouge retaking both Pailin and Anlong Veng within a month. By May 1994, Battambang province was experiencing the heaviest fighting since the withdrawal of Vietnamese troops in 1989. An estimated 40,000 civilians were forced to flee their homes along Route 10 between Battambang and the guerrillas' recaptured base at Pailin. Most foreign aid workers were evacuated from the province. Khmer Rouge forces also managed to sever Route 5, the main road between Sisophon and Poipet. Fighting in Banteay Meanchey displaced a further 10,000 villagers. At the same time, a 400-strong Khmer Rouge unit was reported to have been seen only twenty-five kilometers from Phnom Penh. Also in May, four young foreigners were kidnapped near Sihanoukville, ostensibly by a Khmer Rouge unit, and subsequently were found murdered. Repeated demonstration of the Khmer Rouge's continued ability to wage guerrilla war dealt a serious blow to the confidence and credibility of the Royal Cambodian Armed Forces and also represented a severe embarrassment to the new government.

Besides these major offensives, the Khmer Rouge continued random guerrilla attacks throughout the country. For example, in April 1994 six people were killed and thirty-five others wounded when a train traveling from Phnom Penh to Battambang ran over six land mines and was attacked by Khmer Rouge guerrillas. In September and October 1994, National Army of Democratic Kampuchea (NADK or Khmer Rouge) forces attacked seven districts in Siem Reap province, with fighting also in Kompong Chhnang, Battambang, and Banteay Meanchey provinces in the northwest, as well as in Preah Vihear, Kompong Thom, Kompong Speu, and Kampot provinces. Such attacks involved groups of between 100 and 250 guerrillas each, and resulted in some 120 deaths.

Khmer Rouge attacks on villages and key transportation infrastructure continued through at least mid-1996. The Khmer Rouge also continued to wage a vicious campaign of terror in many parts of the countryside (except for a few bombing incidents in Battambang attributed to the Khmer Rouge, the movement never mounted a campaign of urban-based terrorism). Week by week the Khmer Rouge continued to launch attacks throughout much of rural Cambodia. In addition, heavy fighting continued in Battambang province, with thousands of villagers displaced from their homes.

The Khmer Rouge's new "scorched earth" tactic was a departure from its previous ultranationalist and "hearts and minds" campaign designed to win some measure of support from the rural populace. Some analysts considered the shift in tactics a sign of Khmer Rouge desperation, including its inability to provide food and arms to its guerrilla forces. Others, however, interpreted the village-based attacks as an effective form of intimidation and a clear measure of the Khmer Rouge's continued strength as a insurgent force. While burned villages and the loss of crops might not win the Khmer Rouge popular support, the random exercise of violent force caused nationwide insecurity that challenged the Royal Government and provided the Khmer Rouge with a kind of perverse legitimacy.

The effectiveness of Khmer Rouge tactics, including the murder of three foreigners in Kampot province, the murder of a tourist visiting the monuments in Siem Reap, the early 1996 abduction (and subsequent murders) of an expatriate deminer and his interpreter, and the June 1996 massacre of at least fifteen forest workers in Kampot province, certainly had a negative effect on the reputation of both the Royal Cambodian Armed Forces and the Royal Government. Continued insecurity limited private investment and had a negative effect on the country's growing tourism industry. Reluctant to provide lethal military support to the ill-trained and possibly corrupt Royal Cambodian Armed Forces, donors provided only limited training assistance. Although there was no indication that widespread insecurity directly affected levels of donor funding, donor reluctance to sponsor development or other projects in "insecure" areas necessarily compromised the Royal Government's efforts to end the ongoing civil war through development of the countryside.

As always, the strategy or long-range plans and ambitions of the Khmer Rouge leadership remained a key question. There was no evidence that the Khmer Rouge leadership had given up its quest to return to power in Cambodia. Rather, by establishing its Provisional Government of National Union and National Salvation, the Khmer Rouge indicated its intentions to reassert its control over the whole country. Whatever the actual numbers of its guerrilla fighters, the Khmer Rouge appeared to remain extremely well organized and committed to its struggle, at least at its leadership level.

The guerrilla movement also was thought to be extremely wealthy. For years the Khmer Rouge sold concessions to Thai interests to extract gems and timber from areas under its control. In May 1995, for example, Global Witness, a British environmental group, estimated that the Khmer Rouge earned more than $U.S.10 million a month from the cross-border sale of timber from the 10 percent of Cambodian territory under its control.[36] There was little sign that successive Supreme National Council (SNC) and Royal Government bans on logging or gem mining diminished the exploitation of resources in Khmer Rouge-controlled areas. There also were reports of collusion between the Khmer Rouge and the Royal Cambodian Armed Forces, with continued fighting, though at a fairly low level, seen to be in their mutual interests as a cover for continued and unsupervised exploitation of the country's forestry and other resources.

Such trade was sufficiently lucrative, according to what the *Economist* called "doomsday analysts," to provide the Khmer Rouge with the financial base for a future attempt to retake power in Cambodia. Such analysts believed that despite apparently widespread defections and reported demoralization among the Khmer Rouge rank and file, the leadership of the movement remained intent on returning to power: "They are sitting it out as corruption increases and the political paralysis deepens. They'll wait until political internecine warfare erupts again and the donors withdraw, and then they'll move in."[37]

The defection of much of its military personnel may, indeed, have weakened the Khmer Rouge. After years of guerrilla warfare, Khmer Rouge forces, too, could only be weary of war. Many, seeing only "Khmer killing Khmer," perhaps no longer believed in the movement's virulent anti-Vietnamese propaganda. At the same time, the defection and reinsertion into Cambodian society of large numbers of Khmer Rouge-influenced fighters might well have provided the movement with an incredible base for future propaganda efforts. While, as of end-1996, it appeared that the movement lacked any coherent political program appealing to the population at large, it was important to remember that the Khmer Rouge first came to power as a result of popular disillusionment with the corrupt Lon Nol republican regime. As of mid-1996, many of the same preconditions that contributed to the rise of the Khmer Rouge again seemed to exist in post-UNTAC Cambodia.

In an August 1993 article, Craig Etcheson, a long-time anti-Khmer Rouge activist, proposed the "Sun Tzu" thesis that

Pol Pot is better positioned today for a return to power than at any time since 1979. The Vietnamese are gone. The "puppet regime" is defeated, replaced by an unstable conglomeration. Pol Pot still has his army, and still has highly placed friends in Thailand and China. He is wealthy. He has hugely expanded his territory and population. He has deeply infiltrated the opposing parties, and again has both overt and covert operatives in Phnom Penh. And he has convinced most of the world that the Khmer Rouge threat is no more.[38]

Although the ultimate objectives of the shadowy Khmer Rouge leadership, as well as its strategy in dealing with the Royal Government remained as unclear as ever, it was still far too early to judge the Khmer Rouge a spent force, much less to predict its eventual demise.

In August 1996, however, a surprising and significant split occurred within the Khmer Rouge through the defection of Ieng Sary and a large number of his Pailin and Phnom Malai-based troops.[39] Although Khmer Rouge radio accused Ieng Sary and his followers of embezzling $U.S.16 million from the Khmer Rouge's transborder logging and gem-mining activities, there also were reports that the movement's hard-line leadership had ordered an end to private property in Pailin, specifically motorcycles and cars. Whether occasioned by greed or ideological differences, the split appeared to be further evidence of the waning fortunes of the Khmer Rouge. Although the Ieng Sary faction initially demanded some degree of military and administrative control, the Royal Government firmly rejected any separate military authority but did agree to a "power-sharing" arrangement whereby Ieng Sary loyalists retained some administrative responsibility. On September 16, 1996, Ieng Sary was granted a Royal amnesty. By late October, more than 2,500 dissident Khmer Rouge troops had traded their guerrilla uniforms for those of the Royal Cambodian Armed Forces. The wave of defections left the Khmer Rouge with an estimated military force of some 4,500 battle-hardened troops, including up to 1,000 soldiers in the movement's northern stronghold of Anlong Veng. Several hundred other Khmer Rouge guerrillas held scattered "leopard spots" in the country's northwest and south, although it was expected that as the result of the defections, the Khmer Rouge would have increasing difficulty delivering food and other supplies to its guerrilla forces. In addition, Thailand claimed it would not provide sanctuary to the Khmer Rouge, reiterating official Thai policy to disarm and push back any foreign troops who crossed the border into Thailand.

If the "rehabilitation" of Ieng Sary as a patriot and possible born-again democrat was repugnant to diplomats and other foreign observers, there was grudging acknowledgment that as "unconscionable as they may seem, the talks [negotiations with Ieng Sary] could be the country's best hope of peace."[40] In a similar vein, a *Bangkok Post* editorial rationalized that "Cambodians . . . must choose between seeking justice for the millions who were killed and brutalized, and trying to arrange a peaceful future for the living."[41] Although few—including King Sihanouk, most foreign observers, and probably a majority of the Cambodian population—believed that Ieng Sary had no (bloody) hand in the Cambodian holocaust, his defection and the subsequent amnesty granted him (at the request of the two prime ministers) nevertheless was widely viewed as a necessary and important step toward both "national reconciliation" and the elimination of the Khmer Rouge as a guerrilla force.

Although the mass defection of the Ieng Sary faction, subsequently named the Democratic National United Movement (DNUM), was seen as a significant victory for the Royal Government, the negotiations with Ieng Sary and his followers also widened the rift between the government's coalition partners, with both FUNCINPEC and the CPP criticizing the other's efforts and both attempting to use the ongoing defections of Khmer Rouge guerrillas to their own advantage. Thus, while commenting that the weakening of the Khmer Rouge as a military force might bring peace, the *Far Eastern Economic Review's* Nayan Chanda posited that "it won't necessarily mean an end to the struggle for political supremacy in Cambodia."[42] Indeed, in mid-February 1997 further fighting broke out in Battambang province between military units loyal to FUNCINPEC and the CPP.

Subsequent events in the country's northwest demonstrated the degree of rivalry between FUNCINPEC and the CPP. In late November 1996 at least five civilians were injured in Sisophon as military police aligned with the CPP exchanged gunfire with soldiers loyal to FUNCINPEC. The clash provoked King Sihanouk to warn that mounting tensions between the country's ruling coalition partners could turn "explosive."[43] Indeed, in mid-February 1997 further fighting broke out in Battambang between military units loyal to FUNCINPEC and the CPP. The units were reinforcing allies in rival factions of Khmer Rouge defectors in the region. Both CPP and FUNCINPEC appeared to be courting the estimated 10,000 ex-guerrillas nationwide in a bid to bolster their positions for the legislative elections scheduled for 1998.

Other Cambodia watchers speculated that the purge of the Ieng Sary faction would allow the Khmer Rouge to rebuild: "Some worry that conceding a political role to Ieng Sary's followers may open the way for a return by the Khmer Rouge to the tactics they pursued in the 1960s, when an underground military wing worked in tandem with an above-ground political wing."[44] According to this "politics by other means" theory, the Khmer Rouge's denunciation of Ieng Sary as a traitor was nothing but a strategic ploy, one further tactic in the "fight to the death" promised by the "Radio of the Provisional Government of National Union and National Salvation of Cambodia."

By end-1996 it appeared that what remained of the hard-line Khmer Rouge faction truly was in decline, possibly terminal decline. It remained too early, however, to completely dismiss the Khmer Rouge as a spent force given Cambodia's complicated historical and personal entanglements and the country's still shifting political and economic alliances—particularly in advance of the next national election scheduled for 1998.

During 1997 there was further disintegration of the once monolithic (though schism- and purge-ridden) Khmer Rouge. Having been granted a Royal amnesty by King Sihanouk in late 1996 (at the request of the country's two prime ministers), Ieng Sary, the former Khmer Rouge minister of foreign affairs, established the Democratic National Union Movement (DNUM). This dissident Khmer Rouge faction claimed political, as well as military, neutrality. In exchange for at least tacit support of the (CPP-dominated) Royal Government, Ieng Sary's movement was allowed de facto autonomy over gem- and timber-rich Pailin.

Throughout 1997 both the CPP and FUNCINPEC encouraged further defection of Khmer Rouge rank and file, with most defectors absorbed (and apparently neutralized) into the CPP-dominated Royal Cambodian Armed Forces. Negotiations and bargaining with various Khmer Rouge elements continued, including authorization by Prince Ranariddh of secret and partisan negotiations with the remaining hard-line Khmer Rouge faction based in its northern border redoubt in Anlong Veng. In May 1997 Prince Ranariddh announced that Khieu Samphan wished to break away from the hard-line faction through the establishment of a new political movement, the Khmer Solidarity Party (also called the National Solidarity Party or NSP). The new grouping seemed to exclude Pol Pot and other hard-line figures. In June, reports emerged of a bloody schism within the Khmer Rouge, with Pol Pot himself apparently ordering the execution of Son Sen, a senior Khmer Rouge official, and members of his family. Reports subsequently emerged that Pol Pot and a small group of loyal followers had been forced to flee, and later that Pol Pot had been arrested by what remained of Khieu Samphan's so-called Anlong Veng faction. On June 16, Khmer Rouge radio accused Pol Pot of treason and announced that Khieu Samphan had been named leader of the National Solidarity Party. The radio report also pledged the support of both the NSP and the Khmer Rouge shadow Provisional Government of National Union and National Solidarity (PGNUNS) for the opposition National United Front (NUF). This announcement, formalized in a July 2 agreement between FUNCINPEC and Khieu Samphan, together with Prince Ranariddh's importation of three tons of heavy arms and FUNCINPEC-orchestrated troop movements, was interpreted by the CPP as tantamount to an act of war against the post-UNTAC power-sharing coalition, and served as a pretext for the July 5–6, 1997, coup de force.

In the wake of the coup, which resulted in Prince Ranariddh's ouster and self-imposed exile, he mounted armed border resistance in a loose alliance with Khmer Rouge forces. Democratic National Union Movement President Ieng Sary initially rejected bids by both the Samlot resistance and the government to take sides, expressing neutrality. At the same time, he agreed to try to bring the Samlot rebels—former Khmer Rouge defectors who initially aligned themselves with the CPP—to the negotiating table with the government. Playing a dual track of isolation and intervention, Pol Pot's former foreign minister attempted to present himself as a peacemaker while at the same time preserving Pailin's economic and military autonomy. In October 1997 Ieng Sary traveled to Phnom Penh. During the visit, his first to the capital since Vietnamese forces drove out the Khmer Rouge in January 1979, the former Khmer Rouge leader pledged cooperation with the Phnom Penh government and the Royal Cambodian Armed Forces. He also declared that the July fighting that ousted Prince Ranariddh was not a coup d'etat. In early November Pailin was given municipal status under the control of the Ministry of Interior.

In what only could be interpreted as a last-ditch effort to establish some political legitimacy, the remaining hard-line faction of the Khmer Rouge put an ailing Pol Pot on trial in far northwestern Cambodia in late July 1997. The surreal "show trial," witnessed by *Far Eastern Economic Review* correspondent Nate Thayer, saw the shadowy Khmer Rouge leader denounced by his followers and sentenced to life imprisonment.[45] In a subsequent interview with the former "Brother Number One," Thayer reported that the ailing but nonetheless lucid Pol Pot expressed neither responsibility nor remorse for Cambodia's genocide, blaming instead Viet Nam, Cambodia's traditional enemy.[46]

Rising Political Tensions and Increased Factionalism

As outlined above, in the immediate post-UNTAC period, power sharing between FUNCINPEC and the CPP provided Cambodia with some measure of political stability. Although not anticipated by the architects of the Paris Agreements, the sharing of political power was a necessary accommodation between the results of the 1993 election and the CPP's entrenched control of the country's administrative structures, including the military and police forces. As noted by John McAuliff, executive director of the U.S.-Indochina Reconciliation Project and a long-time follower of Cambodian events: "The genius of the coalition government which was established after the elections was that it brought together formal elected authority with the existing structure of power. Neither could govern the country without the other, either in terms of parliamentary vote requirements or for the implementation of policies."[47]

Although the country still did not enjoy peace, with continued fighting against Khmer Rouge elements as well as other problems of internal security and weapons-related violence, there was hope that the years of fighting and bloodshed might finally come to an end. With massive international technical and financial support, Cambodia also made impressive developmental progress, with significant investment in infrastructural rehabilitation, capacity building, and rural development as well as impressive levels of domestic and foreign investment in the country's productive sectors. Although some human rights and other abuses continued, including several incidents of political intimidation and state control of the country's media, there similarly were signs that some of the elements or trappings of a more open or "democratic" society were emerging in Cambodia.

While the post-UNTAC relationship between FUNCINPEC and the CPP, the Royal Government's main coalition partners, had never been easy, the early months of 1997 saw heightened political tension within the government, particularly between Prince Norodom Ranariddh, the country's first prime minister, and Hun Sen, the second prime minister. Although electorally the senior partner in the coalition, FUNCINPEC had failed to make inroads into the country's administrative structures, particularly at the provincial and district levels. By 1997 FUNCINPEC became increasingly frustrated by the CPP's dominance of the Royal Government's bureaucracy, and also threatened by the CPP's commanding control of the country's military forces. Having been forced into a power-sharing accommodation because of its lack of an effective administrative base, by early 1997 FUNCINPEC had come to realize that the (unequal) sharing of political power was no guarantee of any sharing of political control.[48]

In addition, there were signs that FUNCINPEC, through lack of leadership and organization as well as reports of the corrupt practices of some senior party officials, had lost significant electoral support in urban areas, the base of FUNCINPEC's support. FUNCINPEC also had failed to establish an effective network of provincial and district offices, further undermining its ability to mount a credible campaign in advance of the national election scheduled for 1998.[49]

A March 30, 1997, grenade attack on a demonstration in Phnom Penh led by outspoken opposition politician Sam Rainsy underscored rising political tensions. The attack, outside the gates of the country's National Assembly, killed at least sixteen persons and injured many more. Although neither Hun Sen nor the CPP was directly implicated in the grenade attack, the incident was portrayed by the international media as evidence of the country's political instability and the prevailing state of lawlessness. The incident was seen by many as a heavy-handed attempt by the CPP—or CPP-allied interests—to further limit, if not eliminate, any real opposition voice in the country. The Royal Government's failure to launch a thorough investigation of the attack was taken as further evidence of the fragility of both "the rule of law" and human rights in Cambodia.

The year 1997 also witnessed considerable factionalism and political in-fighting within Cambodia's main political parties. The Buddhist Liberal Democratic Party (BLDP) split into two factions: one loyal to the party's founder, Son Sann (and Son Soubert, his son and political heir), the other taking as its leader Ieng Mouly, the minister of information and culture. Ieng Mouly subsequently launched—and won—a court case permitting his faction to use the BLDP logo in the next general election.

FUNCINPEC suffered an even more serious split with the April 1997 defection of twelve FUNCINPEC members of the National Assembly. The split was led by Siem Reap Governor Tuon Chhay, a former

FUNCINPEC military leader. Although six of the twelve defectors soon returned to the party fold, their action briefly threatened to eliminate FUNCINPEC's small majority in the National Assembly. With the CPP poised to secure a working majority in the assembly, Prince Ranariddh insisted that as FUNCINPEC party leader he had the right to replace dissident FUNCINPEC members of Parliament—a constitutional issue that while not entirely clear, did have precedence in the earlier expulsion from the National Assembly of both Sam Rainsy (the former minister of finance) and Prince Norodom Sirivudh (King Norodom Sihanouk's half-brother—and thus Prince Ranariddh's uncle—who had served as both minister of foreign affairs and secretary general of FUNCINPEC prior to his arrest, conviction, and subsequent exile on a charge of having threatened to assassinate Hun Sen). Thus, rather than Hun Sen being called upon to form a majority government—an accurate reflection of the CPP's political dominance—the uneasy and lopsided power-sharing arrangement continued. In the early months of 1997 the country's two prime ministers met only rarely and criticized each other openly and in the strongest of terms.

By late 1997 there appeared to be at least three FUNCINPEC factions: a group under the nominal leadership of Ung Huot, appointed as first prime minister following the July coup de force; a faction led by Siem Reap Governor Tuon Chhay (whose group continued to use the FUNCINPEC banner and which, following the July coup, took control of FUNCINPEC's party headquarters in Phnom Penh); and a small group still loyal to Prince Ranariddh. The latter group joined the prince in self-imposed exile following the July coup and subsequently attempted to mount armed resistance against the CPP-dominated Phnom Penh government under the banner of the National United Front (NUF), a CGDK-type alliance with the Son Sann faction of the BLDP, Sam Rainsy's Khmer Nation Party, and the remaining hard-line Khmer Rouge.

The year 1997 also witnessed the emergence of new political movements and alliances that further threatened the continuation of the FUNCINPEC-CPP coalition government. In June, Pen Sovan, the People's Republic of Kampuchea's first prime minister, announced the formation of Uphold the Cambodian Nation Party (UCNP).[50] Although initially it appeared that the UCNP leaned toward FUNCINPEC, Pen Sovan's party subsequently indicated its alliance with the CPP. In an effort to broaden its electoral appeal, the CPP also forged links with at least six small parties, including the Khmer Republican Democratic Party.

FUNCINPEC, too, tried to forge new political alliances, notably by joining Sam Rainsy's Khmer Nation Party (KNP) in the formation of NUF. As just noted, the agreement under which the Anlong Veng Khmer Rouge agreed to join the front, thus reconstituting a CGDK-style alliance, sparked the July 5–6 coup de force.

The establishment of new political alliances in anticipation of the 1998 general election and then the July coup seemed to signal the end of the country's post-UNTAC coalition government. However, the selection by Cambodia-based FUNCINPEC party officials of Ung Huot as party leader and the National Assembly's eighty-six to ten secret ballot vote (with three spoiled ballots and twenty-one absentee members—all Ranariddh supporters) to accept Ung Huot as Cambodia's first prime minister seemed to resuscitate the ruling coalition. After months of political stand-off, the machinery of government, including the country's National Assembly, again began to function. Although critics saw the renewed coalition, as well as the apparently cordial working relationship between Ung Huot and Hun Sen as a regrettable accommodation by one FUNCINPEC faction to the CPP's entrenched power, Ung Huot remarked that "two [prime ministers] are better than one in the sense that they work together. If the two leaders are against each other, it's worse. Over the past three years, the two heads worked in different directions. When the heads work in different directions, it's a negative. The two prime ministers in this government will achieve positive things for the country."[51]

As of end-1997 it remained too early to tell whether the renewed coalition would continue to the national election scheduled for May 1998, much less whether a coalition or power-sharing form of government might emerge from the next polls in a further effort to share political power and to achieve a true government of national reconciliation. Although the Ung Huot-Hun Sen coalition definitely served the CPP's interests, particularly with respect to retaining at least a veneer of democratic practice in the face of overwhelming international criticism following the July coup, it was unclear whether the renewed coalition also might allow FUNCINPEC opportunity to reunite a badly splintered party so as to mount a credible election campaign against Hun Sen and the Cambodian People's Party. Because of the various FUNCINPEC factions, as well as continued recognition by King Sihanouk as well as many Western donors of Prince Ranariddh as the duly elected first prime minister, Ung Huot's long-term leadership of the "parliamentary wing" of FUNCINPEC remained far from clear. Nor was it certain what might happen with the criminal charges against Prince Ranariddh (relating to collusion with the Anlong Veng Khmer Rouge, unauthorized troop movements and infiltration by Khmer Rouge elements, and illegal arms importation), and whether Hun Sen might bow to international pressure to allow Prince Ranariddh to return to Phnom Penh, possibly under a royal pardon, in order to contest the 1998 general election.

As of late 1997 FUNCINPEC's ability to mount a credible national electoral campaign was in doubt. Besides being badly fractured, it appeared to have only a limited organizational and financial base and no coherent party "platform." In addition, FUNCINPEC's poor performance in the post-UNTAC period may have tarnished its previous strong identification with both King Sihanouk and the Golden Age of Sihanouk's *Sangkum Reastr Niyum* (usually translated as the "People's Socialist Community").[52] In stark contrast, the CPP appeared organizationally and financially ready to run a national electoral campaign.

Thus, while FUNCINPEC's splintered and weak state seemed to favor the unified and organizationally strong Cambodian People's Party, politics—and particularly Cambodian politics—always remains beyond prediction. Despite its firm political, administrative, and military control as well as its long experience in government, as of late 1997 popular support for the CPP was surprisingly low, as was Hun Sen's personal popularity. Even post-coup efforts to improve internal security, including through the elimination of police checkpoints, brought Hun Sen domestic criticism. In addition, real economic difficulties resulting from cutbacks in foreign direct investment and international development assistance and sharply reduced tourism receipts in the wake of the July coup, as well as crisis in the region's financial markets, were blamed on Hun Sen. Thus as of late 1997 it was premature to predict any massive CPP victory in any future election, especially a "free and fair" election in which the electorate was allowed to express its unhappiness with Cambodia's continued turmoil. There also remained the possibility that King Sihanouk, Prince Ranariddh, Prince Sirivudh, Sam Rainsy, or even Ieng Sary's Democratic National Unity Movement might challenge the CPP's entrenched political control through the establishment of a new, untested (and therefore not discredited) political movement that might win support from Cambodia's disgruntled electorate.

The July 1997 "Coup de Force"

A surprising, although not entirely unanticipated series of events led to the July 1997 ouster of Prince Norodom Ranariddh and his replacement as first prime minister by Ung Huot, the FUNCINPEC minister of foreign affairs.[53] The ouster, effected over a weekend of fighting, resulted in as many as 150 deaths and also saw considerable loss of property because of widespread looting. The weekend's fighting, limited almost exclusively to Phnom Penh, was followed by the extrajudicial killing or disappearance of several senior FUNCINPEC military and security personnel. The July events received extensive international coverage and were widely condemned as a coup d'etat. Major newspapers claimed that the coup represented the death of democracy in Cambodia.[54] In the days following the "coup" some governments chose to evacuate their nationals while several others suspended their development assistance to Cambodia as a rebuke to what was commonly reported as "Hun Sen's bloody seizure of power."

Although it was condemned as a coup d'etat, Prince Ranariddh's ouster possibly was more an opportunistic coup de force, with the CPP taking advantage of a series of tactical errors made by Prince Ranariddh and his senior military advisers. In particular, it appeared that the prince's military advisers convinced him that FUNCINPEC, through force of arms, might redress the imbalance of power suffered by the party in the post-UNTAC period despite its narrow electoral victory in the May 1993 UNTAC-sponsored election. Although it remained somewhat unclear whether it was FUNCINPEC or the CPP who actually provoked the July 1997 military confrontation, Hun Sen's forces were able to take advantage of the situation and, through superior military force, assume even greater control of both the government and the country. Prince Ranariddh (who actually left Cambodia just before the outbreak of fighting) and a group of loyal supporters had to flee the country. In the months following the coup, troops loyal to the prince once again took up position along the Thai-Cambodian border to fight against the Phnom Penh government.

An extraordinary document—in English—released jointly by the Ministry of Foreign Affairs (headed by a FUNCINPEC minister) and the Ministry of Information and Culture (headed by a BLDP minister) within only a few days of the July events presented a quite different account of the coup than was reported in the international press. According to the government's White Paper the July events were the result of a "policy of provocation" adopted by Prince Ranariddh and his military advisers. Such a policy included a deliberate campaign to antagonize Hun Sen so as to provoke him into taking drastic action likely to draw national and international condemnation.[55]

As outlined by the White Paper, the FUNCINPEC strategy of provocation included a secret military buildup by FUNCINPEC military commanders loyal to Prince Ranariddh. Although such a buildup may at first have been merely part of the policy of provocation, the White Paper suggested that such a policy took on a life of its own as Prince Ranariddh was given exaggerated accounts of FUNCINPEC's military strength. Without sanction of the Ministry of Defense, FUNCINPEC commanders subsequently moved redeployed security forces to Phnom Penh and also built up existing military units with Khmer Rouge elements. According to the White Paper FUNCINPEC's military buildup presented three key threats to the continued existence of the coalition government:

> First was the unauthorized expansion and redeployment of FUNCINPEC security forces to Phnom Penh. Second, there was the establishment of illegal garrisons around the capital. Third, there was the deployment of Khmer Rouge soldiers from the northwest to Phnom Penh, intended to both be integrated into existing FUNCINPEC units and to infiltrate the city. The importance of the militarization of the Khmer Rouge and their introduction to Phnom Penh by Prince Ranariddh's military advisors cannot be minimized. For the first time since 1978, armed Khmer Rouge soldiers were present in the streets of Phnom Penh.[56]

The White Paper also alleged that Prince Ranariddh was directly involved in the strategy of provocation, including through the illegal importation under false bills of lading of some three tons of sophisticated weaponry labeled "spare parts."

As documented by the White Paper, in the latter stages of the strategy of provocation

> Prince Ranariddh engaged in the most dangerous tactic of all: he secretly and unilaterally began negotiations with the remaining Khmer Rouge hardliners at Anlong Veng. Hoping to add their military assets to the growing FUNCINPEC military forces, Prince Ranariddh was willing to deal with the last Pol Potists, who remained dedicated to the destruction of his coalition partner, the CPP. . . . Thus you had the unseemly action of

Prince Ranariddh in trying to forge a military and political alliance with the last Khmer Rouge holdouts at the very time that those hardliners remained publicly dedicated to the destruction of one-half of the government. This last action was tantamount to announcing that the coalition government was being terminated. The military build-up and the alliance with the Khmer Rouge was virtually a declaration of war.[57]

On July 3, 1997, Prince Ranariddh—on behalf of the National United Front (NUF)—signed an agreement with Khieu Samphan—the apparent leader of the remaining hard-line Khmer Rouge—through which the Khmer Rouge joined the front. This political, and presumably, military alliance—bringing together FUNCINPEC, Sam Rainsy's Khmer Nation Party, the Son Sann/Son Soubert wing of the BLDP, and the Khmer Rouge—essentially recreated the Coalition Government of Democratic Kampuchea in clear opposition to the CPP.

Although not widely reported, Prince Ranariddh left Cambodia on July 4 on the advice of his senior military advisers. He left the country without official notice to either the government or senior FUNCINPEC officials. Also not widely reported was the fact that on the following day pro-Ranariddh forces occupied and began the looting of Phnom Penh's Pochentong Airport, which provoked CPP troops to move to inspect the Tang Krasang FUNCINPEC military base across from the airport. Fighting thus erupted, without apparent move by Hun Sen or the CPP to specifically seize power.[58]

The fighting, though often intense, was limited almost exclusively to Phnom Penh and was mostly over in less than forty-eight hours. Some provinces were put on alert, with expectation that the fighting would spread. In other provinces, military commanders from both FUNCINPEC and the CPP decided to take no action so as to avoid a spreading military confrontation. By Monday, July 7 the CPP had firm control of all of Phnom Penh, with many FUNCINPEC military officials having to flee for the Thai border and FUNCINPEC personnel and their families taking refuge in the Cambodiana Hotel or other "safe houses." An uneasy calm returned to Phnom Penh, though most residents stayed at home, and banks and most ministries remained closed. In the wake of the coup, some embassies arranged the evacuation of their nationals. International television coverage of such evacuation by military aircraft gave the false impression that fighting and a general state of lawlessness continued in the days following the "coup."[59]

The total number of military and civilian casualties resulting from the weekend of fighting is not known, although estimates ranged up to 150 deaths. Many senior FUNCINPEC military officials were reported as killed or otherwise missing (some having fled to the Thai border), with several having been tortured and executed.[60] In addition to damage from shelling and other military action, the coup sparked widespread looting of Pochentong Airport, car dealerships, petrol stations, factories, and shops, as well as opposition party headquarters and the personal residences of senior FUNCINPEC officials. Damage was estimated to be in the millions of dollars.

The adoption by Prince Ranariddh of a deliberate "strategy of provo-cation" was corroborated in an extensive September 1997 interview in the *Phnom Penh Post* of Tony Kevin, the out-going Australian ambassa-dor to Cambodia. In the interview, Ambassador Kevin said

> But there was another current of events happening late last year which caused us a great deal of concern and that was the breakdown of the relations between FUNCINPEC and the CPP in government and the in-creasingly clear evidence that FUNCINPEC had decided to pursue a pol-icy of building up its military strength and if necessary entering into a military alliance with the Khmer Rouge. . . .You had a great deal of arms importation into Phnom Penh, you had the three tons of anti-tank weap-ons allegedly brought in by Ranariddh, you had the very assertive attempt to negotiate between Ranariddh and Khieu Samphan and the KR in Anlong Veng which didn't even give the appearance of being in the spirit of national reconciliation. You had an increasing militarization of the top echelons in FUNCINPEC. . . . You had the emergence of what an academic colleague has described as two rival party states cohabiting uneasily on the same territory and really getting ready to go to war with each other.[61]

According to the Australian ambassador

> what happened on July 5 and 6 [1997] was not a *coup d'etat* by a military oppressor against a defenceless, unsuspecting rival, . . . What happened . . . was a trial of strength between two sides who had decided to have it out. Now of course, FUNCINPEC say we had no choice, we had to defend ourselves because the CPP was starting to take our forces and it would have left us defenceless. But . . . what were they doing accumulating weapons for an attack on a legally constituted state in the first place? There is no defence for what FUNCINPEC was preparing to do and that was to

take on the state in a military way. . . . The fact [that] the fighting was precipitated by the Hun Sen side seizing FUNCINPEC weapons, to me does not make this a *coup d'etat*, it makes it a trial of strength in a uniquely unstable situation where the relationship between the two sides of government had broken down irretrievably.[62]

In his statement to the opening of the Eighth Session of the National Assembly, Chea Sim, acting head of state (and leading CPP official) placed full blame for the July events on Ranariddh and his military advisers, stating as follows:

The events of 5–6 July took place as a result of actions taken by a handful of extremist elements, in close alliance with the Khmer Rouge from An-long Veng. These extremists ventured to use military force of the outlawed Khmer Rouge and provoke internal conflict, with the ultimate aim of overthrow[ing] the Royal Government and ignit[ing] the fire of urban terrorism in order to generate an adverse climate preventing the organization of the forthcoming elections. The swift, highly efficient retaliation and operation by the government's force bears no characteristics of a coup d'etat. It was not an armed confrontation between political parties. The operation was the Royal Government's effort to enforce the law against the illegal force which spread anarchy. . . . It was within the domain of the government's responsibility to prevent and put a check on illegal armed elements and to act against the clandestine outlawed elements of the Khmer Rouge which had been brought in secrecy into Phnom Penh in order to wage an internal war.[63]

Chea Sim also reported, "Now that this brief and bitter event has subsided, national institutions have resumed their operations; life has rapidly returned to normal. The Constitution, other laws in force, democratic principles and human rights observance continue to be enforced responsibly. The people, as well as our political leaders, political parties, human rights organizations, associations, the media and foreign residents now enjoy full freedom in conducting their activities without restriction, suppression, and without threat. They are receiving protection from our competent authorities."[64]

In the wake of the coup, the National Assembly endorsed—by secret ballot—the nomination of Ung Huot, minister of foreign affairs (FUNCINPEC) as the country's first prime minister. Although King Norodom Sihanouk, as head of state, signed a letter acknowledging the

National Assembly's selection of Ung Huot as first prime minister (Ung Huot also retained his post as minister of foreign affairs), the king let it be known that he still considered his son, Prince Ranariddh, to be Cambodia's duly elected first prime minister. Nonetheless, Ung Huot's nomination represented the continuation of the coalition-style government that had emerged from the UNTAC-sponsored election, though with significantly decreased sharing of power between the CPP and what remained of the badly splintered FUNCINPEC.

Frustrated by his inability to end Cambodia's ongoing conflict, King Norodom Sihanouk in late 1997 again threatened to abdicate, saying, "I sincerely desire to abdicate, but I am waiting for Hun Sen, our strongman, to give me the 'green light' for this abdication."[65] With no clear successor, particularly given that two of the king's sons, Prince Norodom Ranariddh and Prince Norodom Chakrapong, as well as the king's half-brother, Prince Norodom Sirivudh, remained in political exile as of end-1997, Hun Sen was not prepared to accede to the king's expressed desire to abdicate. More important, Hun Sen and the CPP may have feared that King Sihanouk might abdicate as a constitutional monarch who reigns but does not rule in order to reenter active politics as the nominal leader of FUNCINPEC, the royalist party Sihanouk founded and, to many, still symbolized.

After spending two months in Cambodia after the coup—in Siem Reap rather than the Royal Palace in Phnom Penh—the king returned to self-imposed exile in Beijing in order to continue long-term medical treatment for a variety of ailments. As he left Cambodia, the aging and clearly dispirited monarch suggested that he might never return to his country. In an October 25 message marking his seventy-fifth birthday, the king claimed, "My role as 'Father of all Cambodians' has been diminished, and I can only observe with deep anguish and desperation the conflict engulfing our homeland and our international isolation."[66]

The Impact of the "Coup"

After months of heightened political tension, the July coup permitted some return to normalcy. The post-UNTAC coalition government was restored, the National Assembly was reconvened, and the business of government was conducted with renewed dedication and less overt partyism. Internal security also improved throughout the country as the result of Hun Sen's eight-point security program, including the nation-wide elimination of military and police checkpoints that, whatever their security function, had allowed underpaid security personnel to increase their earnings through unofficial tolls.[67]

On July 10 ASEAN foreign ministers decided to "postpone" Cambodia's entry as a full member of the regional organization. Such a decision was the result of too little time following the coup, significant U.S.-led international protest against the coup, and Hun Sen's refusal to accept any ASEAN intermediation of the dispute between the continued Phnom Penh-based coalition government and Ranariddh's "government in exile." The reversal of the earlier decision that Cambodia would join ASEAN at the same time as the Lao People's Democratic Republic and Myanmar was a blow to the Phnom Penh government. The later decision by the UN Credentials Committee to leave vacant the Cambodian seat at the United Nations represented an even greater blow to the legitimacy of the CPP-dominated government in Phnom Penh. As the result of this decision, determined largely through American veto power, Cambodia joined Afghanistan and Sierra Leone as the only countries in the world without accredited representation at the United Nations.

In the months following the coup, Prince Ranariddh attempted to win international support for the prince's "government in exile." The return to the days when FUNCINPEC, as a member of the Coalition Government of Democratic Kampuchea, fought against Hun Sen's Phnom Penh government was completed with actual military confrontations along the Cambodian-Thai border, as well as Ranariddh's claims that Viet Nam had invaded Cambodia and that strongman Hun Sen was a "communist" and a "puppet of Hanoi." As the result of the fighting, up to 60,000 Cambodian civilians again sought refuge in Thai border camps, once more hostage to Cambodian political and military overlords. Both FUNCINPEC and the CPP-dominated Royal Government attempted to win support from the various Khmer Rouge elements and factions. Toward the end of 1997, there was no end in sight to Cambodia's civil strife, with Khmer continuing to fight and kill Khmer.

Internationally, the coup was criticized widely, with Hun Sen, the "CPP strongman," particularly subject to attack. The accounts of his "bloody seizure of power," however, ignored the fact that neither he nor the CPP had ever really relinquished power and that Ranariddh's political supremacy in the postelectoral period—by virtue of his party's slight plurality at the 1993 polls, had never been more than illusory. International reports of the July coup rarely examined the events that led to military confrontation, including Ranariddh's alliance with the Anlong Veng Khmer Rouge, and neglected to mention that at least the form of Cambodia's flawed democracy—that is, the coalition government formed as the result of the 1993 election—survived the July coup de force.

The event clearly presented a dilemma for the international community. On the one hand, the coup and a return to factional fighting symbolized the failure of the UNTAC-led peace process as well as a failure to cultivate democracy in Cambodia. On the other, the coup ended a mostly cosmetic and increasingly untenable alliance between Prince Ranariddh and Hun Sen. While the post-UNTAC sharing of power had been politically expedient, and initially had provided reasonable government, four years after the end of the UNTAC operation the very solution to competing political interests had come to work against good governance.

Given Cambodia's not insignificant (though decidedly uneven) progress in the post-UNTAC period—politically, socially, economically, and developmentally—the international community's response to the coup de force was disappointing. Because of previous international involvement in Cambodia's internal affairs, as well as because of the important stake the international community felt it had in the country because of the Paris Agreements and the UNTAC operation, the international response to the coup stood in marked contrast to comparable situations in other countries.

Despite the coup de force, continued fighting, ongoing human rights abuses, inadequate "rule of law," and insufficient transparency in governance, Cambodia in late 1997 was more democratic than some of its immediate neighbors, and certainly more so than many other countries around the world. Similarly, in 1997 many other countries witnessed far more serious human rights abuses than Cambodia, with far greater acts of terrorism and violence than what was experienced in Cambodia in the post-UNTAC period.[68]

Although in no way condoning or excusing abuse of power and other excesses in Cambodia, there seemed to be little international recognition that despite the UNTAC operation, war-torn Cambodia remained a transitional society, and that the country's further progress, particularly its further political development, would inevitably be hard won.

Rather, Cambodia was made to suffer for having failed to meet unrealistic expectations. Rather than acknowledging the country's many achievements and working constructively to address areas requiring further improvement, such as legal reform in support of an improved environment for the rule of law, it appeared that the international community was, to some extent, "giving up" on Cambodia—at least until the country had an elected government more in favor with the world's power brokers.

This dogmatic attitude was reflected in international demands that Prince Ranariddh be allowed to return to Cambodia to participate in the electoral campaign without any acknowledgment of the criminal charges against the prince or the fact that following Prince Ranariddh's self-imposed exile his badly fractured party had, by a somewhat open process, chosen to replace him as party leader.[69]

If the international community's concerns with respect to the Electoral Law, including the membership and neutrality of the Electoral Commission, were not without substance, such concerns were raised as demands rather than as part of a constructive dialogue to help Cambodia build and strengthen its emerging democracy. Thus, as with American pressure on Iraq's Saddam Hussein, the foreign policy goal for Cambodia seemed to be "to seek to coerce compliance" rather than to build upon the democratic foundation already laid by the Paris Agreements and UNTAC.

Although Phnom Penh-based diplomatic staff, including both the American and Australian ambassadors, provided reasoned analysis of the July events, and recommended at least tacit acceptance of the CPP's political and administrative dominance, such counsel was ignored, particularly by Washington's political establishment. The United States thus led efforts to punish Hun Sen and to restore Ranariddh to power. Unfortunately, however, such efforts again focused on isolation of the Phnom Penh government, including through the cessation of nonhumanitarian assistance. A number of key donors followed the American lead, resulting in the loss of tens of millions of dollars in much needed financial assistance.[70]

The economic fall-out from the coup, in investor confidence and cutbacks in donor assistance, was severe. In October 1997 the *Phnom Penh Post* suggested that "Cambodia's economy faces a 'very real' prospect of disaster, pressed by a serious budgetary shortfall and a massive downturn in foreign aid and investment."[71] In October 1997 Keat

Chhon, minister of finance, stated that the government, which relied on aid for more than 40 percent of its total revenue, stood to lose more than $U.S.100 million in 1997 alone through suspended aid programs. Investor confidence also faltered in the wake of the July fighting, with estimates of foreign direct investment (FDI)—originally pegged at up to $300 million for 1997—slashed by one- third.[72] By late 1997 Cambodia faced a $U.S.58 million budgetary shortfall.[73]

International coverage of the July coup and persistent and negative reports of the country's instability also affected Cambodia's key tourism industry. The government's 1997 revenue from tourism was expected to fall by as much as 25 percent from the 1996 level of $U.S.100 million.[74]

In the wake of the coup the United States and Germany suspended their assistance programs. By late 1997 the impact of cutbacks in donor assistance was being felt. While the American government pledged to continue to provide "humanitarian" assistance to Cambodia, it terminated its support to the Cambodian Assistance to Primary Education (CAPE) project, a $U.S.26 million, five-year program that was in its first year of operation. The project involved the establishment of 315 resource centers in cluster schools across the country and the training of up to 40,000 primary school teachers. As the result of the U.S. decision, more than 40 expatriate and 115 local and provincial staff were dismissed, while 300 Ministry of Education staff who were receiving salary supplements to work as teacher trainers returned to their previous ministry functions. The suspension of U.S. assistance also saw the termination of a $U.S.10 million village roads project in the northwest, a $U.S.3.2 million environmental management program, as well as a number of projects and programs implemented by American and other nongovernmental organizations, including a $U.S.3 million girls' and women's educational project and a $U.S.1.3 million child survival project.[75]

The German government similarly suspended more than 31 million deutsche marks (some $U.S.18 million) in aid activities, including $U.S.9 million in financial support for the procurement of essential drugs, a $U.S.8.5 million rural telecommunications project, road building activities, a credit scheme, and six technical assistance projects. The scaling down of German assistance necessitated a one-third cutback in the country's procurement of essential drugs, affecting national tuberculosis, malaria, and HIV-AIDs programs. As noted by a Ministry of

Health official, "We don't want to add health problems to political problems. We will suffer a lot from this decision. We only want to help the poor people."[76]

The American-led response to the July coup de force, and particularly cutbacks in development assistance, stood in marked contrast to the kind of response recommended by the NGO Forum on Cambodia. In a statement issued within days of the coup, the NGO Forum appealed to the international community to avoid taking sides with parties to the conflict and to pursue all efforts toward constructive dialogue and negotiation. The NGO Forum also urged that continued development and humanitarian assistance be provided to the Cambodian people:

> We have seen, in Cambodia as well as in other parts of the world, that it is ordinary people who are the most vulnerable and who suffer most when punitive measures are imposed. . . . The isolation of Cambodia would be counterproductive and would further undermine all that has been achieved to date. . . . We once again urge donor governments and the international community to continue the work they have started in support of Cambodian people and not to again use the withdrawal of humanitarian and development aid as a political tool.[77]

Chapter 4

Rebuilding Cambodia: From Rehabilitation to Development

The newly established Royal Government of Cambodia articulated its vision for the future of the country through its *National Programme to Rehabilitate and Develop Cambodia*. Prepared with technical assistance from the United Nations Development Program (UNDP) and involving participation of eleven interministerial groups, the program was presented to the international donor community at the March 1994 meeting of the International Committee for the Reconstruction of Cambodia (ICORC-2). According to the document, "The overriding objective of the Royal Government is to achieve a fair, just and peaceful society and, through accelerating the rate of economic growth, to raise the living standards of all Cambodians. In short, the Government is striving to achieve sustainable growth with equity and social justice."[1]

Although billed as an integrated "program," the *National Programme* in fact consisted of a statement of general principles combined with a catalogue of national development priorities that together were to provide a framework for the Royal Government's broad, holistic, long-term vision for the country's reconstruction and development. It promised to lay the foundations for a sustained development effort, including the development of human resources, the streamlining of state finances, the rehabilitation of essential physical infrastructure, the establishment of the rule of law, and the promotion of entrepreneurship with the state as partner of the private sector. In particular, the document committed the Royal Government to

—Reform the State, its institutions, and its Public Service so as to attain political and socioeconomic priorities;

—Rely on private entrepreneurship and the market as engines of growth;

—Double gross domestic product (GDP) by 2004 in real terms and place heightened emphasis on harnessing Cambodia's agricultural, industrial, and tourism potentials;

—Extend health, educational, and social services to the entire population so as to ensure, within the decade, a substantial improvement in the standard of living;

—Improve rural living by promoting rural development as a central feature of the government's development priorities;

—Ensure that the pattern of development is sustainable socially, politically, fiscally, and environmentally; and

—Strengthen domestic self-reliance and thus reduce the current dependence on external financial and technical assistance.[2]

Besides emphasizing a commitment to the establishment of a fully fledged market economy, the *National Programme* also clearly indicated the Royal Government's intention to serve as "a strategist and manager of development . . . working with the private sector as a full partner in the rehabilitation and development of the country."[3] The document further stated that "capacity-building is a major undertaking which can only be realised in full cooperation with private investors and the international community."[4]

While acknowledging the many challenges faced by the new government, the *National Programme* was resolutely upbeat and was carefully crafted to elicit financial support from the international donor community. In particular, the document pledged that the Royal Government would pursue economic and financial stability as well as high growth through a combination of fiscal and monetary policies supported by structural reform (backed by the International Monetary Fund). The document further promised that the government's investment budget would target carefully selected priority areas and that, for stability's sake, the fiscal deficit would be kept to what could be externally financed.[5]

The Royal Government committed itself to a three-year Structural Adjustment Program (SAP), drawn up with the IMF and the World Bank, which was implemented over the 1994 to 1996 period.[6] As noted by K. P. Kannan, the "SAP basically addresses issues in macro-economic management with clear targets for reducing the budget deficit, for monetary and financial reforms, liberalisation of external trade and investment, and for public sector reform. Its long term objectives of economic growth are anchored in the development of the private sector and in restricting the role of the public sector."[7]

If the *National Programme* constituted little more than a statement of intent for the Royal Government's utilization of domestic and external resources for national rehabilitation, reconstruction, and development, it did provide a conceptual framework for the transition from rehabilitation to sustainable development and also focused attention on the necessary institutional underpinnings for such transition. Through the national program the Royal Government pledged to address those structural weaknesses that constrained the country's rehabilitation and development. The Royal Government thus undertook to strengthen the base for a market economy, increase absorptive capacity, and prioritize sector-based initiatives. The document also promised due attention to rural development and the development of human resources as key components of the Royal Government's commitment to "stability and security."[8]

Although the Royal Government relied heavily on UNDP technical assistance in the preparation of the *National Programme*, the program's schematic overview reportedly was devised by Keat Chhon, senior minister in charge of rehabilitation and development (figure 4-1). If somewhat simplistic, the overview graphically depicted the main thrusts of the program as well as the interrelationship among the key elements of Cambodia's rehabilitation and development. The overview also grounded Cambodia's rehabilitation and development on a necessary foundation of rural development. The *National Programme* also attempted to give a clear time frame to the rehabilitation and development process: "The period 1994–95 should thus be seen as a period in which the Government, with the assistance of contributing countries and agencies, will continue to implement critical rehabilitation and development projects, and to continue to consolidate past gains. It should be seen, however, as a crucial preparatory period to a comprehensive programme of development."[9]

In outlining sectoral programs, however, the document was somewhat short on detail. Rather, it provided a long wish list of things to do, achieve, or accomplish, all geared "to provide," "to improve," "to foster," or "to upgrade." An annex, Sectoral Programme Highlights, pro-

FIGURE 4-1.   *Schematic Overview of the National Programme to Rehabilitate and Develop Cambodia (NPRD)*

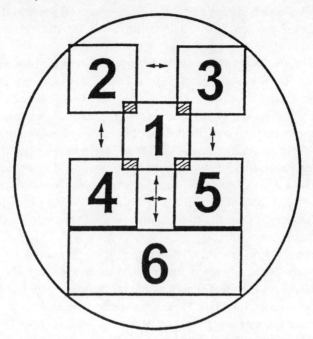

1. *Etat de droit*
Manager of development
Partnership with the private sector

2. *Economic stabilization and structural reforms*

3. *Human resources development*
Health, education
Change of behavior

4. *Rehabilitation and construction of physical infrastructures and facilities*

5. *Integration of Cambodian economy in the region and world economy*
Private investment in agriculture, industry, tourism
Foreign trade

6. *Rural development*
Optimalization of natural resource and environment management

↔ The arrow represents inter-relationship.

○ Security environment
Political stability
Social stability
The well-being of the people is both an objective and a means.

▨ The highlighted areas at the intersection of the five squares represent the interaction of the private sector and the state.

Source: Kingdom of Cambodia, *National Programme to Rehabilitate and Develop Cambodia* (Phnom Penh, February 1994).

vided indicative cost estimates for a range of rehabilitation activities, some quite specific (for example, $U.S.205,000 for a "survey of existing nonformal education activities") but most extremely general (for example, $U.S.150 million for "rehabilitation of 5,000 kilometres of rural roads").[10]

The *National Programme* was very straightforward about the Royal Government's need for substantial foreign development assistance. While promising the "necessary political initiatives," it noted that development assistance would be crucial to the achievement of the Royal Government's many goals, including political reconciliation and overall stability. The government's development vision, as presented through the national program, was well received by the donor community. Delegates to ICORC-2 praised the clear direction set by the document and pledged a total of $U.S.658 million for 1994–95 in support of the Royal Government's plans to promote economic growth, social equity, and political stability.[11]

In February 1995 the Royal Government of Cambodia revisited its plans for the country's rehabilitation and development through a follow-up document entitled *Implementing the National Programme to Rehabilitate and Develop Cambodia*.[12] Like the earlier *National Programme*, the follow-up document was prepared with the assistance of UNDP. *Implementing the National Programme* restated the Royal Government's long-term development vision, including a commitment to sustainable development with equity and social justice. Prepared as the Royal Government's main submission to the March 1995 meeting of ICORC (ICORC-3), the document took stock of the previous year's performance so as to draw lessons learned and to identify the prerequisites for continued and sustainable development, including the further establishment of sectoral policies and priorities over the following eighteen to twenty-four months (that is, to the end of 1997). By elaborating more detailed plans, the government hoped to move beyond rehabilitation and reconstruction to sustainable development.[13]

To achieve such a transition, *Implementing the National Programme* identified six interrelated objectives:

—The rule of law, including the need to promote good governance and the creation of a legal and institutional framework conducive to the emergence of a liberal market economy;

—Economic stabilization and structural reforms (including measures to reduce state expenditure, control inflation, stabilize the domestic currency, privatize state-owned enterprises, increase tax revenues, and balance the national budget);

—Human resource development, including building the capacity of human resources through technical and professional training and the improvement of basic education and health services;

—Rehabilitation of physical infrastructure and facilities;

—Closer integration of the Cambodian economy into the regional and world economies, including further opening of the country to international trade and private foreign investment; and

—Rural development (provisions for food, water, de-mining, credit, shelter, access to markets) and the sustainable management of natural resources.

The follow-up document reaffirmed the Royal Government's determination to improve the well-being of the population, particularly the 85 percent of the population living in rural areas. The document stated that development of the rural economy was the Royal Government's "primary objective," claiming that "the development of Cambodia depends on the development of the countryside" (translation from French) and that rural development would give meaning to the strategic thrusts of the *National Programme*.[14]

Besides outlining the Royal Government's several achievements over the course of its first year as "manager of its own development," the new document highlighted the magnitude of the problems still to be addressed:

> transforming an entire government administration to ensure good governance; establishing a legal base and the means to enforce it; rebuilding a devastated infrastructure; recreating health and education facilities; containing armed insurgency and banditry; rekindling personal trust and social cohesion; consolidating macroeconomic stability and growth; alleviating poverty; and eliminating hunger.[15]

As noted by the document, "tackling any one of these would be difficult enough; tackling all of them simultaneously is positively daunting."[16]

At ICORC-3, the Royal Government of Cambodia asked the donor community to reaffirm its long-term commitment to the government's national reform measures and development programs, as well as to assist in establishing some basic principles to guide the future actions of all concerned. The donor community again responded positively to the Royal Government's stated intention to guide the country toward sustainable development with further financial pledges totaling $U.S.473 million for the 1995–97 period.

At the March 1995 ICORC meeting it was decided that coordination of external assistance to Cambodia, in the future, might be better achieved through a more regular, technical mechanism, with ICORC continuing to act as a periodic forum to discuss other broad issues to reinforce international support for Cambodia. As the result of this decision, the Royal Government asked the World Bank to help organize a Consultative Group (CG) Meeting for Cambodia in mid-1996. A further Cambodia Consultative Group Meeting was held in Paris on July 1–2, 1997.

In addition to reviewing the government's further progress in achieving its broad development objectives, the July 1996 Consultative Group Meeting, held in Tokyo under the cochairmanship of the World Bank and the government of Japan, was presented with two new program areas: civil service reform and reintegration of demobilized military personnel, with tabling of specific costed program proposals. The CG Meeting, which focused on "technical matters" only, provided opportunity for formal presentation of the Royal Government's *Socio-Economic Development Plan (1996–2000)* and a rolling three-year *Public Investment Programme (PIP)*, both prepared with assistance from the Asian Development Bank. The five-year *Socio-Economic Development Plan* outlined the Royal Government's overall development objectives, reiterating its earlier commitment to the achievement of "a fair, just, and peaceful society and, through acceleration of the rate of economic growth, to raise the standard of living of all Cambodians."[17] The plan provided the medium-term policy framework from which indicative sectoral investment levels and specific project proposals might be derived. As Chea Chanto, minister of planning, explained at the May 1996 Donor Consultation Meeting, the focus of the plan was "poverty alleviation, preservation of the environment, human resources development, infrastructure expansion, public administration reform, and a market approach to development through the active promotion by the Government of the comparative advantage of the public and private sectors."[18] The *Socio-Economic Development Plan*, then, represented a continuation and elaboration of the Royal Government's *National Programme to Rehabilitate and Develop Cambodia*.

As a direct complement to the plan, the Public Investment Program detailed the Royal Government's sectoral strategies and policies and the public investment programming process and also provided a list of some $U.S.1.6 billion in public investment projects requiring external support (capital investment, capital investment-related technical assistance, and free-standing technical assistance). The investment program also included project descriptions with project costs, financing requirements, and existing funding pledges. The investment program was to provide a consistent medium-term prioritization of the Royal Government's investment plans and capital financing needs. As stated by the minister of planning, "These public investments have been carefully programmed to fit within the domestic and external resource envelope, while at the same time encouraging additional private investment."[19]

By providing the donor community with a comprehensive catalogue of development projects, the Royal Government hoped to secure sufficient external assistance to complete the transition from rehabilitation to reconstruction so as to be able to focus future efforts on the achievement of sustainable development.[20]

Toward Sustainable Development

According to the commonly held notion of a relief-to-development continuum, the destruction of Cambodia's physical infrastructure and human capital during the Khmer Rouge regime, followed by more than ten years of isolation, deterioration, and neglect, demanded that Cambodia undergo extensive rehabilitation and reconstruction before the country could proceed on a path to sustainable development. Yet in Cambodia everything was seen as a priority, with everything needing to be done at once, and everything dependent on something else. The combination of a lack of resources to meet the country's many needs, insufficient human resources, and an inadequate or absent institutional and administrative framework provided the context for Cambodia's transition from rehabilitation to reconstruction to development.

Given this context, the framework provided by the *National Programme for the Rehabilitation and Development of Cambodia* was well accepted by the international donor community. The document openly and honestly presented Cambodia's many development problems and needs, clear-sightedly outlined the Royal Government's development objectives, and gave priority to key sectors or initiatives. According to

John McAndrew of the Cambodia Development Resource Institute, donor acceptance stemmed from the *National Programme's*

> ability to incorporate elements from several different approaches to development. . . . Whatever the particular donor emphasis, the *National Programme* has sketched the parameters of the development debate in Cambodia. It has also provided an arena for Cambodians and donors of various backgrounds and experience to experiment and work out the contradictions and trade-offs inherent in concrete models of development.[21]

This may, however, be a too charitable view of donor interest and behavior in Cambodia. The program attracted no objections precisely because it served as an all-inclusive statement of intent. Drafted as it was with external technical assistance, the *National Programme to Rehabilitate and Develop Cambodia* said all the kinds of things donors like to hear, using appropriate and developmentally correct jargon. And because it excluded virtually no type or kind of assistance, it allowed donors to provide whatever assistance they wanted and in the form or manner most acceptable to them as donors rather than responding more directly to the priority needs of the country or the wishes of the Cambodian authorities.[22] Hence, it allowed the government of Japan, Cambodia's most generous donor, to continue with the construction of turn-key capital assistance projects, mostly in and around Phnom Penh. Equally, the French government was free to provide support to tertiary training and other institutions using, quite naturally, the French language and French models and systems. Other donors similarly found their niches and provided large amounts of funding, all content that they were contributing to Cambodia's rehabilitation, reconstruction, and development.

In the three years following the end of the UNTAC operation few, if any, real development "choices" were made by the Royal Government (or, indeed, by Cambodians); rather, such choices were made largely in donor capitals or by legions of expatriate technical advisers. Furthermore, because "everything is needed" and given the (very understandable) Cambodian penchant to refuse nothing on offer, no pledge of assistance was refused and the Royal Government's many development priorities remained, for the most part, unranked. The lack of prioritization, beyond such catch-alls as "rural development" or "human resources development," together with the scope of Cambodia's overwhelming need, made it difficult indeed to track or otherwise monitor progress in achieving the Royal Government's broad development objectives.

The lack of choice and absence of Cambodian control over key inputs into the development process were key features of the post-UNTAC "aid market." It was particularly regrettable that despite the *National Programme*, despite the Council for the Development of Cambodia, despite ICORC and other donor consultation mechanisms, external assistance in support of the country's rehabilitation, reconstruction, and development remained, for the most part, quite uncoordinated. At the same time, it is to be recognized that the dynamics of the Cambodian "aid market" also contributed to competition among the Royal Government's main coalition partners.

Given that the country started near one end of the so-called development continuum, given the number of actors, the volume of external assistance resources, and an abbreviated time frame of only a few years, much was quickly achieved toward Cambodia's reconstruction. This is not to say, however, that the coordination of external assistance could not have been managed better or that development resources allocated during the 1992–97 period could not have been employed more efficiently and with greater developmental impact. Nevertheless, Cambodia in the post-UNTAC period made a great leap forward on the transition from rehabilitation to reconstruction and development.

Although rebuilding the country, including its human resource base, might take as much as a generation, post-UNTAC Cambodia was demonstrably on a path toward some form of development—even if the path or its ultimate destination was not necessarily the choice of the Cambodians themselves.

What was clear from the immediate post-UNTAC period was that the Royal Government needed to assert greater control over the country's development future. As emphasized in a January 1996 Working Paper from the Cambodia Development Resource Institute, the overall development framework provided by the *National Programme* needed to be translated into "a more detailed, operational plan for development."[23] The completion in early 1996 of both a five-year Socio-Economic Development Plan and a three-year rolling Public Investment Plan was expected to contribute significantly to the operationalization of the Royal Government's development vision. A major test of the Royal Government's resolve to take greater control of its own development path, however, was its willingness and ability to turn down offers of assistance for activities not specifically included in the investment plan. Similarly, the Royal Government needed to commit itself to realistic performance targets against which it was prepared to be measured, including areas of most interest to the donor community, such as legal and judicial reform, improved revenue collection, civil service, and administrative reform, as well as the observance of human rights and increased transparency in governance.

Chapter 5

The Cambodian
Aid Market

The UNTAC-led peace process led to the establishment of a dynamic "aid market" in Cambodia.[1] From the situation prevailing throughout most of the 1980s, when what little Western assistance as was provided to territorial Cambodia was channeled through a handful of nongovernmental organizations (NGOs) and two or three UN agencies, Cambodia quickly became a focus of international donor assistance. The reasons for such a focus are several.

First of all, the *Declaration on the Rehabilitation and Reconstruction of Cambodia* was an integral part of the *Agreements on a Comprehensive Political Settlement of the Cambodia Conflict*, and the exponential increase in development assistance was intended to promote and reinforce the peace process. (At the same time, it can be argued that however committed to the Paris Agreements, the donor community never really "bought in" to the rehabilitation program outlined through the *Secretary-General's Consolidated Appeal for Cambodia's Immediate Needs and National Rehabilitation*, choosing to ignore a framework of rehabilitation priorities in favor of a broader and self-selected range of activities in what was supposed to be the foundation-laying transitional period.)[2]

A second reason lay in the country's obvious and many needs and the long suffering of its population—both within the country and in the Thai border camps. Few countries had such a tragic, and bloody, recent history. That international power politics had contributed to the Cambodian conflict, and that the problem had so long been allowed to fester, also focused donor attention on Cambodia—if somewhat belatedly. To some extent, the influx of aid resources beginning with the UNTAC period can best be understood as "blood money," expiating guilt over what the international community had wrought in Cambodia.

Another reason, no more salutary, was the fact that Cambodia represented virgin territory for players of the "aid game." Unsullied by previous developmental mistakes (at least at the hand of Western aid practitioners), Cambodia was wide open to new projects, programs, and development experiments. In addition, the preelection absence of a legitimate or recognized government and the inherent weakness of the power-sharing Royal Government which emerged as a result of the UNTAC-sponsored election offered considerable scope for donors to implement a range of activities without government "interference." Aid markets are dynamic; the ready availability of financial resources tended to draw new agencies to undertake new activities or to implement the programs of others. Careers were to be made in Cambodia.

Whatever the reasons for Cambodia's sudden attraction, beginning with the transitional period

> The donor community effectively took possession of the stage. Implementing agencies, which in the past had been strictly controlled by the PRK government, were to all intents and purposes free to take up projects of their choice in just about any part of the country. . . . A country-wide *network system of sub-contracting* between major aid agencies and the NGOs developed. Aid became "competitive" as new donors and implementing agencies entered the scene, carving out their particular niche, at a time when Government counterpart organizations were extremely short of skilled personnel, and absorptive capacity at an ebb.[3]

Underlying such development anarchy was a marked tendency of newly arrived agencies, and most donors, to either assume that Cambodia was without established institutional structures or to explicitly reject such structures as had been put in place by the State of Cambodia (SOC) as somehow illegitimate or invalid. Much of the UNTAC operation similarly had demonstrated a decided anti-SOC bias. Confronted by only one entrenched and functioning "existing administrative structure" rather than the fiction of four equal parties, and extremely conscious of the need to be seen to guarantee a "neutral political environment," UNTAC demanded, expected, and suspected much more of the State of Cambodia than the other three Cambodian factions.

In development terms, this knee-jerk tendency to disregard everything pre-UNTAC resulted in the rejection of much of the hard-won experience of the 1980s, including the resourcefulness and dedication applied to nation building (or rebuilding), training and capacity-building efforts, as well as rural development models piloted with the support of international NGOs. Such disregard also allowed donors and other "purveyors of aid"—as well as FUNCINPEC—to ignore existing (that is, SOC government) mechanisms in favor of direct and often self-styled delivery of programs and services. The UNTAC-led focus on the resettlement and reintegration of returnees and the internally displaced also resulted in a concentration of aid activity in the northwestern provinces. Other needs and other areas of the country, including provinces with a high population density, were all but ignored.

The uncertainties of the UNTAC period resulted in the immobilization of government in Cambodia. As noted by a Swedish International Development Authority (SIDA) evaluation mission (headed by Bernt Bernander, previously director of UNTAC's Rehabilitation Component):

> At provincial and district levels of government, the reduced status of the SOC, the hand-to-mouth budgets and the overwhelming UNTAC presence combined to produce an unprecedented state of disorganization and demoralization, which rendered the government structure incapable of contributing to the relief and rehabilitation effort. A patchwork of interventions by NGOs and international organizations virtually operated in an institutional vacuum.[4]

Importantly, the particularities of the UNTAC-led peace process *created* the institutional vacuum by further diminishing or otherwise handicapping already weak institutional structures. That the SOC's existing administrative structure was, to some extent, put on hold during the transitional period made it all the more difficult to "kick-start" a process of rehabilitation and reconstruction in the post-UNTAC period. The Royal Government's lack of effective control of the development process also was a legacy of the UNTAC rehabilitation experience.

Although the UNTAC period saw the beginning of significant flows of external assistance to Cambodia, the UNTAC Rehabilitation and Economic Affairs Component failed to exert any real influence or control over the rehabilitation process. Its lack of staff and lack of field presence rendered it unable to monitor, much less direct, rehabilitation efforts.

Similarly, the Rehabilitation Component was ineffective in promoting a greater degree of donor coordination and had no mandate to develop any Cambodian aid coordination capability. Despite the elaboration of the *Secretary-General's Consolidated Appeal* and various UNTAC- and UNDP-led efforts toward donor coordination, the major donors rapidly chose their own sectoral priorities, projects, and programs, as well as their own implementation mechanisms and structures.[5]

As for the post-UNTAC period, the SIDA evaluation mission noted as follows:

> In terms of the articulation of development policies and the coordination of external aid, the build-up of government decision-making is necessarily a slow process. The preparation of documents and position papers submitted to ICORC [the International Committee for the Reconstruction of Cambodia] is largely in the hands of the World Bank and UNDP, and the Council for the Development of Cambodia (CDC) created by the new government will only progressively be able to assert its coordinating role.[6]

Given such a "slow process" and particularly given the many anomalies of the UNTAC era, the judgment of the SIDA evaluation mission that "since the demise of the PRK, the government has failed to exercise a coordinating role" seems somewhat harsh.[7] The SOC's central and provincial agencies were not *allowed* to play a role prior to their more or less wholesale transformation into institutions of the Royal Government of Cambodia. Such circumstances, including continued insecurity and ample political ambiguity, made it no surprise that the Royal Government proved incapable of "delivering the goods" with respect to successful or effective management of the rehabilitation and reconstruction process.

Donors were equally, if not more, to blame for the lack of effective coordination. As a whole, donors showed a marked lack of interest in either coordination or being coordinated. Various efforts at coordination permitted the valuable exchange of information, particularly in technical areas such as the energy sector. But the post-UNTAC period featured remarkably little discussion of lessons learned, much less real effort to ensure that donor-funded projects and programs were, as much as possible, congruent or complementary. While the Royal Government could be criticized for not having established a coherent policy and coordination framework for specific sectors or activities, donors made only limited efforts to avoid duplication of effort, much less the elaboration of competing or contradictory programs and activities. Although considerable attention was given to the form of coordination through sectoral and other coordination meetings, there was less attention to the substance of coordination, or what might be called donor "discipline." The lack of such discipline—meaning a real commitment to effective coordination—can be seen as another legacy of the UNTAC (Rehabilitation) experience. At the same time, ineffective coordination and an absence of donor discipline is hardly unique to Cambodia. Rather, coordination of external assistance is something that is often proposed if little practiced.[8]

If the lack of commitment to aid coordination was evident in Phnom Penh, it also extended to the periodic meetings of the International Committee for the Reconstruction of Cambodia (ICORC). These donor meetings proved highly successful in reaffirming donor commitment to Cambodia's reconstruction and development through generous pledges of financial and other assistance. The meetings also provided the opportunity for the Royal Government to signal its plans, achievements, and remaining challenges. The ICORC meetings, including preparatory meetings in Phnom Penh, were far less successful in initiating any real discussion on the direction of Cambodia's development path, much less bringing to the fore particular donor concerns, such as transparency, good governance, and progress toward the rule of law. With a focus on "technical issues," the Consultative Group Meeting held in Tokyo in July 1996 failed to introduce any greater degree of real dialogue on the country's progress toward development and stopped far short of imposing (positive) conditionalities or performance targets on the Royal Government.

Although the Royal Government, with extensive external support and technical assistance, made major steps in developing plans and priorities and elaborating strategies in the post-UNTAC period, such effort "cost" the Royal Government very little. The donor community was exceedingly generous to Cambodia and, at least as of the end of 1996, had demanded very little from the Royal Government in terms of its performance.[9] Without clearly articulated performance targets, however, there was the danger that a donor or donors might suddenly change the "rules of the game."[10]

The relative absence of coordination served donor interests; beginning with the UNTAC period donors largely supported or funded whatever they wanted. The lack of effective coordination also was somewhat advantageous to the Royal Government, in that the laissez-faire approach kept donor assistance flowing and demanded relatively little from the government. The danger, of course, was that donors, who are fickle at best, might suddenly make their aid conditional, introduce new performance criteria, might simply decide to allocate their assistance to other countries or regions with more "strategic" importance than Cambodia, or might choose to focus on different development priorities or dictate new implementation practices.

The pressure to disburse aid funds, combined with the country's lack of absorptive capacity—particularly the shortage of trained government counterparts—conditioned the way in which donors programmed assistance. The Japanese, for example, focused mostly on large-scale, turnkey capital investment projects. Other donors resorted to "project implementation units" or PIUs to facilitate implementation of externally financed activities. Such PIUs had mixed success, to some extent in direct proportion to the size of the project or program being implemented in that larger projects, and larger project budgets, commanded greater profile or attention from recipient ministries.

Most PIUs, however, required the designation of competent and sufficiently senior Cambodian counterpart staff, preferably on a full-time basis. The lack of such staff, or the fact that a single counterpart might be assigned to a number of projects or donor PIUs, further compromised the effective implementation of donor-funded programs. As noted below, separate or parallel implementation structures do not, generally, contribute to capacity building. Rather, they promote the development of parallel structures as well as aid dependency.

The peculiar, double-headed nature of the Royal (coalition) Government also conditioned the manner in which external assistance was used in the post-UNTAC period and also must be factored into any examination of the Cambodian "aid market." As a consequence of power sharing, all ministries and government institutions were bifurcated, some to a greater extent than others, depending on particular interpersonal relationships. In a few cases, ministers and their secretaries of state (from an opposing political party) worked reasonably well together. Normally this meant that a FUNCINPEC minister or secretary of state adopted a low-key or noninterfering role, leaving much of the technical work of the ministry to his CPP colleague and the CPP-dominated administration. In other cases, however, politicians of different parties refused to talk to one another and surrounded themselves with their own set of advisers and policymakers, including foreign-funded technical assistance personnel. In such cases, all policy and all work, including "development work," was highly politicized, with less attention to the impact on or contribution to the country's development objectives than to narrow or short-term political benefit.

Trends in External Assistance

The Royal Government of Cambodia's *Development Cooperation Report 1994-1995* provided interesting information about trends in external assistance pledged and disbursed during the 1992–95 "rehabilitation" period. The *Report*, prepared with assistance from UNDP but issued by the Council for the Development of Cambodia, summarized all multilateral, bilateral, and nongovernmental assistance provided to Cambodia from 1992 to 1995.[11] Updated "Summary Tables" from the 1995–96 version of the *Report* were provided to a Donor Consultation Meeting held in Phnom Penh in May 1996 in preparation for the July 1996 Consultative Group Meeting in Tokyo. Whereas the 1994–95 *Report*, issued in June 1995, projected disbursements to the end of 1995, the "Summary Tables" provided actual reported disbursement figures for the 1992–95 period. Unless otherwise noted, the figures used in the following paragraphs are taken from the tables.[12]

According to the "Summary Tables," donor *pledges* over the four-year period totaled some $U.S.2.29 billion. Total *disbursements*, however, represented only 61 percent of total pledges at some $U.S.1.394 billion.[13] Such disbursements included $U.S.962 million (69 percent) from bilateral donors, $U.S.398.5 million (28.5 percent) from multilateral organizations, and $U.S.33.6 million from nongovernmental organizations (2.5 percent). Although the average rate of disbursements to pledges by bilateral organizations was some 71 percent, the disbursement rate by multilateral organizations over the 1992–95 period was only 41 percent (table 5-1).

In terms of types of assistance, the tables indicated that investment project assistance represented the largest single category of assistance, with $U.S.391.6 million or 28.1 percent of total disbursements (table 5-2). When taken together, the categories "food aid" and "emergency and relief assistance," however, accounted for an almost equal amount of external assistance, with $U.S.360 million in disbursements over the

TABLE 5-1.   *External Assistance Disbursements by Donors, 1992–95*

Thousands of $U.S.

Donor	1992	1993	1994	1995	Total
Bilateral	207,571	251,796	225,878	277,391	962,636
Multilateral	45,396	71,209	108,952	172,940	398,497
Nongovernmental organization	1,068	5,322	17,949	9,259	33,598
Total disbursements	254,035	328,327	352,779	459,590	1,394,731

Source: Kingdom of Cambodia, *National Programme to Rehabilitate and Develop Cambodia* (Phnom Penh, February 1994).

1992–95 period, nearly half ($U.S.167.7 million) disbursed during 1992 alone, presumably in support of the UNTAC repatriation operation.

"Free-standing technical cooperation," at $U.S.345.9 million, accounted for 24.8 percent of total external assistance disbursements. When combined with $U.S.75.4 million in "investment-related technical cooperation (5.4 percent), technical assistance—largely constituting the salaries and benefits of expatriate technical assistance personnel—represented almost the same volume of assistance as had been directed to each of the investment project assistance and the food aid and emergency and relief assistance categories. The remaining category of assistance, budgetary aid/balance of payments support, accounted for a total of $U.S.221.7 million or 15.9 percent of total external assistance disbursements over the 1992–95 period.

Besides the total percentage allocation by category, it is interesting to note how these allocations changed over each of the four years. Although four years is too short a time period to confirm any real trends in the allocation of external assistance to Cambodia, the significant reduction in the amount of assistance directed to the food aid and emergency and relief assistance categories—from 66 percent of total disbursements in 1992 to only 11.4 per cent in 1995—provided some evidence of a shift from emergency or rehabilitation-type assistance toward donor support of activities promoting longer-term reconstruction and development.

Disbursement figures also revealed that external assistance had not been allocated equally among the country's provinces or regions. The capital, Phnom Penh, with approximately 10 percent of the country's

TABLE 5-2. *External Assistance Disbursements by Category, 1992–95*
Thousands of $U.S.

Type of assistance	1992	%	1993	%	1994	%	1995	%	Totals 1992–95	Overall percentage allocation
Investment project assistance	32,758	12.89	67,471	20.56	122,511	34.73	168,901	36.75	391,641	28.08
Free-standing technical cooperation	43,289	17.04	79,040	24.07	97,619	27.67	125,974	27.41	345,922	24.80
Emergency and relief assistance	128,499	50.58	69,704	21.23	31,756	9.00	48,670	10.59	278,629	19.98
Budgetary aid/balance of payments support	1,410	0.56	73,486	22.38	69,170	19.61	77,671	16.90	221,737	15.90
Food aid	39,227	15.44	26,034	7.93	12,394	3.51	3,728	0.81	81,383	5.84
Investment-related technical cooperation	8,855	3.49	12,589	3.83	19,333	5.48	34,644	7.54	75,421	5.41
Totals	254,038	100	328,324	100	352,783	100	459,588	100	1,394,733	100

Source: Kingdom of Cambodia, *Development Cooperation Report 1995–1996*. The *1995–96 Report* "based on information submitted to donor agencies as of 30 March 1996" indicated a $U.S.28 million increase in total disbursements over the four-year period compared with the end-1995 projections of the preceding *Report* (the *1994–95 Report* was released in July 1995 with total disbursements projected to the end of 1995). More surprisingly, the *1995–96 Report* indicated considerable variation in total disbursements by type or classification of assistance. For example, whereas the *1994–95 Report* projected that disbursements for "free-standing technical assistance" would total $U.S.266 million by end-1995, the *1995–96 Report* gave a figure of $U.S.345.92 million, a difference of nearly $U.S.80 million. Similarly, the *1994–95 Report* projected $U.S.259.75 million in disbursements for "budgetary aid/balance of payments support"; the *1995–96 Report*, issued only nine months later, indicated that total "budgetary aid" disbursements were only $U.S.221.74 million, a decrease of some $U.S.38 million.

population, received nearly one-third (30.8 per cent) of total external assistance in 1994, and as much as 37 percent of total assistance in 1995.[14] Countrywide programs or activities supported through donor assistance (which to a considerable extent were staffed and managed from the capital) accounted for 53 percent of total external assistance in 1994 and only 47 percent of total disbursements in 1995. Apart from Phnom Penh, only Battambang and Siem Reap provinces received more than 2 percent of total external assistance disbursements in 1995, with fourteen of the country's twenty-one provinces and municipalities receiving less than 1 percent of total disbursements—some considerably less than 1 percent.[15]

In its presentation to ICORC-3 in March 1995 the World Bank signaled the impact of the skewed distribution of external assistance, citing as an example the fact that in 1994, 43 percent of donor assistance to the health sector had been directed to Phnom Penh. According to the World Bank's calculations, per capita health spending in Phnom Penh in 1994 was $U.S.36.00, compared with only $U.S.5.00 in neighboring Kandal province or the northwestern provinces of Battambang and Banteay Meanchey. Donor assistance to the health sector in the rest of the country—representing some 80 percent of the country's total population—was less than $U.S.2.00 per person. The World Bank similarly found that twice as much international assistance to the education sector had been directed to tertiary education (almost exclusively focused in Phnom Penh) compared with allocations for primary education, with virtually no donor resources having been directed to the secondary school level.[16]

Despite the skewed allocation of external development assistance, by 1996 there was considerable evidence of rehabilitation, reconstruction, and development activity throughout the country—even if much of this activity was focused in provincial capitals or other "urban" areas. Nowhere was such "development" so apparent, however, than in Phnom Penh. The construction boom that began in anticipation of the UNTAC operation continued beyond UNTAC, including the wholesale demolition of older buildings and the construction in many parts of the city of office buildings, commercial buildings, and luxury villas, as well as scores of hotels. Although much of Phnom Penh's former colonial charm had forever vanished, the capital's broad, tree-lined boulevards—supplemented by new, landscaped parks bearing the names of the country's leading politicians—proclaimed the city's once and future glories.

Surveys indicated that more than 67 percent of Phnom Penh's inhabitants used at least some electricity, compared with only 3 percent of rural inhabitants. By the end of 1996, however, no fewer than eleven major electricity projects were projected to come on-stream in Phnom Penh. Although a planned citywide grid distribution system was not expected to be put in place before the end of 1997, Phnom Penh—formerly subject to frequent power interruptions or dependent on stand-alone (and noisy) generators—promised soon to be awash with electrical power.[17]

Whereas in the late 1980s the most common traffic on the capital's streets was Chinese-made bicycles, in the post-UNTAC era the city's main avenues were clogged with motor vehicles, including many luxury cars competing with motorcycles, bicycles, and *cyclo-pousses* (bicycle rickshaws). The range of consumer goods available—at least for those with money (that is, $U.S.)—was astonishing. Mini-marts and restaurants had proliferated. The narrow isthmus beyond the Changwar Bridge ("the broken bridge," restored after the May 1993 election with Japanese grant assistance) was once farmland; with the reopening of the bridge in 1994 it became Phnom Penh's restaurant district, with literally hundreds of restaurants, including many that would not be out of place in any modern Asian capital—and all filled with customers.

A 1993–94 socioeconomic survey indicated that the average monthly household expenditure in Phnom Penh was a startling $U.S.365, more than twice Cambodia's estimated yearly per capita income.[18] Such a figure showed how skewed were the benefits of development in Cambodia. The monthly expenditure figure for Phnom Penh also suggested huge income disparities in the capital. Although Cambodian households typically have earned income from a variety of sources, a government worker in 1996 was only able to contribute a salary of some $U.S.30-40 a month to the household income. A *cyclo-pousse* driver earned only a fraction of that. A 1994 survey similarly demonstrated that expenditure on education and cultural services was twice as high in Phnom Penh as in the countryside, with a comparable disparity for years of schooling.[19]

In 1996 the concentration of development activity—and wealth—in the capital was symbolically displayed by the night-time beacon atop the Malaysian-owned *Naga Island* casino-boat moored behind the Cambodiana Hotel at the confluence of the Mekong, Tonle Sap, and Bassac rivers. The beacon nightly advertised Phnom Penh's resurgent affluence. It remained unclear, however, whether it signaled a bright future for Cambodia and all Cambodians, or whether it in fact was a harbinger of growing class-based disparity as well as a distancing of Phnom Penh and its inhabitants—including the country's politicians—from the realities of rural Cambodia and its people.

The skewed allocation of external assistance, however, was not a new phenomenon for Cambodia or, indeed, for many developing countries. Throughout most of the 1980s, much of the very limited Western assistance was concentrated in Phnom Penh and a few key provinces. Such concentration was the result partly of access (by virtue of government policy, the poor state of the country's transportation infrastructure, and, in many provinces, continued insecurity) and partly because of the necessary focusing of limited resources in support of national institutions and nationally directed programs. The 1994 SIDA evaluation mission noted the following:

> The imbalance in the dispensation of aid was supposed to end with the peace accords in October 1991, but in fact continued, with most donors concentrating their assistance on the western parts of Cambodia, and areas where most of the refugees planned to resettle. . . . Even after the signing of the peace accords, which called for balanced assistance to those most in need throughout the country, these imbalances continue, carried forward by their own momentum.[20]

Although noting the particular political antecedents for a geographically skewed distribution of foreign development assistance in Cambodia, the SIDA mission suggested that such imbalances are inherent in the provision of international development assistance as a whole with a decided tendency to favor urban areas over rural or to fund tertiary educational institutions rather than primary schools.[21]

As was pointed out in the 1994–95 *Development Cooperation Report*, the skewed pattern of external assistance disbursements ran counter to the Royal Government's stated rural development priority—and the needs of 85 percent of the Cambodian population living in rural areas. Fearing the negative effects that could result from these regional imbalances (such as a rural exodus to urban areas, reduced productive activity, reduction of trade, increased unemployment, and so on) the Royal Government called on donors to "quickly prioritize the reallocation of external assistance to the benefit, notably, of rural development (such as for basic infrastructure for transportation, farm-to-market roads, irrigation systems, basic education and health services)."[22] As is examined below, however, the Royal Government allowed donors, more by conscious decision than by default, to plan and implement rural development interventions, including the range of activities and the selection of target areas.

A 1996 examination of bilateral and multilateral emergency and development assistance undertaken by the Cambodia Development Resource Institute (CDRI) in collaboration with the Cooperation Committee for Cambodia (CCC) suggested that the geographical imbalance of aid in Cambodia could be at least partly explained by adherence to an open-market strategy that concentrated infrastructure development in growth centers like Phnom Penh to attract private investment, with expected spin-offs in terms of employment creation, the expansion of local markets, and the creation of capital for further investment. As noted by the study, however,

> Coordination between public investment and private investment in Cambodia is weak and donors may be unwittingly subsidizing investment activities that do not produce long-term and broadly based benefits. The impact of investment projects on job creation, local market expansion, capital generation for in-country re-investment, and environmental degradation needs to be carefully addressed.[23]

In addition to maldistribution by geographic area, the allocation of external assistance to the country's different sectors also was skewed. According to the 1995–1996 *Development Cooperation Report*, "Summary Tables," between 1992 and 1995 nearly one-fifth (19.65 percent) of all disbursements were directed to the humanitarian aid and relief sector. Although significant disbursements to the transport sector (13.51 percent) and the economic management sector (10.21 percent) were understandable given the priority attached, in practice, to rehabilitation of key transportation infrastructure and macroeconomic stability by both the Royal Government and the donor community, disproportionately small allocations to the education and human resources development (8.39 percent) and health sectors (6.38 percent) were somewhat surprising given the stated emphasis on capacity building as well as the acknowledged need for improved social sector services. Whereas the 1994–95 *Development Cooperation Report* indicated that only $U.S.147.7 million or 10.65 percent of total projected disbursements had been directed to area-based or rural development, the summary tables indicated that $U.S.178.1 million or 12.96 percent of all external assistance had been directed to rural development activities over the 1992–95 period, reflecting a slight shift in favor of rural (or, rather, nonurban) projects and programs (table 5-3).

This imbalance partly reflects the priorities contained in, and accorded to, the Structural Adjustment Program (SAP). Although the SAP was fairly successful in controlling inflation, stabilizing the exchange rate, and stimulating short-term economic growth,[24] by eliminating monetary financing of the budget deficit (that is, through the printing of money), it restricted the already extremely low levels of government expenditures on basic public services and rural assistance programs. It might be argued, therefore, that the SAP may have served to undermine the goals of human development outlined in the *National Programme to Rehabilitate and Develop Cambodia*, which emphasized rural development and the extension of health, education, and social services.[25]

It also is to be noted that with major rural development initiatives funded by UNDP/ OPS/ CARERE, the European Union, the World Bank, and other donors, a further increase in disbursement to the area/rural development sector was anticipated for 1995–96. Similarly, large multilateral loan disbursements to the education and health sectors were expected to alter the pattern of external assistance allocations by sector. At the same time, because a large proportion of externally funded projects and programs consisted of Phnom Penh-based technical assistance, an appreciable lag time was likely before changes in sectoral allocations might be translated into effective development at a provincial, much less a grass-roots, level (table 5-3).

Technical Assistance

A 1996 assessment of technical assistance posed the question: "Does technical assistance/technical cooperation help Cambodia?"[26] Given the sheer volume of technical assistance as a percentage of total external assistance disbursements, as well as the different forms of technical assistance and widely different implementation arrangements, the effectiveness of technical assistance and its overall impact for indigenous capacity building became perhaps the paramount issue of the Cambodian "aid market."

TABLE 5-3. *External Assistance Disbursements by Sector, 1992–95*

Thousands of $U.S.

Development sector	1992	1993	1994	1995	Total disbursements	Percentage allocation
Humanitarian aid and relief	141,058	53,756	47,548	27,630	269,992	19.65
Transport	8,682	45,126	57,743	74,021	185,572	13.51
Area/rural development	35,103	43,651	28,542	70,806	178,102	12.96
Economic management	542	2,352	72,738	63,405	139,037	10.12
Development administration	9,937	71,965	17,160	23,142	122,204	8.90
Education/human resources development	15,763	28,834	28,818	41,871	115,286	8.39
Agriculture, forestry, fisheries	16,875	27,528	24,269	34,600	103,272	7.52
Health	15,483	28,867	20,788	22,451	87,589	6.38
Social development	5,571	15,782	27,095	37,667	86,115	6.27
Energy	1,057	7,498	23,702	38,707	70,964	5.17
Communications	860	1,350	2,086	3,635	7,931	0.58
Natural resources	315	1,236	1,541	1,035	4,127	0.30
Disaster preparedness	2,359	220	0	0	2,579	0.188
Domestic trade	300	0	297	273	870	0.063
Industry	132	10	7	0	149	0.011
International trade	0	0	0	58	58	0.004
Totals	254,037	328,175	352,334	439,301	1,373,847	100.00

Source: Kingdom of Cambodia, *Development Cooperation Report 1995–1996*. As discussed in the source to table 5-2, the two successive *Development Cooperation Reports* demonstrated significant unexplained variations in total disbursements by development sector. For example, the 1995–96 *Report* recorded a $U.S.30.37 million increase in disbursements for "area/rural development" compared with the end-1995 projections in the earlier *Report*. Other development sectors showed similar wide variations, including "economic management" (a $U.S.20.92 million decrease), "transport" (a $U.S.12.30 million decrease), and "social development" (a $U.S.10.07 million increase). In addition, the 1995–96 *Report* provided no explanation as to why there was a $U.S.20 million difference between total disbursements by type of assistance ($U.S.1,394,733,000) and total disbursements by development sector ($U.S.1,373,847,000).

In considering the effectiveness and impact of technical assistance in post-UNTAC Cambodia, it is necessary to consider the types of technical assistance provided to the country. In its *Development Cooperation Report*, the Royal Government made a distinction only between "free-standing technical cooperation" and "investment-related technical cooperation" and appeared less interested in the amount or effectiveness of such assistance than in the terms under which it was provided, stating a clear preference for technical cooperation through grant assistance rather than as part of concessional loans.

Further and more important distinctions can be made based on the specific purposes of technical cooperation and the nature and scope of work performed by expatriate technical assistance personnel. In post-UNTAC Cambodia, donors provided at least three different types of technical assistance: substitution technical assistance, policy-related technical assistance, and technical assistance for institutional development. None of these different types of technical cooperation are mutually exclusive; indeed, policy-related and institutional development technical assistance are differentiated largely by the degree to which they involve counterpart training or other aspects of capacity building.

As implied by its name, *substitution technical assistance* is intended to substitute for a perceived lack of national capacity. Such assistance, then, is used to address gaps in national capacity by providing technical expertise to undertake specific tasks or to oversee certain processes. In Cambodia, substitution technical assistance was used to guide the overall rehabilitation and reconstruction process, to support the implementation of public sector programs, and to plan and manage specific donor-funded activities. Substitution technical assistance also was used to undertake sectoral reviews and to assist in the development of policy frameworks; examine institutional structures, including the establishment of new institutions (for example, the Council for the Development of Cambodia); draft legislation or other implementation regulations, and develop standards or protocols for certain activities. Substitution technical assistance similarly was utilized in the establishment and operation of project management units or other similar bodies charged with the execution of donor-funded activities.

Although "substitution" implies replacement at some point in time as national (counterpart) capacity is trained or otherwise developed, in the immediate post-UNTAC period much substitution technical assistance focused on day-to-day project implementation. Inadequate attention to counterpart training and capacity building perpetuated the need for further technical assistance, resulting in further lucrative consultancies for legions of (mostly Western) technical assistance personnel. The rapid postelection scaling up of donor-funded project and program activity also necessitated increased amounts of such assistance. As expatriate technical expertise does not come cheaply, technical cooperation absorbed nearly a third of all external assistance disbursements in the post-UNTAC period.

A variant of substitution technical assistance, focusing on policy or strategic options, was relatively absent in post-UNTAC Cambodia. Such assistance is used to provide specific, often very technical, expertise as well as to present policy options or "best practices." In the case of Cambodia, however, the Royal Government felt the need to proceed quickly and also lacked sufficient institutional strength to request or manage policy-based expertise or assistance, as well as to use specific policy advice to develop its own programs or activities. In the post-UNTAC period, then, the Royal Government relied mostly on substitution kinds of technical assistance, with a marked tendency to defer, with little question, to the recommendations of donor-funded advisers with little weighing of options or consideration of alternative courses of action.

Technical assistance for institutional development, or IDTA, is necessarily more long term in that such assistance is directed to the establishment or upgrading of institutions through institutional reform and capacity building. As noted by the World Bank, "the emphasis of IDTA is on longer-term goals (such as the training of individuals and the transfer of knowledge) which are time-consuming and for which progress is uneven and difficult to measure."[27] IDTA normally includes a strong training component, including off-shore training of specialized personnel, and features what could be considered nurturing support of indigenous capacity. For the most part, Cambodia as of 1997 had not yet graduated from direct, hands-on substitution technical assistance to the more sophisticated or advanced IDTA, partly because of the country's extremely low level of human resources and partly the postelection imperative to demonstrate rapid progress along the "relief to development continuum."

As outlined above, nearly a third of all external assistance disbursements between 1992 and 1995 constituted technical cooperation, with 24.8 percent of total disbursements directed to free-standing technical assistance and 5.4 percent to investment-related (that is, project-specific) technical cooperation activities. As shown in table 5-1, disbursements for technical cooperation showed steady growth over the four-year period. Such growth was consistent with the development and implementation of bilateral and multilateral programs of assistance as well as Cambodia's progress from relief to reconstruction and development activities. The concentration of donor assistance in the technical assistance sectors also was consistent with Cambodia's lack of trained human resources, widely recognized as the country's chief constraint to long-term, sustainable development—apart, of course, from the need for ever-increasing amounts of development financing.

In recognizing Cambodia's human resources gap, the 1994–95 *Development Cooperation Report* suggested

> It may be advisable for donors to continue, over the next 3-5 years, with direct delivery of services and direct execution of projects either by donor staff or by NGOs, while Cambodian counterparts are still in the process of enhancing their own knowledge and implementation skills. In the same vein, donors should progressively involve their national counterparts in the initial design, development, presentation for approval, and in the final implementation and evaluation of investment projects and other funded programs.[28]

This statement is interesting in at least two ways. First, it implicitly acknowledged that as of mid-1995 "national counterparts" had not been involved in the design, approval, or implementation of donor-funded activities. Second, it demonstrated a surprising but nonetheless very real disconnection between the continued direct delivery of projects and services by external actors and a process of indigenous capacity building. How could Cambodians be expected to enhance their "knowledge and implementation skills," much less ownership of the country's development process, if not through active involvement in ongoing development activities? The *Development Cooperation Report* thus almost suggested that capacity building was a process separate from the delivery of external assistance, and that Cambodians would only be able to become fully involved once they had magically assumed the necessary knowledge and skills. The disappointing adoption by the Royal Government of such a paternalistic and patronizing approach to capacity building well reflected the kind of dependence which results from a too-sudden flow of external assistance.

To enhance capacity building, the *Report* called for "fast-track" train-ing and education of selected Cambodian counterparts as part of for-eign-funded project design and cost structures. Given that lack of capacity had long been identified as a key, if not the key, development constraint in Cambodia, it was surprising as well as disappointing that the Royal Government felt the need to suggest the importance of such training and education or that donors should not have more promi-nently and explicitly provided for such capacity building as part of their support to the newly established government.

It should be noted that the UNTAC experience set the stage for reliance, if not dependence, on foreign technical assistance. Although the Supreme National Council, including representatives of the four warring Cambodian factions, was vested with the sovereignty of Cam-bodia during the transitional period, the United Nations Transitional Authority in Cambodia itself was very much an externally imposed and foreign-driven operation. UNTAC had no specific mandate to train or otherwise build the capacity of the "four existing administrations" or Cambodian nationals. Any training that took place during UNTAC was narrowly directed to the various components of the UNTAC operation, with little thought to the country's longer-term human resource needs. Furthermore, there was a decided tendency during the UNTAC period to avoid being seen to favor in any way the State of Cambodia admini-stration—the only one of the four existing administrative structures with any real administrative capacity and experience. Based on the false premise of equality among the four factions, and charged with ensuring a neutral political environment, UNTAC both expected and demanded more of the State of Cambodia, including a far greater degree of both "direct" and "indirect" control and oversight, than was exercised over any of the other three factions. Although justified in terms of a "free and fair" electoral result, it can be argued that the externally driven peace process penalized the State of Cambodia for its proven administrative strength without any clear understanding or acknowledgment that the duly elected government would of necessity depend heavily on the SOC's administrative structure to carry out the business of government, including the implementation of any program of rehabilitation and development.

The UNTAC experience, then, combined with postelection uncer-tainty pending the emergence of a new political order, had the un-wanted effect of diminishing the capacity and confidence of an administration already suffering a critical lack of trained and qualified human resources. Such a situation, compounded by profound mutual distrust among the new government's coalition partners, paved the way for uncritical acceptance of massive amounts of foreign technical assistance.

Using the World Bank's timeframe and phasing, the immediate post-UNTAC or recovery period demanded substantial substitution technical cooperation, with expatriate "advisers" undertaking the implementation of specific technical tasks, including routine administrative tasks, program delivery, and the planning and execution of policy studies and analysis, including sectoral analysis. Substitution technical assistance was particularly important in this early period to help the Royal Government, as well as the donor community, become better informed about the country's rehabilitation and development needs, information not necessarily readily available because of the country's long international isolation and the peculiarities of the UNTAC mandate. More important, expatriate technical assistance was required to translate such needs into language and project formats understood by donors. The prime example of such substitution technical cooperation was UNDP's provision of technical assistance in the elaboration of the *National Programme to Rehabilitate and Develop Cambodia*. Similarly, substitution technical assistance was used to plan and undertake several sectoral reviews that were used—chiefly by foreign advisers—in the development of policy and program frameworks. Examples of such policy development, all completed before the March 1995 ICORC Meeting, included an Agricultural Development Options Review, a position paper for the Development of the Energy Sector, and the Asian Development Bank-led review of Cambodia's education sector, including the development of a Basic Education Investment Plan.

In its report for the March 1995 ICORC Conference, the World Bank cautioned, "At present, the Government and its international partners are still largely in the difficult first phase where so much needs to be done and there is a danger that too much will be attempted."[29] The World Bank also noted that substitution technical assistance was essential to the launching of an effective rehabilitation and reconstruction program:

In the first phase, substantial substitution technical assistance will continue to play a critical role, as will related mechanisms such as project implementation units or other special and temporary administrative ar-rangements—many of which will be supported by donor funding. The creation of these enclaves within the public sector is inevitable in the present context in order to achieve the needed policies, programs, and other outputs. Given the lack of skills and the working conditions of the civil service, an enclave approach complemented by extensive substitution technical assistance and training is essential and will still be needed, on a reduced and more intermittent basis, after the capacity building phase has begun.[30]

The World Bank's 1995 report noted that the Royal Government "continues to depend heavily on outsiders funded by foreign agencies to both spearhead the recovery program and perform routine tasks."[31] Although acknowledging that the Royal Government had begun to plan for the medium-term to long-term transition to a self-sufficient bureaucracy and a revitalized private sector, it suggested that Cambodia would require substantial substitution technical assistance "for a long time." Indeed, the World Bank proposed an indicative strategy for capacity building based on a three-phase, fifteen-year time horizon. In the first, or "prerequisite phase," substitution technical assistance would be used to identify and meet the country's most basic and es-sential economic, social, and administrative needs as well as to de-velop an agenda for the next, "capacity building and institutional development phase." Only during the final, "consolidation phase" would the Government begin to manage its own development at all levels.[32]

The fifteen-year time horizon suggested by the World Bank probably represented a realistic, although still ambitious, time frame; Cambo-dia's twenty years of destruction, isolation, and neglect could not be remedied overnight. Development, and particularly institutional devel-opment, is necessarily a long process that can take decades. Even if such a process can, to some extent, be accelerated through key interventions, it cannot be abbreviated or condensed in the absence of several precon-ditions, including a sound human resources base. In the case of Cambo-dia, the fifteen-year time frame might well prove overly optimistic should the Royal Government not urgently undertake a comprehensive examination of the country's mid- to long-term human resource devel-opment needs, and then—with assistance from its development part-ners—specifically and systematically begin to address those needs.

According to the World Bank's 1995 assessment, within a period of a few years the prerequisites for successful capacity building would begin to be in place, particularly within those individual administrative units that had benefited from donor-funded substitution technical assistance. Then, suggested the Bank, substitution technical assistance gradually could be reduced in favor of technical assistance for institutional development as the Royal Government became more responsible and accountable for the implementation of donor-funded development activities.

Unfortunately, however, as of late 1996 there was little evidence that donor-funded technical assistance had included much in the way of counterpart training or other capacity building, with much greater resources having been invested in substitution technical assistance. If the need for such assistance was obvious, given the need to launch a program of rehabilitation and reconstruction, it highlighted an essential paradox: as much as Cambodia urgently required external technical assistance because of the extremely low level of its own human resources base, any delay in training, upgrading, and capacity building of indigenous capacity would further delay the country's ability to take charge of its development.

There could be no argument that Cambodia in the post-UNTAC period required—and would continue to require—considerable substitution technical assistance. At the same time, it was necessary to consider the cost and consequences of such assistance, particularly with respect to Cambodia's development needs.

As already noted, technical cooperation absorbed nearly a third of all external assistance disbursements over the 1992–95 period. Totaling more than $U.S.421 million, such assistance represented a key contribution to Cambodia's rehabilitation, reconstruction, and development. At the same time, the post-UNTAC onslaught of externally funded technical assistance personnel raised several questions. Given the almost unlimited scale of Cambodia's many needs, how much more technical cooperation could have been used, particularly in the face of Cambodia's supposed problem of absorptive capacity? Might such resources, in many cases amounting to $U.S.150,000 or more per expatriate technical adviser, have been better used to service other priority needs? Could less technical assistance have been used more effectively and to greater effect? Who determined the need for such assistance? Who identified and recruited the technical assistance personnel? To what extent were the Cambodian authorities involved in decisions concerning technical assistance personnel? How well developed were individual terms of reference and with what performance criteria? What degree of oversight was provided for technical assistance personnel and under whose responsibility?

These are pertinent questions, but questions without easy or definitive answers. It must be noted, however, that the provision of technical assistance to post-UNTAC Cambodia was uncoordinated in the extreme. In the immediate postelection period, donors began to place technical assistance advisers in ministries and other key institutions. Although such substitution technical assistance was key to the launch of donor-funded initiatives, the recruitment and fielding of expatriate personnel was undertaken with little consultation with the Cambodian authorities, in the absence of any kind of strategy, and with little or no coordination between and among donor agencies. One senior Cambodian official was quoted as complaining, "Most donors, on their own, project our needs, fix time-schedules and assign technical advisors. We face considerable difficulties to convince the donors on the specifics of our needs and the sequencing of that support."[33]

In many cases, there appeared to have been virtually no consultation with the Royal Government—advisers were introduced (and expected to be accommodated with offices and counterpart staff) as they arrived in-country. Many donor-funded advisers were appointed with only limited terms of reference and thus had to create their own job descriptions and workplans in a complicated, often byzantine, and increasingly politicized environment. With their salaries and generous benefit packages fully funded by donor agencies, not all had resources at their disposal for counterpart training so as to be able to even begin to transfer their skills. And although well meaning, many donor-funded substitution technical advisers were narrowly charged with the planning and implementation of specific donor-funded activities almost independent of the larger work of the development of sectoral policy orientations and national program frameworks.

The uncoordinated character of substitution-forms of technical assistance provided by donors in the post-UNTAC period represented perhaps the most prominent feature of the Cambodian "aid market." The presence of so many well-paid and presumably well-qualified and experienced technical assistance personnel—the overwhelming majority of whom were based in Phnom Penh—quickly created its own dynamic, a frenzied subculture of missions, meetings, and project documents. Just as the UNTAC "occupation" produced the desired result of an internationally recognized Cambodian government, so the "invasion" by an army of technical assistance personnel resulted in innumerable position papers and strategy documents and "national programs" directed to Cambodia's rehabilitation and reconstruction. What was disturbing about the hectic pace of such activity was that it remained, to a great extent, externally driven and externally controlled. And, in some aspects, it was divorced from either the Royal Government or Cambodians, with the legions of expatriate advisers spending more time meeting and dealing with one another than with their Cambodian counterparts.

As of mid-1996 the Council for the Development of Cambodia, charged with oversight of the rehabilitation and reconstruction of Cambodia, had established no registry or list of donor-funded technical assistance personnel assigned to ministries and other government bodies. Nor had the Royal Government made any effort to review, in any systematic fashion, the terms of reference of externally provided technical assistance. No system was in place to monitor the work of such personnel, including any measurement of success such as skills transfer or counterpart training. No effort was made to evaluate the costs and benefits of technical assistance against the country's other priority needs.

In his January 1996 assessment of external development assistance to Cambodia, development analyst John McAndrew stated:

> The provision of expatriate technical assistance has the potential to equip Cambodians with the technical and managerial skills needed to undertake development activities in the short-term. It also holds the potential to stifle local initiatives or simply to be irrelevant. For these reasons the effectiveness and appropriateness of expatriate assistance have to be assessed on a regular basis. Equally important as expatriate advice is the provision of technical assistance as educational and training opportunities. This form of technical assistance has the capacity to equip Cambodians with knowledge and learning for long-term, self-reliant development.[34]

Insufficient counterpart training resulted in the failure, or at least only limited success, of some donor-funded activities. One development analyst suggested that "the 'graveyard' of failed technical assistance/technical cooperation is now filled with projects and programs where counterparts have not sufficiently picked up skills to sustain—and it would be difficult to fund such projects one more time to 'train' the nationals."[35]

Training in the post-UNTAC period also was clouded by language. In most cases, "training" meant instruction in either English or French. This considerably limited the potential pool of trainees and also encouraged donor competition, including language-based support to different sectors and institutions. Even when provided, training often pulled key officials from their jobs for extended periods. There also was little effort to ensure that the right people were being trained, that training was appropriate to their job-related responsibilities, or that key personnel would stay in their positions long enough to utilize their newly acquired knowledge and skills.

In some cases, donor-funded technical assistance personnel in the post-UNTAC period were rendered ineffective through the lack of counterpart staff, or, in cases where counterpart staff was indeed designated, by having such staff pulled in different directions by competing teams of foreign-funded advisers. In a few cases expatriate technical advisers allowed themselves to be drawn into the political process by supporting one power-sharing faction against the other or by engaging in divide-and-rule tactics between both Cambodian civil servants and donor agencies through selective sharing of information. This was particularly true of the education sector, where the Asian Development Bank too aggressively tried to exert leadership in a field crowded with other actors, many of whom were significant "players" with long(er) experience in Cambodia. According to well-placed observers, AsDB-funded technical advisers acted in a highly partisan manner and, by dint of the significant financial resources on offer by the AsDB, ruthlessly pursued their own program agendas.

Given the Royal Government's inability to manage external technical assistance, or, perhaps, because of such inability, it is not surprising that the 1994–95 *Development Cooperation Report* asserted that "an increased proportion of assistance needs to be allocated towards Free-Standing and Investment-Related Technical Cooperation, in order to enhance national capacity for development policy formulation and to facilitate implementing Investment Project Assistance."[36] It is significant, however, that the *Report* also suggested that it was equally important that the donor community allocate "increased external assistance to investment projects to meet the objectives of the Government in rebuilding devastated infrastructure and to respond to the huge needs in the social sectors especially in education and health."[37] These two statements almost seemed to contradict each other were it not understood that the Royal Government was not really expressing the desire for less of one kind of assistance in favor of another—rather, it sought more of everything so as to better pursue its ambitious—although rarely clearly defined—development objectives.

Although the Royal Government in the post-UNTAC period appeared to do little to manage or otherwise guide the provision of technical cooperation—at least with respect to foreign-funded advisers—it was not unaware of its deficiencies in this area:

> Technical assistance provided by donors in the areas of national policy planning, sectoral policy development and planning activities for the various sectors have been reduced or were not appropriately utilized. The lack of this type of assistance has affected the institutionalization of sectoral plans and programs within government ministries, as well as actions that could be taken by government leading to project prioritization and programming of available funds, and in making defensible decisions on funds and resource allocation.[38]

In response, then, the Royal Government in 1995 requested that donors "reinforce the transfer of knowledge and technology in order to ensure and guarantee the enhanced implementation of development programmes, and increase the involvement of Cambodian counterparts in project design and implementation."[39]

Based on Cambodia's post-UNTAC experience, it was clear that increased emphasis needed to be given to institutional development, including capacity building. Indeed, many of the problems encountered in the rehabilitation and reconstruction "phases" could be attributed to the country's weak institutional base. Much effort, including many millions of dollars and thousands of person-months of expatriate technical assistance, was devoted to what essentially were the effects or symptoms of Cambodia's weak institutional base. To move beyond reconstruction to sustainable development, it was evident that the Royal Government would require further support in the development of a sound institutional framework.

Although more than 98 percent of technical assistance to Cambodia in 1994 and 1995 was provided on a grant basis, Cambodia in 1995 assumed loans of some $U.S.2.5 million for technical assistance, the

bulk of which ($U.S.2.044 million) was for free-standing technical coop-
eration. The 1994–95 *Development Cooperation Report* deemed it "satisfac-
tory" that most technical cooperation contributions had been in the
form of development grants, saying, "This pattern must continue in
order to enhance the Government's operational capacity, ensure human
resource training, and support the good delivery of all development
programmes at the lowest cost to Government, at this stage of Cambodia's reconstruction."[40]

A December 1995 review of Asian Development Bank activities in
Cambodia revealed that its lending program ($U.S.141 million to the end
of 1995) had required a substantial amount of technical assistance. According to the review, such assistance had been necessary to assist line
ministries to carry out their tasks as well as to follow standard AsDB
lending procedures. The AsDB had found, however, that owing to the
lack of qualified counterpart staff and weak institutional mechanisms,
project implementation often took longer than scheduled. Such delay in
the implementation of AsDB-funded activities resulted in the need for
additional amounts of technical assistance. While acknowledging Cambodia's unique development circumstances, the Asian Development
Bank as a matter of policy indicated that in the future it would not be able
to provide all necessary technical assistance on a grant basis.[41]

Absorptive Capacity

Closely connected to the matter of technical assistance in post-
UNTAC Cambodia was the country's overall absorptive capacity.
Every document and every meeting directed to Cambodia's transition
toward sustainable development highlighted the country's lack of absorptive capacity. While there was a tendency to explain this problem
as a function of the acute lack of managerial and administrative personnel in the country's public sector, the international community bears
some responsibility for Cambodia's human resources constraints. The
way in which the SOC administration was weakened during the
UNTAC period and the limited attention that many donors subsequently placed on meaningful forms of "training" already have been
noted. Furthermore, the Structural Adjustment Program that was designed in agreement with the IMF and the World Bank prevented any
significant increase in extremely low civil service salaries, contributing

to such problems as corruption, absenteeism, and moonlighting, which affected most government agencies and which further constrained the country's absorptive capacity.

In his opening remarks to the March 1994 ICORC meeting (ICORC-2), the conference chairman, Tsutomu Hata, Japanese deputy prime minister and minister of foreign affairs, stated:

> This ICORC meeting should focus on the efforts to be made by the Cambodian side in order to accelerate the implementation of aid projects and programmes. The chair would like to be informed and inspired by the experiences and lessons which the donors have acquired while implementing their respective aid projects and programmes. Proposals on concrete measures to improve the aid absorption capacity of Cambodia are welcome. . . . In connection with the above, ICORC should continue to put particular emphasis on the importance of Cambodia's national capacity building including the improvement of its aid absorption capacity. The chair would like to invite discussion on how to better coordinate technical assistance to Cambodia in different sectors.[42]

A year later, in a position paper submitted to the March 1995 ICORC meeting (ICORC-3), the Royal Government freely acknowledged the difficulties the government had experienced in implementing the *National Programme to Rehabilitate and Develop Cambodia*. The government's position paper, "Issues in Implementing the National Programme to Rehabilitate and Develop Cambodia," noted that while most of the difficulties encountered derived from the country's weak absorptive and management capacities, others stemmed "from the procedures and practices of our partners which serve to compound our own inherent weaknesses."[43] The position paper proposed the establishment of an International Working Group, to be chaired by the Royal Government, to address a number of "intractable" issues, including commodity aid and budgetary support, incentive practices (for example, salary supplements), operational planning and monitoring, and skills development. Besides coordinating donor-funded initiatives in these areas, the position paper proposed that the Working Group "address the need for further financial and technical assistance in such areas as administrative reform and the demobilization of the armed forces, and thus to recommend implementation strategies that meet internationally-acceptable standards of propriety, and that accommodate the national and institutional interests of our partners."[44]

The Royal Government's proposal represented an attempt to begin to address some of the capacity-related problems affecting the implementation of the government's ambitious, donor-funded development strategy. The proposal also represented an attempt to engage or otherwise co-opt donors toward greater coordinated effort. That such a Working Group was not established by ICORC says less about the need for such a group than it does about the donor community's real commitment to either aid coordination or the improvement of Cambodia's absorption capacity.

It is without question that the Royal Government, in the post-UNTAC period, lacked the necessary technical and managerial skills to effectively plan and manage the development process or to coordinate external assistance inputs. It equally was clear that Cambodia's primary and insistent human resources constraint could only be addressed over time through concerted training, upgrading, and capacity-building efforts, as well as through experience, again acquired over time. A somewhat different issue, and one that was largely overlooked in the discussion of absorption capacity, was Cambodia's tremendous development needs and the fact that the country clearly could have absorbed much greater amounts of certain kinds of assistance, for example, more wells, expanded irrigation infrastructure, essential drugs and immunization supplies, condoms, textbooks, fertilizer, and so forth.

The oft-repeated assertion that the country's limited absorption capacity constrained Cambodia's reconstruction and development effort bedeviled the Cambodian authorities in the post-UNTAC period. On the one hand, it was clear that the lack of managerial skills and prowess inhibited the implementation of the country's development programme, including the implementation of some types or forms of development assistance. On the other hand, given Cambodia's many needs as well as its very limited financial resources, the country could have benefited from an almost infinite amount of financial and other forms of assistance, including capital-intensive turn-key projects, balance of payments support, commodity aid, debt swaps, or other forms of debt forgiveness (including, for example, the country's debt to the former Soviet Union), assistance in support of civil service reform and demobilization, as well as major education, training, and scholarship programs—all forms of assistance that would not necessarily have placed additional burdens on the country's admittedly overstretched administrative capabilities.

As noted by Robert Muscat, donors also could have done much to minimize demands placed on Cambodia's still-weak administrative capability, including avoidance of "specious data requirements and exactitude in programme and project planning . . . as well as complexity and duplication in coordination and execution arrangements." Muscat further suggested the following:

> Documentation requirements should be simplified and fulfilled as much as possible by the aid agencies themselves. Projects should be packaged so as to reduce to a minimum the number of management units for which Cambodian managers will be responsible. To avoid adding excessive complexity or proliferating options that could diffuse administrative attention, it may be wise to limit the numbers of models or pilot schemes and to focus on proving out limited numbers of interventions and approaches, and on testing replicability and scaling up. Another economizing principle should be to limit the creation of new institutions, phasing in such entities over time so as to avoid excessive pressure on management cadres while such cadres are still in short supply.[45]

Although further prioritization of Cambodia's reconstruction and development needs would not, in itself, have addressed the continuing problem of indigenous capacity, such prioritization might have served to alert donors to those areas and sectors deemed most important so as to concentrate effort, including efforts directed to capacity building. The Royal Government, its development partners, as well as the (World Bank-led) Consultative Group, ICORC, and other donor forums also should have given greater attention to those implementation strategies and forms of assistance that would not have further taxed Cambodia's still-limited administrative and managerial capacity. Donors also could have been more sensitive—and responsive—to the management capabilities of specific administrative entities. Alternatively, as was requested by the Royal Government, donors could and should have provided increased amounts of (substitution) technical assistance linked clearly to training and capacity building, including counterpart training.

In addressing the issue of Cambodia's absorption capacity, the 1995 SIDA evaluation report gave particular attention to local cost or counterpart funding as well as the widespread practice of salary supplementation. According to the SIDA evaluation, "Paying of salary supplements and other honoraria to government counterparts . . . goes very much further than taking on responsibility for local costs. This is a very serious problem that has unintended implications for capacity-building."[46] As noted by the report, "The widespread practice of paying salary supplements is not conducive to sound capacity-building, and also fosters relationships between donor and recipient analogous to those that prevailed in colonial times."[47] Besides provoking jealousy among those civil servants not receiving salary supplements or other "top-ups," the SIDA report also suggested that the practice had resulted in further demoralization of an already dispirited civil service as well as significant competition among donor agencies for qualified or experienced Cambodian staff.

As perhaps "the most vexing issue confronting the donor community," the SIDA evaluation indicated that the matter of salary supplementation could only be addressed over the long term in the context of government revenue generation and public administration reform, including downsizing of both the civil service and the military establishment. The SIDA evaluation thus called for "a concerted effort" by the donor community "not only to establish the scale and impact of this practice but also to devise joint remedial action" through "imaginative solutions" including, possibly, the establishment of a special central fund "to provide payments to selected civil servants according to preset criteria . . . over a transitional period."[48]

Pending resolute action by both the Royal Government and the donor community, however, the SIDA report resignedly concluded: "In the meantime, international organizations and NGOs will have to live with an unsatisfactory situation, where there is little genuine participation by the government in the delivery of aid, except on the part of officials beholden to the munificence of the aid agencies."[49]

Overcoming Aid Dependence

In its examination of the process by which war-torn societies can be rebuilt, the United Nations Research Institute for Social Development noted the "proportionately large" danger of overdependence on external actors and of loss of control over the reconstruction process:

In theory, there seems to be agreement that external assistance should be subsidiary to local efforts, and that the main responsibility and control should ultimately remain with local actors. External assistance, after responding to immediate emergencies, should limit itself to reinforcing local coping mechanisms, institutions and capacities in order to promote a self-reliant and sustainable pattern of development. In practice, however, external assistance, rather than being subsidiary to local efforts, becomes a substitute, and worse, destroys local coping and resistance mechanisms and controls emerging local institutions and solutions.[50]

That Cambodia, in the post-UNTAC period, demonstrated many of the characteristics of aid dependency is hardly surprising. As noted by *Facing a Complex Emergency*, SIDA's 1995 evaluation of external assistance to Cambodia, "Various forms of dependency become inevitable in a situation where a country covers almost half its budget expenditures from external financing."[51] In particular, the SIDA evaluation stressed the negative consequences of insufficient involvement of Cambodians in the planning and implementation of reconstruction and development activities.

In post-UNTAC Cambodia, the lack of indigenous capacity resulted in extensive use of substitution technical assistance as well as the employment of various implementation structures or mechanisms to supplement, if not replace, normal administrative structures and implementation channels. Project implementation units, or PIUs, became a common, donor-funded feature of many of Cambodia's ministries. It can be argued that such PIUs, including their heavy dependence on expatriate technical assistance, worked against the development of government capacity by setting up parallel and nonsustainable structures and by diverting the energies of the country's too few qualified staff from other equally important tasks. In addition, a too-narrow focus on project implementation may have precluded effective counterpart training. PIUs by their very nature have an impact on the development of overall sectoral policies, and rather than reinforcing the capability of the government, can remove responsibility for the articulation or development of policy from the government. In such a situation, the government at best becomes a rubber stamp for a policy process—and resultant policies and programs—not firmly under its direction or control.

Besides running counter to self-reliance, the lack of control over the country's rehabilitation and reconstruction breeds lack of confidence that in turn spawns even greater dependence. As a consequence, sustainable and self-directed development becomes even less an achievable goal.

Without question, Cambodia in the post-UNTAC period was dependent on high volumes of external financial support and technical assistance. But the portrayal of Cambodians as helpless and hapless mendicants did them great disservice and also credited the donor community with far more than it had done to help individual Cambodians.

While the post-UNTAC period provided ample evidence of Cambodia having either ceded or lost control of the rehabilitation and reconstruction process as well as other manifestations of aid dependence, by 1997 there was some evidence that the Cambodian authorities had developed greater confidence and that they were prepared to reassert control over the country's development path. Some of this newfound confidence may have been simply misplaced bravado or naiveté. Belligerent, almost antiforeigner, statements by senior government officials demonstrated this new self-confidence, although such statements certainly were not without domestic political content. The second prime minister's early 1996 assertions that donor countries should not meddle in Cambodia's internal affairs were not without point. Cambodia's rulers, however, may have seriously underestimated just how dependent Cambodia had become on continued flows of foreign assistance. The decision by some donors to suspend aid to Cambodia in the wake of the July 1997 coup, and the severe negative impact of such cutbacks on key development programs, demonstrated the country's continued dependence on external financial support.

Other, more positive indications of this new self-confidence also had emerged by 1997. In the pre-UNTAC period, the Ministry of Health was considered one of the country's weaker ministries. A UNDP- and ODA-funded technical assistance project helped to restructure the ministry and to facilitate a comprehensive planning process. By 1997 the Ministry of Health appeared to be more in control of donors and donor-funded initiatives than most other ministries. As one expatriate advisor commented, "The Ministry is realistically facing problems rather than saying everything is fine. Ministry staff are swamped—but they're keeping their heads above water."[52] Similarly, the Ministry of Labour and Social Action, another critically weak ministry with an impossibly large mandate, in March 1996 refused the offer of UNICEF support for a new program initiative: "No, we cannot, we have no capacity to do it the way we should. Thus, reluctantly we must say no."[53]

There also was evidence that the apparent passivity of the Cambodian authorities, including "the impression that they are comfortable in leaving the initiative to outside organizations"[54] also had begun to change. Although the Council for the Development of Cambodia remained extremely dependent on foreign technical assistance, there was some indication that the Royal Government had internalized its own *National Programme to Rehabilitate and Develop Cambodia*. In April 1996 the Ministry of Interior introduced legislation that required the registration of all nongovernmental organizations, local as well as international, including the provision of budgetary information. The ministry also was expected to instruct all provincial governors to prepare an annual report on the activities of all development and religious organizations operating in their jurisdiction. Although some NGO and human rights analysts denounced the move as further evidence of the Royal Government's authoritarian tendencies, others noted that the government, through its Ministry of Interior (Home Affairs) had every right and, indeed, obligation, to monitor externally funded activities as part of taking responsibility for the country's further development.

Private Investment and Development

A key tenet of the Royal Government's *National Programme to Rehabilitate and Develop Cambodia* was reliance on private entrepreneurship and the market as engines of growth. The document pledged that the state would promote private investment, with the state serving as a partner of the private sector in the realization of the country's further reconstruction and development. The commitment to private sector development was seen as an important means "to accelerate the rate of economic growth, to raise the living standards of all Cambodians, [and] . . . to achieve sustainable growth with equity and social justice."[55]

Early efforts by the Royal Government to promote private sector investment included the passage of a liberal Investment Law in August 1994. An attractive package of investment incentives included duty-free imports, export tax waivers, seventy-year land leases, and tax holidays of up to eight years. The Royal Government also established the "one-stop" Cambodian Investment Board (CIB), the private sector arm of the Council for the Development of Cambodia (CDC). An international media campaign was launched to inform the world that Cambodia was "open for business" and to change perceptions of the country as an unstable, hostile place still riven by civil war. Senior government officials toured regional and Western capitals to promote investment.

By early 1995, the Cambodian Investment Board claimed more than $U.S.625.4 million in "invested capital" with a further $U.S.1.55 billion in "approved projects." Such investment promised more than 32,500 new jobs. In the first five months of 1995 the board approved thirty additional projects worth more than $U.S.374 million, with prospects of a further 8,500 jobs.

In his statement to the May 1996 Donor Consultation Meeting, Keat Chhon, minister of economy and finance and senior minister in charge of rehabilitation and development, claimed that increased investor confidence in Cambodia's future had been manifested in over $U.S.2.3 billion in commitments of foreign direct investment. According to the minister's statement, total investments within Cambodia reached $U.S.587 million in 1995, representing more than 20 percent of the country's GDP, compared with only $U.S.123 million in 1990 (12 percent of GDP).[56]

If the Royal Government's promotional efforts had resulted in increased levels of direct foreign investment, such investment was skewed to certain sectors. For example, of the more than $U.S.2 billion in investment projects "approved" in the months after the promulgation of the Investment Law, investment in the primary sector (livestock, crops, forestry) accounted for only $U.S.44 million or 2 percent of projected investment, promising the creation of only 8,300 jobs. Investment in secondary activities (transportation, telecommunications, energy, and industry) was somewhat stronger but still accounted for less than 30 percent of total planned investment. As of early 1995, the bulk of approved investment activity was in the tertiary tourism and services sectors. Such investment, however, was expected to result in fewer than 2,000 permanent jobs.[57]

By mid-1996, there was some evidence that despite investor concern about continuing political instability, Cambodia had begun to attract the type of long-term, productive investment that would contribute to job creation and further economic growth. Whereas much foreign direct investment in the UNTAC and immediate post-UNTAC periods had been concentrated in the natural resource and service sectors, particularly the hotel and tourism sector, as of 1996 there was increased investment in the agricultural, agro-industry, and manufacturing sectors. Besides several large-scale projects, including a number of electricity generation plants financed by the private sector, there were many smaller investments geared to the local and export markets. Cambodia's investment climate soured in 1997, particularly following the July 1997 coup de force. In addition to heavy fighting, the coup was accompanied by looting and major loss or destruction of property. The July events hardly dispelled widespread perceptions of Cambodia's instability and lawlessness and thus had a further negative impact on investor confidence. The Asian financial crisis, including significant currency devaluations in Indonesia, Malaysia, South Korea, and Thailand, also negatively affected foreign investment in Cambodia.

Foreign direct investment in Cambodia also was skewed to certain countries of origin, with Malaysia and other Asian "tigers" assuming a dominant position (at least before the Asian financial crisis). Prior to the UNTAC operation much of Cambodia's foreign investment came from Thailand. In the post-UNTAC period, however, Malaysian commercial interests were particularly aggressive. In the five months following the passage of the 1994 Investment Law, the Royal Government signed contracts with seventeen Malaysian companies valued at some $U.S.1.6 billion, including the Sihanoukville-based Naga Island Resort project as well as investments related to a vast logging concession, garment factories, petrol stations, palm oil plantations, a power plant, office blocks, a winery, a golf course, and a race track and theme park.[58] Investment from China also was significant, although somewhat hidden in that much of the investment was directed through the highly entrepreneurial Cambodian Chinese community.

A June 1996 issue of the *Phnom Penh Post* gave extensive coverage to the growth in foreign private investment, including feature articles on a fifty-three-person delegation from the Federation of Korean Industries and the return to Cambodia of the American petroleum giant Caltex with an initial $U.S.20 million investment.[59] According to one of the articles, South Korean investors had leased more than 200 square kilometers of land in Kompong Cham and Mondulkiri provinces to mine gold, copper, and other mineral resources with promised investment of as much as $U.S.25 million a year. The article reported that another Korean company was in the process of acquiring 100,000 hectares of land to grow cassava to produce wine. The same company planned to establish a factory to make bottles for its wine to be shipped to the South

Korean market. As a further example of South Korean investment interest, the *Phnom Penh Post* cited the plan of industrial giant Hyundai to establish a cement factory in Battambang on a joint venture basis with a Cambodian company.[60]

The June 1996 Cambodia Roundtable Investment Conference similarly demonstrated investor interest in Cambodia. The conference, organized by the Economist Group, allowed 120 delegates from some 80 blue-chip companies to discuss investment possibilities with senior Royal Government officials. Although investors expressed concern about the country's political stability as well as the ongoing security problem, many indicated a sense of optimism about investment prospects in Cambodia, particularly given the country's cheap, if relatively unskilled labor force, its liberal investment regime, and the prospect of Cambodia being granted most favored nation (MFN) trading status by the United States.

In the post-UNTAC period, the Royal Government welcomed any investment in the country's further development. The government thus adopted the same laissez-faire stance toward direct foreign investment as it took on external assistance. Just as donors were allowed free rein to direct economic and technical assistance to those sectors or activities in which they were most interested, so the investment community was assured that the country was "open for business." Understandably, the Royal Government encouraged as much investment as possible in any and all sectors so as to promote as rapid as possible economic growth. Similarly, it is recognized that the Royal Government ultimately had little sway over investment choices by external actors. Nevertheless, it was disappointing that the Cambodian authorities did not make any real attempt to secure direct foreign investment that built upon the country's comparative advantages or that promoted value-added manufacturing and employment creation. It similarly was disappointing that the Royal Government did not make a more determined effort to link private sector investment with its *National Programme to Rehabilitate and Develop Cambodia*.

A March 1996 "Policy Position Paper for Sectorial Investment in the Industrial, Energy, and Mineral Sectors" claimed that the Ministry of Industry, Mines and Energy (MIME) was the principal catalyst within the Royal Government to create the necessary atmosphere conducive to the industrial and economic development of the kingdom, while safeguarding the welfare of the people and the environment. According to the position paper, the ministry was "charged with promoting industrial activity in order to create jobs as a matter of priority and to attract foreign investment." The ministry's "industrial development and investment strategy," however, represented less a strategy than a statement of the kind of industrial activities and sectoral investment required in the development of a modern industrial sector:

> Cambodia's industrial development requires expansion of] export oriented industries; high labour-intensive enterprises; the selective exploration and exploitation of natural resources; import substitution of consumer goods; promotion of industry in rural and provincial areas; development of a sound entrepreneur base in the country; growth in the micro-enterprise and informal sector which provides the vast majority of employment; promotion of tourism-related industries; and in the longer term, industries based on oil and gas. An important feature of the industrial development strategy will be creating growth centres strengthened by infrastructure development, industrial zoning, and establishing export processing zones in Phnom Penh and Sihanoukville. Some larger population centres also will be targeted as trade and market centres.[61]

To serve such ambition, the Ministry of Industry, Mines and Energy identified four critical sectors for investment, especially foreign investment: the fuel and energy sector, capital-intensive and high energy consumption industries, labor-intensive and value-added industries, and "sectors of higher need" such as agro-manufacturing and consumable goods production.

While the policy statement outlined most of the preconditions and goals of a robust industrial sector, including the effective but sustainable use of existing natural resources, the attraction of greater foreign investment, the promotion of technology transfer, and enhanced human resources development, it was markedly bereft of measures to achieve such objectives.

By late 1996 the Royal Government had imposed no conditions nor offered additional investment incentives targeted to private sector investment in training and other forms of human resources development. The lack of specific attention to skills training and human resources upgrading was particularly unfortunate in that both Cambodia and the donor community fully recognized that the country's weak human resources base would continue to be the chief constraint to Cambodia's further progress toward sustainable development.

Although the Royal Government had committed itself to the establishment of the rule of law, the relative absence of a legal and regulatory framework and a weak banking sector constrained direct foreign investment in the post-UNTAC period, particularly investment by well-established international companies. The same lack of regulation, however, encouraged the rapid growth of illegal or questionable business activities, including money laundering, gambling, prostitution, and, reportedly, significant trafficking in drugs and weapons. The proliferation of such activities worked against the kind of image Cambodia tried to present to the outside world, including both donors and investors. The exponential growth of corruption and other forms of rent-seeking at all levels, even at the highest levels of government, discouraged legitimate business interests and entrepreneurs from investing in Cambodia. With contract signing bonuses and other forms of payments reported to amount to millions of dollars, investors committed themselves only to the most lucrative of investment projects, projects not necessarily in the best or long-term interests of the kingdom and the people of Cambodia.

Chapter 6

Civil Society in the Post-UNTAC Period

It is a truism to say that development is conditioned by the particular cultural and institutional environment in which such development is prosecuted. In Cambodia, as well as other war-torn societies, the development process is made more complicated and more difficult by the fact that the process of reconstruction and development extends beyond mere rehabilitation of infrastructure or the establishment of institutions to the very recreation of many aspects of traditional society. Indeed, the Royal Government claimed that a necessary condition for the successful implementation of its *National Programme to Rehabilitate and Develop Cambodia* was "the need to motivate and change the behaviour patterns, attitudes, and mentalities of the people, including those of government officials and civil servants."[1]

Because of Cambodia's long international isolation, less is known about Cambodia's sociocultural environment than most other developing countries: for nearly twenty years it was impossible to conduct baseline anthropological or other research, particularly at the village level. And if no society is static, Cambodia and its people have been subjected to particularly dramatic changes, having suffered war, the extreme privations of the Khmer Rouge period, massive population movements, international isolation, a protracted peace process, the UNTAC "occupation," and, in the post-UNTAC period, accommodation to a new set of political and economic circumstances. During the last several years, Cambodia has had to "confront the special challenge of making the difficult 'triple transition' from war to peace, from state and party organization to liberal civil administration, and from economic underdevelopment to development."[2]

Although Cambodian society remains understudied, by 1997 there was a growing body of literature examining contemporary Cambodian culture and society.[3] Some of this literature dealt with specific aspects of Cambodian culture or society, such as the changed and changing role of women, particularly women-headed households. Other studies began to document the incredible changes wrought upon traditional Cambodian society or to interpret how traditional values affect, or are affected by, the process of rapid political, economic, and social change. It was unfortunate, however, that most of the post-UNTAC research into sociological change in Cambodia was undertaken by non-Cambodians. Although external perceptions and comparative approaches are useful, a full understanding of social change and the consequences of such change requires explication by those rooted in the particularities of the culture, including the process of change itself.

Available research into social change in Cambodia, including the review of previous anthropological and sociological research in light of the country's much changed circumstances, shed some light on the several processes of change in Cambodia. Although inconclusive, such research needed to be more carefully considered as part of the development of plans and programs, particularly plans that involved the Cambodian peasantry as partners, agents, or beneficiaries (or, less optimistically, as victims) of whatever development process was under way in post-UNTAC Cambodia.

Existing research overwhelmingly emphasized that the hierarchical, almost feudalistic, nature of traditional Cambodian society continued to underlie social relations in Cambodia, including political relationships. According to Cambodia scholar Serge Thion, "The backbone of the traditional [Cambodian] political structure was the patron-client system of dyadic relationships."[4] As explained by anthropologist Lindsay French, this has meant that

> political power and control traditionally has involved the accumulation of
> an entourage of assistants, employees, and loyal followers who provide
> support in exchange for various forms of protection and assistance. These
> people in turn build up their own patronage networks with the resources
> provided by their patrons. . . . The basic dynamic of patron-client relations,
> in which a structurally less powerful person submits to the authority of a

more powerful other in exchange for protection and/or material support, is an aspect of virtually all reciprocal hierarchical relationships in Cambodia, kin and non-kin alike.[5]

An understanding of such well-entrenched and well-accepted hierarchies helped to explain Cambodian deference to authority, including absolutist forms of authority.

French, citing a 1977 article by James Scott and Benedict Kerkvliet, suggested that certain political conditions reinforce and promote patron-clientism: marked inequalities of wealth, status, and power that are accorded a certain legitimacy; the relative absence of effective impersonal guarantees such as public law for physical security, property, and position; and the inability of kinship units or traditional village communities to serve as effective vehicles for personal security or advancement.[6] A 1995 SIDA-sponsored examination of social organization and power structures in rural Cambodia noted that all these conditions existed in contemporary Cambodia. The SIDA study also suggested the following:

> The analytic description of these conditions also contains the recipe for the dismantling or defusing of patron-client relationships: promotion of economic, social, and political equality; adequate enforcement of adequate civil and criminal laws; creation of kinship and village solidarity. Unfortunately, the combination of privatization of land, economic liberalization (capitalism), absence of state fiscal control and inability to ensure discipline within the armed forces and police does not seem conducive to the attainment of these goals.[7]

In her examination of social dynamics in the Thai border camps French found constant "wheeling and dealing": "as the political landscape shifted people rushed to position themselves favorably relative to each new configuration of power. The result was that people's commitment to each other, as patrons and as clients, was often rather shallow. People made their commitment to the main chance."[8] Such opportunism, entirely understandable in the context of Cambodia's recent history, also characterized much post-UNTAC Khmer social behavior. If opportunism is indeed a defining characteristic of Khmer society, such attitudes and "me first" behaviors can be expected to provide arid soil for either democracy or good governance.[9]

In considering the cumulative impact of Cambodia's recent history, more attention has been devoted to the symptoms of social malaise than to its longer-term or societal consequences. Commentators have noted the high incidence of mental health problems, particularly among adult women: "Knowledgeable observers report the presence of similar psychosomatic symptoms that could well be contributing to the disadvantaged position of Cambodian women and widow-headed households."[10] Although there has been no systematic study, particularly within Cambodia, survivors of the Cambodian holocaust are widely reported to suffer sleep disturbances, memory difficulties, poor concentration or difficulty in focusing on specific tasks, depression, apathy, aggressiveness, violent behavior, as well as the emergence of what has been termed a "dummy personality" (mistaken by Western aid providers as Khmer "toughness," "stoicism," "callousness," "dishonesty," or "corruptness").[11]

In the absence of hard data, it can only be assumed that Cambodia and its people continue to suffer the effects of mass post-traumatic stress syndrome. For example, a UN Border Relief Operation (UNBRO) –sponsored psychological assessment predicted that many people in the Thai border camps would experience severe difficulties following their eventual return to Cambodia:

> Many Khmer now stable in Site Two [border camp] will experience psychological collapse when they are resettled or repatriated. Present resettlement experiences are a harbinger of the future emotional stress and social disability which they will experience once they leave Site Two. Forced dependency [on outside aid] and ongoing Khmer coping strategies for dealing with conditions in Site Two (for example, dummy personality) have failed to provide them with the skills necessary for adapting to the pressures of "normal" existence.[12]

Such difficulties indeed did emerge, although measured more by economic criteria, including food security, than on the basis of psychological adaptation. A 1995 survey of the resettlement and reintegration of the returnee population revealed that up to 40 percent of returnees were "not coping" in an economic sense. The survey also outlined some social difficulties faced by returnees, including the inability to rely on family or neighbors for long-term support (owing in large part to their own struggle to survive), lack of acceptance or trust as "new people," as well as certain expectations concerning behavior, including deference as "new-comers."[13]

Although it is widely accepted that the traumas of the previous twenty-five years have profoundly affected all Cambodians, little is really known about the extent of such effects, their continuing impact on individuals as well as Cambodian society as a whole, or what new social structures or coping mechanisms have developed as a result of, or in response to, such social strains.[14] Of such effects, the most important that have been cited are a generalized lack of trust, a related lack of social or community cohesion, and difficulty in concentrating or focusing on anything other than the present moment.

The lack of trust is considered a particular consequence of the Khmer Rouge period, when the very bases of traditional Cambodian society were destroyed, families were fractured, "old people" were turned against "new people," and families, friends, and neighbors were forced to spy on one another as a matter of survival. Lack of trust similarly was a characteristic of life in the Thai border camps and also was a key factor in the UNTAC-led repatriation and reintegration process.[15] Cambodians of all ranks, levels, and locations have bemoaned the lack of trust that characterizes contemporary Cambodian society at the village level as well as in the political realm. Such lack of trust obviously has had a significant and negative impact on the country's social cohesion.

As for the ability of Cambodians to plan for the future, the SIDA evaluation mission noted, "Living with profound insecurity for so long, Cambodians have developed an understandable propensity to think for the short term, an attitude that has constricted the planning perspectives in the government service."[16] However, the inability to plan is more a function of uncertainty and lack of control over events and circumstances than actual physical insecurity. Life in rural Cambodia always has been uncertain and highly subject to the vagaries of nature, with regular occurrence of flood or drought, often one hard upon the other. Physical insecurity resulting from the ongoing civil war, however, certainly has had a major effect on societal attitudes, as have the political ramifications of the war, both resulting in massive population displacements. Uncertainty about all aspects of life has negatively affected Cambodians' ability to hope and plan for the future.

In the case of government planning perspectives, the lack of control over resources, particularly financial resources, has made planning very difficult. In the pre-UNTAC period, the country's almost total isolation and lack of financial resources, together with uncertainty connected with the peace process, rendered any attempt at long-term planning somewhat futile. The UNTAC period established a definite planning framework, but with its own objectives, timeframe, and operating procedures. As indicated in chapter 5, planning in the post-UNTAC period similarly was dominated by foreign technical advisers, with most rehabilitation and development activities still conditioned by the flow of donor funding. In addition to contributing to dependence, the lack of control by Cambodians over their own future can be seen to have contributed to a kind of passivity often misinterpreted as an inability to plan.[17] The SIDA evaluation mission noted the "seeming passivity of national officials, and the willingness to cede to outsiders aspects of programme management and administration that customarily fall on the shoulders of national authorities."[18] The apparently willing abdication of responsibility can be seen as further evidence of ingrained deference to authority and/or power (including economic power, superior education, and so on) as well as a lack of self-confidence, such a lack again stemming from the country's collective recent experience.

Robert Putnam, a Harvard professor of government, has suggested that democracy is the product of "a quality that Machiavelli called *virtu civile* (civic virtue)—an ingrained tendency to form small-scale associations that create a fertile ground for political and economic development, even if . . . the associations are not themselves political or economic."[19] According to Putnam, good government is a by-product of such associations: "Civic virtue both expresses and builds trust and cooperation in the citizenry, and it is these qualities . . . that [make] everything else go well."[20] Examining differences in "social capital" between southern and northern Italy and the effect of such differences on the practice of democracy, Putnam found:

> In southern Italy, the southern system stressed "vertical bonds": it was rigidly hierarchical, with those at the bottom dependent on the patronage of landowners and officials rather than one another. In the north small organizations such as guilds and credit associations generated "horizontal bonds," fostering a sense of mutual trust that doesn't exist in the south.[21]

Rather than southern Italy, Putnam could have been describing contemporary rural Cambodia, both in terms of traditional patron-client relations as well as the lack, certainly in the post-Khmer Rouge period, of horizontal bonds.

In Cambodia there is an assumption of an implicit and close relationship between the establishment of the trappings of democracy and the (re)emergence of civil society as well as between civil society and development. The belief that such relationships are symbiotic or mutually supportive is a key element of the Royal Government's *National Programme to Rehabilitate and Develop Cambodia.*

The entire object of the internationally supported Cambodian peace process, of course, was the establishment of a "legitimate" multiparty liberal democracy through a free and fair electoral process. That the seed of democracy was to be sown in soil unused to anything akin to Western-style democratic principles or practices did not concern the architects of the Paris Peace Accords. Some international observers took the overwhelming electoral turnout in May 1993 to be proof that democracy had indeed taken root in Cambodia. Other more pragmatic observers, however, suggested that although the UNTAC-sponsored election represented a promising start, it was far too early to tell whether democratic principles and practices had been successfully grafted onto Cambodia's political culture and that, at best, it would take many years of careful nurturing before democracy in Cambodia might flourish and bear fruit.[22]

A 1996 SIDA-sponsored study noted that the establishment of "democracy" in Cambodia through the UNTAC-led electoral process resulted only in a "partial democracy" in that the UNTAC-sponsored election focused on the creation of a Constituent or National Assembly without any form of representational government at a provincial, district, or local level.[23] As already noted, efforts by FUNCINPEC to extend power sharing to the district level as well as preparations for local elections initially planned for 1997 served to politicize governance at the local level, but quite likely without any real impact on popular participation. Instead of "democracy" and responsibility, it was more likely that any politicization at the local level only reinforced traditional patron-client networks and linkages as well as increased opportunities for rent-seeking behavior.[24]

Despite such reservations, considerable efforts continued to be devoted to the establishment of democracy in Cambodia. In the post-UNTAC period donors, chiefly the United States, supported a range of activities promoting democracy and democratization.[25] The Royal Government's *SEILA* program, to be implemented initially in five provinces through the UNDP-supported Cambodian Resettlement and Reintegration program (CARERE), proposed, in essence, the exercise of democracy at the village level through the election of village and commune development councils and the establishment of a bottom-up planning process to target development efforts to local needs and local resources (see Appendix).

To outside observers, a key measurement of Cambodia's post-UNTAC progress toward democracy was the Royal Government's adherence to those democratic principles enshrined in its Constitution. The government committed itself to democracy as well as good governance. Donor meetings, particularly ICORC meetings, were used to highlight the importance donors attach to good governance, including transparency in government. Given popular perceptions that corruption, including corruption at the highest levels, was endemic in post-UNTAC Cambodia, the issue of transparency in government was a thinly veiled subtext of the July 1996 Consultative Group Meeting. However, as the meeting focused only on "technical matters," the Royal Government's progress toward increased transparency was not specifically addressed and no performance conditions or other benchmarks were established. Donors reiterated their concerns at the July 1997 Consultative Group Meeting, particularly about forestry receipts not passing through Cambodia's national treasury, but again (apart from the IMF) with no firm threat of sanctions.

In addition, there was no clear agreement that Cambodia and Cambodians were ready for full democracy. As noted by Aun Porn Moniroth, a young, Russian-trained political scientist and economist:

> A democratic political system requires that diversified structures of social classes and pluralistic economic and political interests emerge. All these factors are amazingly quite different than what we have in Cambodia. Furthermore, the patriarchal farmer class is not a social class which can appreciate a mentality, a psychology and values of democracy and pluralism. As to the other social class[es] such as the capitalists, the labor, the bureaucrats, the workers, and the intellectuals whose numbers are but a few and newly born, they have yet to detach themselves completely from the patriarchal farmer class in their ways of life, their tradition, their psychology and their moral values. The urban culture and lifestyle whose appearance is quite recent, has not yet completely grown out of the rural lifestyle.[26]

Assuming Aun Porn Moniroth's statement accurately depicted the reality of post-UNTAC Cambodia, a country prone by tradition to patron-clientism and authoritarianism, it also underscored the significant challenge of nurturing any variant of Western-style democracy in Cambodia. Particularly so, when, as also noted by Aun Porn Moniroth:

The majority of people in [Cambodian] society [do] not seem to value social ethics and the respect of law. Law is respected and applied only in instances where one's own interest is protected or enhanced. In many cases, law and social ethics are practically abused almost by everyone and everywhere. Corruption, bureaucracy, nepotism, favoritism and extortion have become a way of life. The powerful officials will squeeze more while the less powerful will squeeze less, respectively. Evidences are staggering, but no one seems to notice them, and when confronted, no one would dare do anything about it. Paradoxically, society seems to treat such persons as wise, smart, and capable. . . . Law-abiding and ethical citizens will live in sheer misery with nothing left but hope for a better life after death.[27]

If it is unrealistic to apply absolutist measurement to Cambodia's success in "growing democracy," perhaps a better way is to assess progress toward the reestablishment of Cambodian civil society. Such assessment, of course, assumes that the organs of civil society and the practice of public participation will necessarily promote or reinforce democracy in Cambodia—as well as a process of rehabilitation, reconstruction, and development.

In its review of Cambodian development history, the 1994 SIDA evaluation mission noted that the Cambodian government has always been a somewhat weak institution, even during Cambodia's Golden Age in the 1960s: "Government officials lacked commitment to involve the poor in their own development. Development was perceived as an act of royal beneficence."[28] Although efforts continued in the post-UNTAC period to promote more participatory or bottom-up forms of development, it remained unclear whether the Royal Government was indeed firmly committed to popular participation or whether such a development model more accurately reflected donor influence as the latest in development fashion. In addition, some of the "old" patterns of governance were reestablished in the country's "Second Kingdom," including distributions by the Royal Palace of rice and clothing to needy peasants and the even more overtly political "hand-outs" of schools and clinics by the country's two prime ministers.[29] Although hard to deny that such assistance was not needed or welcomed by poor villagers, it again reinforced their "traditional" role as supplicants or, equally, as potential electors whose votes could be bought. Deference to authority, particularly senior party officials, also subverted the transparent use of state revenues, including loan-derived funds.[30]

Is civil society emerging in Cambodia? The UNTAC era, as well as the availability of donor funding, saw the creation of many groups, including, certainly, political parties, but also an array of nongovernmental organizations (NGOs); advocacy, watch-dog, and single-interest groups such as professional associations; community groups; credit societies; and users' groups. As outlined in a section on NGOs below, many of these organizations had their roots in the Thai border camps and in the post-UNTAC period were chiefly concerned with the welfare of the returnee population. Many other groups were established under the human rights banner. Still more groups were established to promote community-based development activities or evolved into organizations with a community development focus. Some remained driven by a single individual's vision; others had developed into more mature organizations.

The range of such organizations—most established during or after UNTAC—was impressive and exciting and may give evidence of the emergence of popularly based civil society in Cambodia. At the same time, such organizations had not, at least by end-1996, been recognized by the government or by political parties as having any legitimate political role, either as a voice of people or as a vehicle to address particular social problems. In addition, many of the civil society organizations that emerged during the UNTAC era remained dependent on external funding. Unless donor agencies were extremely sensitive and supportive, allowing for trial and error, the dependence on external funding was more likely to be translated into the adoption of donor agendas, including the kinds of issues, projects, and development approaches favored by donors. As a result, in the period following the UNTAC operation, locally established agencies had some difficulty in articulating their own unique development vision or in developing their own ways of dealing with their grass-roots development partners.

Did such organizations have an impact? Yes and also no. Yes in that there were a greater number of voices and opinion in post-UNTAC Cambodia than at any time in the country's recent past, with some, though limited, civic space permitted (if not necessarily encouraged) under Cambodia's new political order. The human rights umbrella, in particular, permitted the establishment of a number of groups. Although some of the success of these groups could be attributed to the supposed universal nature of human rights as embodied in several international conventions, it was more attributable to the ready availability of donor financial and other support, as well as to the fact that human rights issues remained carefully monitored by donors as well as several international watch-dog or support groups, including the United Nations Center for Human Rights, Amnesty International, and others.

Another sign of positive impact was that by late 1996 several models and experiments were under way, some of which were likely to bear fruit and which could then be transplanted elsewhere in the country. With no clear recipe for developmental success in Cambodia, the development of appropriate and indigenous models and methodologies was an all-essential element of the development process. Some groups, particularly some community development organizations, had made considerable progress toward an authentic Cambodian "voice" or vision. As these organizations matured further, it was possible that they would help to reinforce civil society in Cambodia, particularly if they were able to firmly establish themselves at a village level, including through other, more traditional channels of civil society (box 6-1).

Less optimistically, the Royal Government seemed to have limited tolerance for dissent and by 1996 was demonstrating marked authoritarian tendencies. The concept of "loyal opposition" clearly was not well understood in Cambodia. Furthermore, as has been noted elsewhere, social relations in Cambodia remained functions of power and increasingly of political power. In the country's highly charged political environment all nongovernment groups needed to walk a very fine line indeed to not be perceived as antigovernment and hence a threat. This would explain, to some extent, the absence of indigenous groups with a focus on environmental or other contentious or politically sensitive issues.[31]

Note, too, in that as with all other institutions and sectors, post-UNTAC Cambodia suffered an acute lack of human resources, including gifted social leaders with the necessary skills, training, and political or social connections to allow them to be effective advocates and change agents. The most successful of the new generation of agencies and organizations in post-UNTAC Cambodia had impressive, sometimes charismatic, leadership. Many of these leaders received training or other exposure outside of Cambodia, including in the Thai border camps. The rejuvenation of civil society in Cambodia, however, required many more leaders and social activists, with a broader range of support and funding, particularly locally generated support.

Furthermore, in its research on "rebuilding war-torn societies," the United Nations Research Institute for Social Development (UNRISD)

BOX 6-1
TOWARD CIVIL SOCIETY IN CAMBODIA

Some important roles played by nongovernmental organizations to aid the reemergence of civil society in Cambodia include:

—Encouraging people's participation in the development process and helping increase their awareness so they can understand the situation and the role and functioning of civil society;

—Reducing poverty at the grass-roots level, where the government does not reach, to ensure that all citizens have fair access to the country's resources, aid money, and growing GNP. The approaches for development, in particular community development, used by NGOs also emphasize participation, self-reliance, and justice;

—Participating in activities that promote peace, democracy, and human rights in order to respect human rights and to protect people's rights;

—Assisting in safeguarding the democratic process through lobbying and functioning of democratic institutions;

—Being an observer of elections to ensure they are free and fair;

—Strengthening the government's understanding and knowledge of human rights and lobbying for the implementation of a genuine rule of law and the monitoring of their processes; and

—Seeking dispute-solving mechanisms at the local level whereby civic groups can play a role in mediating on behalf of the citizens.

Source: Adapted from Thun Saray, "The Way Ahead to a Civil Society," *Phnom Penh Post*, January 26–February 8, 1996, p. 7. Thun Saray, president of ADHOC, a local human rights and development organization, in the post-UNTAC period also served as a spokesperson for local human rights groups and other indigenous nongovernmental organizations.

identified several problems resulting from lack of clarity in the roles between external and local actors:

> As a result of its politicization and militarization, humanitarian assistance has taken ever more massive and spectacular forms and tends increasingly to substitute and destroy local resistance and coping mechanisms and institutions rather than to support and reinforce them. The same tendency, on a more general level of international assistance, leads external actors to impose their own solutions, plans and priorities on local societies and actors rather than assisting the latter in gradually rebuilding their societies, polities, and economies themselves.[32]

This was more than true of Cambodia in the post-UNTAC era.

Harvard University's Robert Putnam expressed pessimism about the possibility of establishing "civic virtue" (or, in the case of Cambodia, civil society) where it does not already exist: "Unhappily, from the point of view of social engineering . . . local organizations 'implanted' from the outside have a high failure rate. The most successful local organizations represent indigenous, participatory initiatives in relatively cohesive local communities."[33] Putnam also heartily endorsed a theory from economic history called "path dependence," which he summarized as "Where you can get to depends on where you're coming from, and some destinations you simply cannot get to from here."[34] Such path dependence had obvious implications for Cambodia's post-UNTAC success in achieving Western-style democracy, civil society, and development. Furthermore, some of the social, political, and development experiments undertaken in post-UNTAC Cambodia—mostly with donor funding and heavily dependent on expatriate technical assistance—might well be doomed, if not to failure, at least to less than anticipated success owing to the strength of Cambodia's endogenous social and cultural values, attitudes, and practices.

Toward Restoring Life: Development at the Village Level[35]

That traditional Cambodian society survived in spite of the many traumas of the country's recent past is, of course, indication of the durability of traditional cultural values. There is ample evidence, however, that traditional Cambodian values and cultural practices were greatly weakened by the events of the past twenty-five years. Also, somewhat paradoxically, rather than allowing the ready transplantation or grafting of new values, practices, and institutions, the weakening of traditional life seemed to reinforce or amplify the effects of the dislocations Cambodia and its people have endured. As a result, Cambodia was rendered a badly fractured society, including at the village level, home to some 85 percent of all Cambodians.

As stated earlier, there has been a paucity of village-based sociological or anthropological research into community and family dynamics and on how or to what extent community-level social bonds have been weakened in Cambodia. As of 1997 it was possible to identify at least some of the social changes that had altered Cambodian society, including those induced at the village level. Based on such research as had been undertaken, there were discernible changes in social organization, community participation, and social practices—all evidence of a society in flux.

As just emphasized, a generalized lack of trust is said to be one such effect. Although localized communities remained the basis of both Cambodian social and administrative structures, the traditional bonds that tie villages and communities together were weakened over the past twenty years. As eloquently noted by Meas Nee: "We need to find ways to restore the confidence and trust of individual people, of families, and of whole communities. This is done in the same way that any relationships are made. Slowly."[36] Nee described a contemporary Cambodian village as a basket that had been broken, its pieces scattered:

> Whoever wants to re-weave the basket must understand clearly that the social, cultural and psychological destruction of village life is deep and cannot be ignored. It is not easy for those who do not belong to a community to see this.... You cannot make people co-operate without looking at the trust that was broken. You cannot make people trust. Some small projects will have the objective to build trust and will succeed because the village people are at the centre. Others may hope to build trust but will not understand the informal structure of the village well enough and may inadvertently make trust more difficult to achieve. They have not understood deeply enough.[37]

The 1995 SIDA-sponsored examination of social organization and power structures in rural Cambodia also noted the relative absence of formal organizational structures beyond the level of the individual household, and indeed beyond the nuclear family.[38]

Although the antipathy of villagers toward the communal forms of production imposed during the Khmer Rouge and People's Republic of

Kampuchea regimes has been widely noted, the time-honored practice of "mutual assistance" in rural Cambodia had not been abandoned but rather altered. The labor-sharing practices that emerged since the end of the *"krom samaki"*[39] era—while inegalitarian (demanding a disproportionate share of labor from poor, often women-headed households)—generally conformed to Cambodian tradition. At the same time, beginning with the economic liberalization of the late 1980s, productive relations in rural Cambodia became increasingly monetized. In addition, it can be assumed that Buddhism, formerly the mainstay of traditional Cambodian life, lost some of its influence or authority, including observance of Buddhist-inspired rules governing social relationships and social practices.

The difficulties and challenges that returnees had to face in reestablishing themselves in Cambodia provided further evidence of how Cambodian society had been fractured. Research into the reintegration process revealed that returnees were very conscious of not yet being trusted or accepted into their new communities. Many returnees felt that they had to demonstrate an abnormal degree of deference to "old people" (that is, those who had remained in Cambodia) and that they also were subject to unrealistic expectations of exemplary behavior. A 1995 NGO-commissioned study revealed that up to 40 percent of returnees were "not coping"; notably, however, the study focused on income generation and food self-sufficiency as a measure of coping rather than on more social or psychological-based criteria.[40]

Cambodian society has traditionally been loosely structured, which, according to Robert Muscat, has resulted in little tendency toward the formation of interest groups or other kinds of associations outside the family. The apparent disinterest in spontaneous organization of community activities was reinforced as a result of experience under the Khmer Rouge:

> Fear of unpredictable consequences, uncertainty over who can be trusted, a traumatically engraved passivity as the primary survival skill under a regime in which safety depended on not being noticed, even a kind of internal blankness as a substitute for external passivity—these and other reactions and symptoms of an isolating and depressing character have been assumed to be operating to reinforce the traditional atomistic mores.[41]

The SIDA anthropological study also noted that direct participation in decisionmaking processes at the village level in post-UNTAC

Cambodia remained quite weak. The study ascribed this lack of participation to traditionally held perceptions of power and authority and secondly to the legacy of the centralist socialist system imposed during the 1980s.[42] Well-learned behavior during a succession of regimes, none of them particularly benevolent, has schooled the Cambodian peasantry into least-risk patterns of behavior. Such patterns were unlikely to be altered by the advent of liberal democracy, particularly a democracy based on a single internationally supported election.

The SIDA report, based largely on a sociological study of a village in Kompong Chhnang province, stated that many commune and village chiefs complained that it was impossible to govern because "villagers do not do as we tell them."[43] Such a statement clearly demonstrated the decided authoritarian streak of those with power, which certainly is consistent with Cambodian history. According to the report, however, recalcitrance on the part of villagers had several sources, including a "democratic system which is diffusing the power center and giving an escape way for the ordinary citizen from all comfortable orders. . . . An increased awareness of issues of human rights and law and order of course give the villagers extra strength in refusing to obey the orders of commune officials."[44]

This "I don't have to do what you tell me" attitude represented a new feature of Cambodian life quite opposed to traditional deference to authority. Although such behavior could be interpreted to represent popular demand for more representative forms of governance at the local level, it more likely stemmed from a kind of perverted "civil libertarianism" that emerged during the UNTAC period under the guise of "human rights." It also may be attributed to the lack of social cohesion and the consequent emergence of self-centered and self-interested me-first attitudes, including rampant greed, which also manifested themselves in the post-UNTAC period.

According to the SIDA study, a second reason for the refusal of villagers to comply with orders from commune leaders is the fact that whereas mutual assistance once characterized Cambodian village life, monetized relations became increasingly important, "permeating Cambodian villages." As noted by the report, villagers increasingly were refusing to perform public work, even if such work was of direct personal benefit, without first asking "How much do you pay me?"[45] Such attitudes, if indeed prevalent throughout rural Cambodia, can only have been reinforced by donor-funded labor-intensive rural infrastructure schemes, including food-for-work activities.[46]

Traditionally the Cambodian peasantry has been relatively passive, either by its intrinsic nature, a fatalistic belief in karma, or through deference to more powerful social classes. Just as it was far too early to begin to measure any new sense of empowerment or control at the local level as a result of "democratization" or "community development" efforts, so it was too early by late 1996 to see any conclusive evidence of either the popularization of the development process or the benefits of more open and participatory forms of social organization.

Another potential problem of the post-UNTAC period was the trend toward narrow politicization of the entire process at the local level through the introduction of competitive partyism. In itself, this might have represented the logical extension of democracy to Cambodia. In the country's post-UNTAC political environment, however, it more likely represented the competition for power and control, as well as whatever benefits, particularly economic benefits, might stem from such control.

Worldwide experience in grass-roots development has revealed that although far from static, traditional communities generally are resistant to change. As noted by Muscat, "The way in which village communities function and respond to outside interventions, however benign, will be critical to the feasibility"—and success—of all donor-funded activities targeted to the village level.[47] Handicapped by the lack of Cambodia-specific research, and with pressure of both need and major donor funding, in the post-UNTAC period significant efforts were made to bring development (and change) to Cambodia's overwhelmingly rural population.

If the post-UNTAC focus on rural development was to be welcomed as a means of bringing peace and stability, as well as other social and economic benefits to rural Cambodia, there was a clear danger of too much change, too fast. Community development workers in Cambodia stressed the need for enhanced recognition of the necessarily slow pace of sustainable rural development; they also cautioned that some efforts under way in the post-UNTAC period might serve to further marginalize already vulnerable groups:

> Many of the development models adopted . . . recognize only what is immediately visible, ignoring the less formal networks and mechanisms that have supported the village (particularly the poor) for generations.

There seems to have been no place for them in the new round of Cambodian rural development. And yet these are the conduits most likely to deliver at least some of the ideas, techniques, and implementation opportunities needed to improve the lot of those unable to manage. . . .

There are already thriving community structures both formal and informal. Dramatic change that is not in tune with what currently exists will only serve to rupture further a damaged social structure. Again, this accords with the belief that gradual incremental change from within is required.[48]

Meas Nee further cautioned against village-based community development being undertaken by anyone other than Cambodians:

Even though we all say that we want to empower the people to be self-reliant, sometimes the work in the village begins with a westerner coming in with the Cambodian team. This is not a wise thing to do. White skinned people are seen as rich and naturally the villagers hope they can get something. . . . If a Cambodian goes into a village with a westerner the people will believe that the westerner is the boss.[49]

In reflective fashion, Meas Nee also emphasized that in the rush to bring "development" to rural Cambodia, it was important not to lose sight of what sustainable rural development is all about: "This is not a matter of building rice barns and organizing pig banks. It is a matter of rebuilding spirit, life, and relationships."[50]

Buddhism, the Monarchy, and Social Change

The Buddhist religion, outlawed and all but destroyed during the Khmer Rouge period, made a slow recovery during the 1980s, with Buddhism again becoming the state religion as the People's Republic of Kampuchea was transformed first into the State of Cambodia and then, through the UNTAC-led peace process, into the Kingdom of Cambodia. By 1996 there were more than 3,000 active *wats* (Buddhist temples) in Cambodia with some 30,000 monks, compared with 3,369 *wats* and 65,000 monks before the onset of civil war in 1970. Although Cambodia's "Second Kingdom" saw the restoration of many of the trappings of traditional Buddhist belief and practice, including the reestablishment of religious rites associated with the monarchy, the effect of the

Khmer Rouge period and its aftermath on Cambodian Buddhism was not well studied. Even less was known of the effect of the country's recent history on Cambodia's religious minorities, including the Cham (Muslim) and Christian communities. It is more than likely that the country's recent history resulted in decided generation-based differences in attitude toward religion, with those born after the Khmer Rouge take-over in 1975 less steeped in Buddhist tradition and hence less likely to adhere closely to Buddhist precepts.[51] Without benefit of research, it safely can be assumed that the position and influence of religion in Cambodian society declined as the result of the country's recent past.

Given the importance of Buddhism as a key aspect of traditional Cambodian culture, it is surprising indeed that the Buddhist *sangkha* (clergy) was not given more prominence, including during the Cambodian peace process.[52] Similarly, it is surprising that the Buddhist *sangkha* was not utilized more specifically with respect to community development and social service activities. For example, as much as the lack of social "safety nets" was bemoaned, little effort was directed to one of the most important social service institutions in the country—the community *wat*. As well, in a country with severe human resource limitations, religious institutions could and should have been supported so they could play a more obvious role, whether in conflict resolution, public education, social values and behavior, or developmental change. Public health and family planning, HIV/AIDS, and protection of the environment are three obvious examples of key public issues that could have been promoted more fully through religious institutions. Besides helping to address these social issues, support to religious institutions would have helped to redefine and reestablish such institutions as a vital part of Cambodian civil society. At the same time, initiatives such as the Venerable Ghosananda's dharma peace walks clearly struck a responsive chord among many Cambodians.

In like fashion, it was disappointing that the king, as "father of the nation," was not more active or successful in his efforts to promote national reconciliation. His children (both literal and figurative) proved more than intractable, particularly in political affairs. Although King Sihanouk, to his credit, made typically outspoken statements on the environment, the observance of human rights, and the importance of traditional Khmer values, his considerable influence was not enough to provoke real change in either the political or social realms. Furthermore, rather than setting a positive leadership role model—for example, through committing himself to the wholesale planting of trees as evident counterpoint to the continued destruction of the country's forest resources, or demanding an end to the use of landmines on Cambodian soil—too many of the king's post-UNTAC efforts were charity oriented, reinforcing the traditional traits of unbending deference to power and authority. In this, of course, the king was not alone—public displays of charity or "good works" became a prominent part of the post-UNTAC political process, including through such political largesse as handouts to the poor and construction of "personally financed" schools and clinics. Such practice only reinforced traditional patron-client relationships and contributed little to necessary efforts toward increased self-reliance.

It also was unfortunate that in the post-UNTAC period King Sihanouk spent relatively little time in Cambodia where he commanded respect and possessed some moral authority. Instead, the king chose to base himself more prominently in Beijing, ostensibly to receive treatment for a litany of medical conditions. Reminded on occasion that his role as constitutional monarch constrained his power and influence, the king became increasingly despondent at the course of Cambodian politics, leading him more than once to propose abdication.[53]

Conflict Resolution

Commentators have pointed to the absence of a cultural tradition in Cambodia for the acceptance of differing opinions, much less reconciliation, in the case of dispute.[54] Nonviolent conflict resolution (through negotiation, compromise, or consensus) traditionally has been little practiced in Cambodia. More commonly, problems have been addressed through veiled threat through the "exhibition of the power of the claimant, (or) seeking a more powerful client who can prevail on behalf of the claimant (or), failing all else, withdrawal from the conflict."[55] Dispute resolution in Cambodia often has been a function of power and position, with the more powerful overriding the position of those less powerful. The resort to such zero-sum relationships very much dominated the Cambodian peace process. UNTAC's lack of attention to or effort toward the introduction of new attitudes and behavior in conflict resolution was among the peacebuilding operation's signal failures. Rather than promoting consensus and building on areas

of agreement or mutual interest as a way to achieve national reconciliation, UNTAC's peace-building efforts were more often characterized
by narrowly defined zero-sum politics. Another failure of the UNTAC-
led peace process was its inability to oversee large-scale demobilization
as a step toward demilitarization and the establishment of the rule of
law.[56]

At a village level, problems with dispute resolution in the UNTAC era
were manifest chiefly in conflicts over land. UNTAC officials were surprised that most human rights complaints lodged during the UNTAC
period related to land disputes. Population growth, resettlement, and
the indiscriminate presence of millions of landmines resulted in growing pressure on land, particularly agricultural land. Registration and
titling of land proved to be a necessarily slow process, as well as a
process highly subject to political and other pressures.

Although a few agencies, notably the Cambodia Development Resource Institute (CDRI) and the Cambodian Institute for Peace and
Cooperation (supported by the German-based Friedrich Ebert Stiftung
[foundation]) sponsored a few isolated conflict resolution activities,
these limited efforts did not go far enough, particularly given the traditional lack or weakness of dispute settlement mechanisms within Cambodian society and particularly in face of the country's weak and poorly
developed legal system.

In addition, in the past communities and community leaders had a
particular and traditionally recognized role in the resolution of domestic disputes. In post-UNTAC Cambodia such systems appeared to have
broken down and were neither reinforced nor replaced by new (legal)
measures. As a result, it appeared that Cambodian households—and
particularly women and children—were subject to increased incidence
of domestic violence.[57]

In post-UNTAC Cambodia, the lack of societally accepted or reinforced methods of conflict resolution was exacerbated—or at least made
more violent—by the widespread presence and use of firearms, itself a
function of the country's recent past. If both *bas reliefs* at Angkor Wat
and the Tuol Sleng Genocide Museum provide testament to Cambodia's long familiarity with violence, the *Phnom Penh Post's* "Police Blot-
ter" feature gave ample evidence of the further development of a
"culture of violence."

In 1996 the Cambodia Development Resource Institute established
the Cambodian Center for Conflict Resolution (CCCR) as an inde-

pendent center supporting a community of conflict resolution practitioners with skills training and resources to enhance the capacity of Cambodians and Cambodian institutions to peacefully prevent, manage, and resolve conflicts. The long-term vision of the CCCR includes development of a resource center and research capacity, an education and training unit, provincial outreach, and an extensive network of support.

Nongovernmental Organizations and the Reconstruction of Cambodia

Nongovernmental organizations (NGOs) have made a significant contribution to Cambodia's rehabilitation, reconstruction, and development, beginning with the post-1979 emergency period and extending through periods of international isolation, liberalization, the UNTAC transitional period, and—with the establishment of the Royal Government of Cambodia—in the post-UNTAC reconstruction period.[58]

In the wake of the Khmer Rouge regime's almost total destruction of the Cambodian nation and people, NGOs provided urgently needed humanitarian and relief assistance as part of an international relief operation. NGOs continued to provide such assistance throughout the 1980s and indeed still helped to meet the immediate needs of the country's vulnerable groups in the post-UNTAC period. Throughout the 1980s and into the early 1990s, NGOs also contributed to the delivery of basic services, within the country and in the Thai border camps. In the post-UNTAC period, NGOs continued to support service delivery, especially health and education services, usually through government structures but sometimes directly or in parallel to inadequate or nonfunctioning government services.

Beginning in 1979, NGOs provided essential support to the country's rehabilitation and reconstruction. NGOs provided financial and technical assistance and support to a wide range of training and capacity-building activities, including exposure to best practices and alternative methods. NGOs also helped in the rehabilitation of essential infrastructure and helped to initiate many community development activities in many parts of the country. Beginning with the UNTAC period, international NGOs assisted in the development of local or indigenous NGOs and other civic and community-based organizations.

Some NGOs, or groups of NGOs, also served as effective advocates for the people of Cambodia. NGO advocacy efforts, including sustained lobbying of Western governments and the publication of an influential report, *Punishing the Poor: The International Isolation of Cambodia*, served as an important impetus to what became the internationally driven Cambodian peace process.[59] In the post-UNTAC period NGO groups served as advocates of vulnerable, often voiceless, groups and lobbied the Royal Government and the donor community on important development issues. A small group of NGOs similarly continued advocacy efforts to ensure the nonreturn of the Khmer Rouge to any position of political power, as well as to assist in efforts that might result in the leadership of the Khmer Rouge being brought to trial for genocide and other crimes against humanity.[60]

The role of NGOs in Cambodia's rehabilitation, reconstruction, and development changed over time. Throughout the 1980s, international NGOs had a special role and influence in Cambodia owing to the nonrecognition by the Western world of the Phnom Penh government, including an economic embargo. Apart from very limited funding provided through UNICEF and the World Food Program, the only Western support to the population of territorial Cambodia was channeled through a core group of international NGOs. As noted by Charny, the strengths of NGO work in Cambodia during the 1980s clustered around the traditional strengths of NGOs: "commitment to people, commitment to the development of local capacity, commitment to the provision of assistance using humanitarian criteria even in the midst of civil conflict."[61] Such assistance, however, encompassed activities unusual for NGOs, including major infrastructural rehabilitation, provision of expensive and specialized spare parts, and technical assistance outside the normal realms of NGO expertise. International nongovernmental organizations also found themselves providing assistance directly to the Cambodian government in direct support of government programs and services. In the absence of other Western assistance, international NGOs working in Cambodia throughout the 1980s served as an opening to the outside world; they also became trusted partners of the Cambodian administration and the Cambodian people.

Cambodia's long international isolation ended with the Paris Peace Accords and the subsequent establishment of the United Nations Transitional Authority in Cambodia. As Cambodia again joined the community of nations through the reestablishment of normal diplomatic, economic, and aid relationships, many international NGOs began to take steps toward devolving or otherwise relinquishing some of their nontraditional roles and activities to the newly arriving bilateral and multilateral aid agencies. Beginning with UNTAC, then, NGOs were able to focus more strongly on "traditional" NGO activities, including community-based development. As noted in the NGO statement to ICORC-3:

> With the increased level of international support, NGOs are free again from responsibility for infrastructure and national developments to take up essential development tasks at the village and district level. This means that NGOs are in a prime position to assist the Government and international donors in sensitive and efficient aid delivery. At the same time, NGOs will continue to accept responsibilities at the national and provincial levels, where their extensive experience in field work provides an irreplaceable source of information. Extensive consultation and collaboration between donors and NGOs will be to the great benefit of Cambodia as a whole.[62]

Although some of the roles played by NGOs began to change with the normalization of the country's circumstances and the establishment of alternative sources of external assistance, the search by NGOs for appropriate roles, operational mandates, and activities continued through the post-UNTAC period (box 6-2).

Some international NGOs made the transition more successfully than others. Some deliberately and strategically phased out their support by reducing and later terminating their assistance to certain activities, particularly activities attracting direct bilateral or multilateral assistance. Some focused efforts on community-based activities, including area-based or integrated rural development programs. Some chose to serve as implementing agencies for projects and programs funded by bilateral and multilateral donors. The UNTAC period, in particular, promoted such NGO implementation, owing to the sudden availability of large amounts of external assistance and donor distrust of the State of Cambodia's "existing administrative structure." In addition, major donors had only just begun to establish an administrative presence in Cambodia and had no capacity—or experience—to directly implement projects in Cambodia. As a result, it was expedient to channel funding through the NGO sector, particularly given the imperative—after more than a

BOX 6-2

NONGOVERNMENTAL ORGANIZATIONS IN CAMBODIA: STRENGTHS AND WEAKNESSES

Many of the longer-established NGOs have made a significant contribution to Cambodia's rehabilitation, reconstruction, and development. The Cooperation Committee for Cambodia summed up their strengths as follows. They have demonstrated the concern, flexibility, and experience to respond to humanitarian needs, to manage development projects and contribute to policy formulation. They have helped Cambodian communities articulate their own concerns and have committed themselves to working at the people's level to help meet these needs. They have supported the establishment of local NGOs and have moved to localize their own staffing. They have worked as advocates for Cambodian people, internationally and within Cambodia. They have brought specialist technical skills to Cambodia and invested in the training of Cambodian staff and counterparts. NGOs have also raised key issues of women's rights, sustainability, environmental degradation, community participation, and ownership in the development arena. And they have continued to serve the government's priorities: the development of health, education, and rural development investments in the people of Cambodia, in their rights to improved living conditions and opportunities, their right to live a decent life and achieve their full human potential.

A 1996 independent study of certain NGO projects, commissioned by the NGO Forum on Cambodia and carried out by the

decade of intentional international neglect—to undertake quick and high-impact rehabilitation action.

Other international NGOs chose to support the establishment or growth of local or indigenous organizations, by providing training and other necessary organizational support or by providing funding support. Although some agencies chose to assist local organizations that shared, or adopted, similar sectoral interests and common approaches to development, other, mostly well-established NGOs encouraged local organizations to develop their own identities, priorities, and ap-

International NGO Training and Research Center, INTRAC, stated:

> Most NGOs benefit from the comparative clarity of their objectives . . . even if these are quite limited in scope. Most take some care in designing their interventions, investing time in dialogue at community level and in participatory rural appraisal, though only rarely in wider baseline studies. Performance indicators are sometimes unclear, and the quality of information obtained from beneficiaries often limited. Most international NGOs attach importance to supporting local NGOs, though many do not follow this up in practice and few have well-developed plans for capacity building and institutional support. Many are unclear about their future and have not developed strategies for handover or withdrawal, leaving the sustainability of their programs in doubt. . . . Many . . . find difficulty in giving adequate support to fieldworkers and experience related management problems such as lack of continuity of expatriate staff. Assumptions about developments in Cambodian society are often not made explicit and cause uncertainties, in particular in relation to the desirability or appropriate methods of working with government, where approaches are particularly variable.

Sources: Cooperation Committee for Cambodia, *Annual Report 1995*, Phnom Penh; Cooperation Committee for Cambodia, Phnom Penh, 1995; and Chris Dammers and others, *Differing Approaches to Development Assistance in Cambodia: NGOs and the European Commission* (Phnom Penh: NGO Forum on Cambodia, August 1996), also published by International NGO Training and Research Center (INTRAC), Occasional Paper Series 13, Oxford, UK, August 1996.

proaches. As some of these local NGOs matured, there was a call for further autonomy, including financial independence, so as to promote a truly indigenous form of development free from donor-driven objectives and priorities.

The reaction of the NGO community to Cambodia's much changed circumstances was mixed. With normalization of the country's political, economic, and external assistance relationships, some NGOs—again usually the more established organizations—were relieved to be able to relinquish some of their activities to the new government and its bilateral and multilateral partners. In addition to consciously planning for a hand-over of responsibility, such organizations also began to develop new activities or programs, often community-based activities. Other NGOs had more difficulty adapting to the post-UNTAC environment, somewhat jealously pursuing their same range of activities and trying to retain their former position of influence despite the arrival on the Cambodian scene of much bigger actors. Still others took advantage of the ready availability of external assistance funding to undertake new program activities or to serve as implementing agencies. With certain of the country's priority rehabilitation and reconstruction needs being addressed by other agencies, some NGOs initiated activities in new or less-served sectors, such as ethnic minorities, the environment, HIV/AIDS, street children, child prostitution, and other sectors. Other international NGOs seized the country's new circumstances to indigenize their operations through the recruitment of Cambodian staff, including project and management staff, or they chose to provide financial, technical, or other support to local groups, including local NGOs and community-based groups.

As noted by the NGO Forum, "one of the great challenges facing international NGOs is to genuinely support and foster the development of local organizations which are not simply locally-run versions of international NGOs." Just as many international NGOs were unprepared to serve only as implementation channels for multilateral or bilateral funding, so international NGOs could not expect their local partners, including local NGOs, to serve merely as implementation channels. Rather, more attention was required to developing the capacity of such groups to serve as true partners.[63] Although the relationship between international and local NGOs was, on the whole, very good, the relationship was not without tension, particularly as local NGOs began to acquire experience and a greater sense of their own identities. In an address to the NGO Forum's 1996 annual meeting, a Buddhist monk, the Venerable Moneychenda, himself head of a local NGO, forcefully reminded international NGOs that they should not strive to create local organizations in their own image. Rather, he called on international NGOs to help indigenous groups find their own voices and roles without the creation of long-term dependencies. Similarly, he pointed out that there was need for greater integration of local NGOs into the wider international NGO network to learn from experience elsewhere as well as to inform or witness the Cambodian experience.

Although there was a tendency to group all NGOs together, the NGO community in Cambodia always was somewhat diverse and was particularly so in the post-UNTAC period. As of mid-1996, an estimated 200 international nongovernmental organizations and as many as 130 local NGOs were supporting or directly undertaking a wide range of activities in most of the country's economic and social sectors (box 6-3).[64] The surprisingly large number of NGOs included a core group of international NGOs that had supported projects and programs in Cambodia for several years, some since the 1979–82 emergency period. Another group of international NGOs had established themselves in Cambodia as increased funding became available from UN and bilateral sources as a consequence of the peace process. Many other NGOs had a history of service delivery in the refugee camps along the Thai border and moved to Cambodia in anticipation of the UNTAC-led repatriation process or as part of the process itself. Other international NGOs launched programs in Cambodia in the post-UNTAC period in response to heightened international awareness of the country's humanitarian and other needs or to serve as implementing agencies for donor-funded activities.

Of the country's estimated 130 local or indigenous nongovernmental organizations, only a very few grew out of "people's organizations." Several were established during the UNTAC period in connection with UNTAC-supported human rights activities. Several more originated in the border camps and focused, at least initially, on the reintegration needs of returnees. Some started as one-person efforts to address a particular need or client group; others brought together individuals with similar interests or objectives. Some indigenous organizations were created with the assistance of international NGOs or other external funding agencies; others were established independently of foreign support, although most sought external financial assistance. Although most local NGOs were established with mostly altruistic intentions, undoubtedly some were created with a view to providing employment or to secure available donor funding.

Although some of the local NGOs established during the UNTAC transitional period, including most of the border-related NGOs and those established by expatriate Khmer, may have tended to support a particular political party or political orientation, indigenous NGOs in the post-UNTAC period were surprisingly apolitical. At the same time, many of the indigenous Cambodian NGOs experienced the types of

BOX 6-3
COOPERATION COMMITTEE FOR CAMBODIA

The Cooperation Committee for Cambodia, or CCC, was established in 1990 by NGOs working in the country to help improve their assistance to the Cambodian people by facilitating contacts and coordination among NGOs themselves, as well as by helping forge strengthened links between NGOs and the Cambodian government, international organizations, and other agencies supporting relief, reconstruction, and development efforts.

As of June 1996, the CCC had sixty-two members and four associate members, with the bulk of the organization's membership consisting of international nongovernmental organizations.

CCC-organized activities include the following:

Information exchange

—Distribution of a wide range of information to member and other organizations (for example, quarterly list of agency personnel, an annual Directory of Humanitarian Assistance in Cambodia, a monthly newsletter, a weekly security briefing, surveys of NGO salary rates for Cambodian personnel, a list of meeting details for NGO sectoral groups, and so on);

—Maintaining a resource center with programme information as well as practical information of interest to agencies working in Cambodia. Provision of advice to member agencies in the maintenance of their own resource collections;

—Liaison with other resource centers and libraries both within Cambodia and outside to facilitate networking and the sharing of information resources and skills;

—Provision of a central location where announcements and other important information (for example, details of employment vacancies for expatriate and local personnel) can be displayed;

—Orientation and advice for NGOs establishing and carrying

out programs in Cambodia (for example, advice on government accreditation protocol, recruitment of staff, staff salary levels, and so on);

—An NGO development analyst position to inform development policy through information dissemination, seminars of program quality, community development and capacity building, and NGO input into donor forums; and

—Monthly meetings to discuss common issues or hear presentations by representatives of government departments or other institutions.

NGO coordination activities

—Representation of member agencies to the Cambodian authorities and others on subjects of mutual interest and concern;

—Serve as a point of contact with other institutions, as well as a briefing center for development personnel, journalists, and researchers;

—Serve as a venue and provide support to thirty-nine sectoral groups (for example, health, education, community development, credit, and so on). Such sectoral groups bring together staff of NGOs, international organizations, and related government bodies to discuss and coordinate their work. The CCC gathers and distributes a list of sectoral groups and the details of their meetings;

—NGO input into consultative group and other donor meetings, including specific input from sectoral groups for collective presentation by CCC-nominated delegates; and

—Cooperation with indigenous NGOs, including staff training activities.

As of 1996 the CCC planned to support research activities addressing aid coordination, NGOs adapting to change, and poverty alleviation.

Source: Cooperation Committee for Cambodia, Phnom Penh.

"growing pains" common to such organizations everywhere, including internal power struggles and schisms over leadership, direction, or policy. As elsewhere in Cambodian society, a generalized lack of trust adversely affected the development of cohesive indigenous NGOs. As noted by Thun Saray, a leader of the local NGO community:

> Gaining experience and understanding is a long-term process. We do not yet have sufficient cooperation, neither between NGOs nor different sectors. This lack of cooperation also weakens our efforts to build up a strong society as a counter-balancing power to the government. This situation can partially be explained by our efforts to build up our own organizations and activities which leaves us little time to reflect together on national issues. We also need the time to overcome our distrust of each other stemming from the Khmer Rouge period and its aftermath, in particular, between those who remain[ed] and those who left Cambodia. This is a slow process that cannot be forced. Collaboration is a step-by-step process as mutual trust is built. Sometimes, foreigners find it difficult to understand this situation and try to force cooperation.[65]

At the same time, by end-1996 a handful of local NGOs already had clearly matured into professional, competent development agencies (box 6-4).

Because nongovernmental organizations in Cambodia often were used as channels for other donor funding, or served as executing agencies for donor-funded projects and programs, it remained somewhat difficult to measure the overall contribution NGOs made to Cambodia's reconstruction and development. At the March 1995 ICORC-3 meeting, international NGOs pledged $U.S.75 million in support of Cambodia's further reconstruction and development. According to the statement delivered at the meeting on behalf of the NGO community, "A significant portion" of the funds pledged for 1995 "comes directly from the community in our countries as a concrete expression of people-to-people solidarity with Cambodians."[66]

Although the contribution of NGOs to Cambodia's rehabilitation, reconstruction, and development was widely acknowledged (through, for example, NGO participation in ICORC and other donor meetings), during the transitional period and beyond, more attention was given to large bilateral and multilateral projects and programs than to activities undertaken by NGOs. At the same time, the Royal Government eagerly accepted whatever assistance NGOs were prepared to supply to ensure

BOX 6-4
NGO FORUM ON CAMBODIA

The NGO Forum on Cambodia was established in the mid-1980s as a partnership of several like-minded organizations supporting a range of activities inside Cambodia. Members of the forum undertook joint lobbying and other advocacy work to publicize the many needs of the Cambodian people and to end the country's international isolation. The work of the forum, including the publication of the influential tract *Punishing the Poor*, directly contributed to the Cambodian peace process.

In 1994 the NGO forum was "repatriated" to Cambodia. As of mid-1996, the forum had some forty members, including nine local nongovernmental organizations. As indicated by its mission statement, the NGO Forum on Cambodia was composed of organizations grounded in their experience of humanitarian assistance to Cambodia and existed in order to advocate on issues of concern to the Cambodian people and to NGOs (local and international) working in Cambodia. The forum also indicated its willingness to continue to coordinate and support advocacy activities and to support capacity building of local partners to carry out advocacy while respecting their independence. The NGO Forum on Cambodia noted particular responsibility to highlight the impact of the development process and economic, social, and political change on ordinary Cambodian people, noting "the advocacy agenda of the Forum must be set in Cambodia and be driven by events in Cambodia." One identified role of the forum was to mobilize international support for this agenda and another was to advocate in Cambodia, working as appropriate in partnership with local partners.

As of 1996 the forum focused its advocacy efforts on five main issues areas: development assistance, the international campaign to ban landmines, the environment (jointly with a CCC theme group), the development of civil society, and the nonreturn of the Khmer Rouge.

Source: NGO Forum on Cambodia, *Annual Report 1996*.

maximum "coverage" at the provincial level, thus enhancing its own credibility with the Cambodian electorate. For donors, NGOs remained extremely useful as implementing partners, particularly before the establishment of bilateral aid missions or other implementing capacity. The proliferation of NGOs, especially indigenous NGOs or other locally established groups, was also interpreted by some as a positive indication of the (re)emergence of "civil society" in Cambodia.[67]

According to an analysis undertaken by the Council for the Development of Cambodia (CDC), the Royal Government expected the NGO community to continue to play an important role in the country's further reconstruction and development as "donors, partners in development, coordinators and managers, experts, an arm of government (especially in rural areas), sources of current information and best practice, agents for capacity building within government and communities, researchers, development leaders and supporters, a prototype for government and donors, as partners in the rehabilitation of infrastructure, and as effective providers of emergency and humanitarian assistance."[68]

The Royal Government's *Five Year Socio-Economic Development Plan for Cambodia 1995-2000* similarly stated that the financial contribution by NGOs was

> only one facet of the involvement of NGOs whose work is geared towards empowering people, especially the disadvantaged, to provide themselves a life of dignity and pride. It is anticipated that the long-standing commitment of the international NGO community to the people of Cambodia and to national rehabilitation and development will continue. This commitment will be reinforced by the emergence of people's initiatives and the further development of local NGOs, which are the normal partners of people-centred, non-profit, non-government organizations.[69]

Quoting Cooperation Committee for Cambodia (CCC) figures, the Council for the Development of Cambodia projected that over the five-year plan period, NGOs would implement more than $U.S.375 million in assistance, including "more than 65 health-related projects with a total budget of $U.S.100 million. . . . more than 40 projects in community development with a total amount of $U.S.50 million, and more than 30 projects in agriculture and rural development for a total amount of $U.S.65 million, along with a further $U.S.20 million for water and sanitation."[70]

The CDC analysis also outlined some of the problems confronting local nongovernmental organizations. The CDC report noted that although local NGOs ideally should develop from the collective articulation of community needs and should not necessarily develop in response to funding, in the case of Cambodia.

> If local NGOs want funding from international donors they must meet certain [donor determined] criteria. They must be able to write detailed, structured applications [in either English or the language of the donor, rarely in Khmer]. They must have qualified, competent staff. They must have a record of success and they must meet the development goals of the donor. In other words, if a local NGO wants project funding it must accept the donor's rules and play the donor's game.[71]

The CDC analysis further suggested that local NGOs in Cambodia were compelled to spend considerable time and effort searching for sources of funding. This had the undesired consequence of some local organizations accepting funding for projects not related to the skills, interests, or experience of the local NGO. As the CDC report noted, "Of particular significance at the present moment is the number of local NGOs who were funded by UNTAC Human Rights [Component] and who are now searching for new patrons. Many of these groups may have little development experience and, in some instances, their prime motive is their own survival."[72]

The dependence of indigenous groups on outside financial and other support also was noted with some concern. In his examination of the emergence of civil society in Cambodia, Thun Saray, NGO leader and human rights activist, noted:

> Our emerging civil society is very dependent on outside funding. We hope such dependence is only temporary until Cambodia is able to support its own civil organizations and people have the increased possibility for voluntary work once their own livelihoods are assured. However, there are certain donors who impose models of development on their partners and control their growth and direction. This attitude arises from a lack of trust, and often little effort is made to build up this trust by the foreign donors for whom partnership counts less than their own plans. In many cases the local partners are too weak to understand this process to be able to resist it. In some cases donors have resorted to setting up their own local structures and NGOs rather than entrust tasks to existing genuine local organizations. Is this partnership?[73]

The CDC analysis also pointed to "malaise and fragmentation" within the indigenous Cambodian NGO community, citing as an example the existence of competing umbrella organizations as well as internecine competition for patrons with funds or political influence or both. The analysis further claimed a lack of agreement on an approach to development—or, perhaps more accurately, an unwillingness to recognize the validity of different approaches: "There is also debate as to how development should occur. On the one hand there is the 'we are the educated and expert and powerful and we know best' approach and at the other, the 'we must encourage and support the local community to articulate its own development needs' approach."[74]

Although the CDC report provided no details or examples, it indicated that there also were some "quasi-NGOs," foreign and local, which had been engaged in proselytism for an assortment of religions, a range of small business activities, as well as direct political activities.

In 1995 and early 1996 the CDC's Cambodian Rehabilitation and Development Board, the Ministry of Foreign Affairs, and the Ministry of Interior all initiated plans directed to the registration and oversight of nongovernmental organizations operating in the country. It ultimately was decided that the Ministry of Interior would assume responsibility for registering NGOs and for monitoring all NGO-supported activity. Although some observers saw the Ministry of Interior's involvement as further evidence of the Royal Government's growing authoritarian tendencies, many others saw the government's determination to better monitor NGO activities as a healthy sign of the government's intention to assume greater control of the country's development path. At the same time, there was some concern that greater scrutiny by the Royal Government of NGO activity might limit or otherwise constrain the further development of civil society, particularly on the part of local groups.

The country's vibrant, if as yet unsophisticated or professionalized local press, as well as the proliferation of local nongovernmental groups, was widely taken as evidence of the emergence of civil society in Cambodia. Indeed, the establishment of local NGOs, human rights groups, environmental organizations, trade unions, media outlets, professional associations, religious organizations, and traditional community groups was commonly perceived to be one of the most positive consequences of the UNTAC-led peace process. As noted by Thun Saray:

Professional associations existed before 1975 but NGOs are a new phenomenon in a country where, until recently, the state alone was responsible for all aspects of life and society. There are now over 100 local NGOs and most of them are genuinely rooted in the local communities. Despite the newness of this work and the problems encountered, progress has been made in all sectors. Professional associations are carrying out their activities on behalf of their members and lobbying the government. There is collaboration among the local NGOs. There is also increased understanding of the role of genuine and independent civil organizations that are free from political links. It is also mentioned that up to now the government and the general public have not opposed, and in some cases have actually been supportive of, the emergence of civil organizations and activities. This is despite the political difficulties at the national level.[75]

As of 1997 it was too early to tell whether Cambodia's nascent civil society might provide a necessary counterbalance to the role of the state. Pessimists were quick to cite the intimidation and even murder of prominent press critics as ample proof of the unwillingness of the country's politicians—and particularly Second Prime Minister Hun Sen—to brook any opposition. As already noted, many similarly interpreted efforts by the Royal Government to better regulate the NGO sector as a threat to the further development of civil society in Cambodia. At the same time, the sheer numbers of local groups and organizations established in the country, the breadth of their involvement in most sectors of Cambodian society, and the courage with which many continued to speak and act was a clear sign that at least some of the international community's hopes for a pluralistic Cambodia had indeed found root in Cambodian soil (box 6-5).

There also was increasing evidence that local groups were having a real impact, with "development" occurring at many levels and in most parts of the country. For example, a May 1996 report demonstrated the effectiveness of NGO-supported court defenders' activities: "It might not seem like it, but there are signs that the rule of law is gradually being embraced in Cambodia. According to one NGO, the Cambodian Defenders Project, in the past sixteen months public advocates have secured acquittals or dismissals in 37 percent of criminal court cases where they represented the accused."[76] Similar small but important victories were being achieved throughout the "Second Kingdom," offering hope that civil society—and the benefits of expression of popular will—would continue to grow.

BOX 6-5
PONLEU KHMER

Ponleu Khmer was established in 1993 to permit popular input into the drafting of the country's new Constitution as well as policies of the newly established Royal Government. The organization later attempted to serve as a funding agency for local NGOs. After considerable soul searching, the organization by 1996 was attempting to speak on behalf of local NGOs in the same way the CCC served international NGOs.

In 1996 Ponleu Khmer had a membership of some twenty local NGOs, serving as "a Federation of Cambodian Associations and NGOs working together to reconstruct and develop a society broken up by two decades of war and human suffering. . . . The reconstruction of such a society requires . . . the full and productive participation of its citizens . . . and should be based on the principles of human dignity and human rights."

Source: Ponleu Khmer, Phnom Penh, 1996.

Corruption

In a June 1994 diplomatic cable subsequently leaked to the press, then-Australian Ambassador to Cambodia John Holloway stated:

Corruption at every level of society has again become a way of life in Cambodia. Every business deal must have a cut for the relevant minister (or Prime Minister) and every transaction involves a percentage for the relevant official in a situation where most government ministries are barely working. . . . Cambodian public servants on an average salary of $U.S.28 per month [an ordinary policeman or soldier received only $U.S.14 per month] are only motivated to attend their offices at all by the possibility of making some extra money. Where it is a matter of facilitation, Cambodians are more or less accepting. Where police, army, or local officials take bribes or illegal imposts, however, there is high level of resentment building up.[77]

In late 1994, the *Economist Intelligence Unit* similarly stated, "Corruption in Cambodia is endemic, and there is little or no prospect of this changing. . . . the distribution of 'largesse' is an activity common to nearly all politicians in Cambodia, including even those termed reformers."[78] Although not a uniquely Cambodian problem, corruption and other "rent-seeking behavior" was a very prominent feature of the post-UNTAC period.[79] Indeed, of the country's many problems, stemming the tide of corruption may have been among the greatest challenges facing the Royal Government as well as Cambodian society as a whole. The scale of corruption in contemporary Cambodia was astounding by any standards. When compared with the absolute poverty of most of the country's inhabitants, the corruption in post-UNTAC Cambodia was nothing less than obscene. In March 1995 Keat Chhon, the country's finance minister and senior minister in charge of rehabilitation and development, estimated that revenue lost through corruption was some $U.S.100 million a year, a sum equal to more than one-third of all internally generated revenue. "It is shameful," he said.[80]

Although no direct evidence was produced, it was well known that senior Royal Government officials had demanded "signing bonuses," often of millions of dollars, as part of the official approval of contracts and other agreements.[81] Regrettably, such "under-the-table" payments ended up in the pockets—or Swiss bank accounts—of senior political officials of both major parties, with no benefit to Cambodia. Such behavior by Cambodia's new political elite contributed to rampant and ubiquitous corruption throughout the kingdom. What was worse, many of the major contracts approved following the establishment of the Royal Government entailed the sale of Cambodia's natural resources—often at fire-sale prices. Corruption, then, not only negatively affected the country's reconstruction, it severely mortgaged the country's future, including through the establishment or reinforcement of a culture of corruption and nepotism.

Such corruption, of course, had a political dimension. Although members of the Cambodian People's Party were far from blameless, in private conversations many Khmer indicated that FUNCINPEC officials very much discredited themselves with their rapaciousness. Unfortunately, cupidity on the part of the country's post-UNTAC leadership only reinforced the low regard most Cambodians had for all politicians.

Corruption in Cambodia was not, however, limited only to senior politicians. Corruption and other forms of rent-seeking behavior became institutionalized at all levels of Cambodian society. To some extent, corrupt practices emerged out of economic necessity as a means to supplement woefully inadequate state salaries. Such petty corruption, including demand for payment for the provision of government services, was expected and accepted by most Cambodians, particularly in the context of well-understood patron-client relationships. Several Cambodian commentators noted that an attitude of "what's in it for me?" had come to permeate most economic as well as many social relationships in post-UNTAC Cambodia. There can be no question that institutionalized corruption limited private investment in the country, or that investments that were made were concentrated in lucrative resource-based activities such as logging, or in casino gambling.[82] It also was no surprise that such an environment allowed the rise of numerous illegal, and hence highly profitable, activities including money laundering, narcotics traffic, and prostitution and trafficking of women and children.

The Royal Government clearly was aware of the problem of all-pervasive corruption, but, with some of its senior officials among the worst offenders, it lacked the political will to really address the problem. In its position paper, "Reinforcing the Rule of Law," presented to ICORC-3 in March 1995, the Royal Government declared that it considered "good governance and the establishment of the rule of law as being central to the evolution of Cambodia's democracy and liberal market economy. It also considers them to be essential to the success of the *National Programme to Rehabilitate and Develop Cambodia*."[83] The Royal Government further committed itself to changing patterns of societal behavior, including by combating corruption, so as to transform "Cambodian society into one which respects fundamental standards deriving from the creation of a body of law, an impartial judicial and enforcement process, and a transparent and accountable public service; and a respect for human rights, social justice, fairness, the immutable sanctity of contracts, and personal honesty and integrity."[84]

The SIDA evaluation report suggested that in war-torn societies like Cambodia "institutions" such as morale or lawfulness are broken down.[85] In Cambodia, the years of war, privation, isolation, unending insecurity, a protracted peace process, and the extraordinary circumstances of the UNTAC transitional period provoked a kind of institutional or moral vacuum that allowed the rapid growth of rent-seeking behavior. As noted by the SIDA report, "The environment of rampant corruption and rent seeking in Cambodia is not only an impediment to effectiveness, but might also have serious political consequences. Even organizations working with labour intensive programmes, and with elaborate control systems established over time, calculate 'losses' of 20-30 percent. The ratio in more rapidly implemented capital intensive programmes is unknown."[86] The SIDA evaluation further predicted, "Rent seeking is likely to be reinforced by the sudden expansion of aid."[87] Following hard upon the overwhelming and profligate UNTAC presence, the post-UNTAC influx of large volumes of both private investment and external assistance contributed to conditions and attitudes conducive to corrupt practices. Private investors certainly had to provide a costly range of "signing bonuses," "contract fees," and other kick-backs. Although the provision of external assistance might have offered less lucrative rent-seeking opportunities owing to more exacting external controls, donors encountered the same "me first" attitude that had come to dominate post-UNTAC Cambodian society.[88]

Although corruption or "the lack of government transparency" in the post-UNTAC period was acknowledged to be a major concern, donors remained surprisingly silent on the issue. Australia, in its statement to ICORC-3 in March 1995, raised the issue of the impact of corruption on the development process. Without support from other major donors, however, the issue was not addressed. Given the entrenchment of corruption at all levels of government and society, it was certain that it would be extremely difficult for the Royal Government to take steps toward "transparency." It also was clear that it would be very difficult to inculcate the necessary change in societal attitudes and behavior within the civil service and the Cambodian population at large. As of 1997, there regrettably was nothing that inspired confidence in the Royal Government's willingness, much less ability, to begin to address the societywide problem of corruption.[89]

Chapter 7

Beyond UNTAC: Rebuilding a Country, Creating a State

The United Nations Transitional Authority in Cambodia signaled a new start for Cambodia. The key elements of the UNTAC operation—peace building; the repatriation of the border population; the electoral process, including basic democracy and human rights training; and the beginnings of concerted effort to rehabilitate and rebuild the country's basic infrastructure and services—all contributed to "Cambodia's New Deal."[1] If the UNTAC operation brought an end to a difficult and often horrific period in Cambodia's recent history, it must be remembered that Cambodia's post-UNTAC future was determined largely outside the country and mostly by non-Cambodians. Imposed, at least initially, by foreign forces, Cambodia's future course was based to a great extent on ideals or precepts alien to the country and its recent history.

Four years beyond the end of UNTAC, a tendency remained to measure Cambodia's progress against the ambitious—and hence not fully realized—objectives of the UNTAC-led peace process. Given the $U.S.2.2 billion cost of the UNTAC operation as well as the fact that UNTAC subsequently was cited as a model of UN-led peace-building efforts, it is important to consider the success—as well as the failures—of the process engendered by or through the United Nations Transitional Authority in Cambodia.

First and foremost, any objective review of UNTAC must note that the operation failed to bring peace to Cambodia. Although the Paris Agreements provided a framework to end the Cambodia conflict, the noncompliance of the Party of Democratic Kampuchea ultimately precluded an effective or lasting cease-fire as well as demobilization and demilitari-zation, much less the achievement of a "comprehensive political settle-ment." If UNTAC can indeed be faulted for not having more successfully dealt with the Khmer Rouge faction, the operation cannot be directly or solely blamed for not bringing peace to Cambodia. The Cambodian fac-tions themselves, the UN Security Council, the signatories to the Agree-ments, and the countries contributing personnel and funding to the UNTAC operation jointly bore responsibility for UNTAC's suc-cesses—and its signal failures. Notably, if the Agreements gave UNTAC considerable authority, the operation never had the capability to even begin to prosecute its wide-ranging mandate. This certainly was true of UNTAC's military and civilian police components, as well as the civil administration and rehabilitation and economic affairs components.

In terms of successes, UNTAC (through UNHCR) did oversee the repatriation of 370,000 Cambodians, many of whom had spent more than a decade in border camps in Thailand. Although faced with the fiction of four equal, and equally capable administrations, and a very hostile political environment, UNTAC did ensure an acceptably neutral political environment for the conduct of a national election. The UNTAC operation introduced and promoted new concepts and forms of behavior, including the observance of human rights, a free press, and multiparty democracy. UNTAC designed a process of rehabilitation and reconstruction that, if not implemented by the donor community, did focus attention on the country's many rehabilitation needs as a foundation for longer-term reconstruction and development. And, of course, UNTAC organized and supervised a "free and fair" electoral process, which ultimately provided Cambodia with an internationally recognized government.[2] Not insignificantly, the internationally led peace process and the UNTAC operation provided a "neutral" (or face-saving) way for Western countries to reverse their foreign affairs, aid, and investment policies with respect to Cambodia. More arguably, international support for the UNTAC operation and rehabilitation ef-forts also afforded some expiation of guilt at what the international community had allowed to happen to Cambodia and its people.

In a 1996 book, *The UN and Complex Emergencies*, Jonathan Moore, former American ambassador to the United Nations, concluded:

> Given that UNTAC was asked to take on much more than it could possibly accomplish, the priorities it followed were admirable, notably throwing its

resources into the elections and not going to war. But it left the country with no real recovery momentum in the countryside, especially needed in the absence of demonstrated coherence and capacity at the centre, along with political stalemate, serious unrest and outright military conflict. Lessons to be drawn about the UNTAC organization itself, apart from political misjudgments in its conception, are that it was much too big and that electoral victories turn up hollow without enough social and economic health to sustain them.[3]

This book has looked beyond UNTAC to focus on Cambodia's difficult and overlapping transitional efforts: the transition toward some form of liberal democracy, including the experience with power sharing as an accommodation between FUNCINPEC and the Cambodian People's Party; economic transition, including a transition from rehabilitation toward development; and the possible beginnings of societal transformation. By exploring the dynamic processes of political, economic, and social change under way in Cambodia, and the role of the international community in support of such fundamental change, this book has attempted to outline some of the influences that will determine the country's future path, as well as the success of what was begun through the UNTAC operation.

Cambodia's Political Transition

Cambodia's many political commentators readily concede that "liberal democracy" cannot be easily transplanted or otherwise grafted to a country lacking any real democratic tradition. At the same time, there has been a tendency to expect too much—and too much, too soon—of Cambodia's transition to liberal, multiparty democracy. The UNTAC-led peace process promised more than it could deliver and raised the expectations of the Cambodian people and the international community. If well intentioned, the imposition of Western-style liberal democracy in Cambodia was compromised by ongoing war (and all that implies in terms of the character of the state) and by features of Cambodian society and history associated with "social relations" and personalized politics. Cambodia's new democracy was not created in a vacuum; rather, it had to adapt to Cambodian political and social realities that in turn conditioned or otherwise intruded on the establishment of liberal democracy.

As noted by Steven Heder, the Paris Agreements did not, in fact, place a high priority on the consolidation of liberal democracy in Cambodia.[4] Rather, the so-called peace process was directed more purposely to the achievement of a new and internationally acceptable political arrangement in Cambodia through a free and fair electoral process. Although some may have hoped that the electoral process would produce a democratic political transition in Cambodia, the UNTAC operation itself invested very little toward ensuring a nurturing postelectoral environment for a fledgling Cambodian democracy.

In a February 1996 statement, Keat Chhon, minister of finance and senior minister in charge of rehabilitation and development, noted that "Cambodia has only recently emerged from long years of traumatic experiences and internal conflict. Democracy is just beginning to take root but is gathering strength. We are now re-establishing the rule of law. As democracy grows in our soil, we seek the understanding of the international community instead of negative and harsh judgments."[5]

According to political scientist Ronald St. John, key elements of political development include an increasing number of contributing citizens, an associated spread of mass participation, and a heightened sensitivity to the principles of equality.[6] Based on these elements alone, the "donor democracy" introduced through the UNTAC electoral process successfully contributed to Cambodia's political development. But as St. John notes, political development "also entails an increased capacity in the political system to manage public affairs, control controversy, and respond to popular demands."[7] As of end-1996, Cambodia's tenuous and personality-ridden coalition government had made little progress in putting high-minded statements about Cambodian democracy into practice.[8] Within a few months, Cambodia's fledgling democracy was further threatened. The rising political tensions and increased factionalism that led to the July 1997 coup de force seemed, to many, to signal the end of democracy in Cambodia.

In addressing the postelection phenomenon of power sharing, this book has suggested that the need for some division of political (and administrative and economic) power should have been anticipated by the architects of the Cambodian peace plan as a necessary accommodation to Cambodian political realities. In hindsight, it became clear that the "democracy" installed through the UNTAC-led electoral process was less a political revolution marking a transition to Western-style democracy than what academic Heder has described as a more transitory set of "conditions in which embryonic and fledgling facsimiles of archetypal bodies of civil society could play a disproportionate and temporarily precocious political role alongside other political forces organized along communist or insurgent military lines."[9] Thus, rather than establishing democracy in Cambodia, UNTAC instead launched a process of political change, including the creation of new political institutions, which ultimately might result in the establishment of a functioning democracy.

Again, in hindsight, it was not surprising that a single foreign-inspired and organized election was unable to much alter the behavior of Cambodian politicians or, at least initially, the country's political traditions. If the UNTAC-led process served to enshrine liberal democratic principles, including pluralism, in the country's new Constitution, the departure of UNTAC permitted a return to many of the (political) practices of Cambodia's near past. In an indictment of Cambodia's post-UNTAC leadership, St. John pointed out that those in power in post-UNTAC Cambodia "mostly have continued to practise politics as usual, often evidencing the familism, cupidity, narrow horizons, and reluctance to absorb or tolerate opposing points of view prevalent in the Sihanouk and Lon Nol periods."[10]

In a similar vein, Heder concluded that the "absence of socio-economic pre-conditions favouring liberalization and democratization in Cambodia was matched by the presence of traits of a political culture which are antithetical to them."[11] Thus, the political turmoil of the post-UNTAC period, including the uneasy coalition between FUNCINPEC and the CPP as well as ongoing efforts to court or co-opt other political groups, including dissident elements of the Khmer Rouge, was a reflection of "the general refusal of [Cambodian] elite culture to recognize the legitimacy of difference and opposition."[12]

At the same time, although power sharing in the post-UNTAC era did not produce true "national reconciliation," the political dichotomy at least initially permitted more political stability than might have been expected given the country's tortured political past or the lack of alternative coalition-style models by which power, and the benefits that accrue from such power, might be shared.

Apart from the powerful concept of a god-king (which is fundamentally oppressive and structurally limiting) Cambodia never has had a common vision or conception of governance. With the arguable exception of Sihanouk's *Sangkum Reastr Niyum*, contemporary Cambodia has seen no leadership that has mobilized masses of people in the country-side to rally for modern change.[13] The UNTAC-sponsored election was seen to voice popular demand for peace and change, but did little to develop a popularly led process of democratization, much less to entrench the corresponding institutions that would guarantee such a process. The lack of an effective social contract between the Cambodian people and the new government left the country again subject to highly personalized politics.

As of the end of 1997, armed resistance in border areas continued, resulting in a new wave of refugees and the reestablishment of refugee camps across the Thai border. Continued fighting and political factionalism raised serious concerns about the health and future direction of Cambodia's nascent democracy and the country's further progress toward the rule of law. The country's future also appeared threatened by the preponderant power of Hun Sen and the Cambodian People's Party, doubts about the timing and conduct of the national election scheduled for July 1998, uncertainty about succession to the throne and the role or scope of future Cambodian monarchs, the National Assembly's continued weakness, ongoing problems with freedom of the press, continued human rights violations and misunderstanding of the basic principles of human rights, the remaining influence of the Khmer Rouge and former Khmer Rouge elements, the political resolution of the "practices of the recent past," lack of effort to limit or control the arbitrary exercise of power by the country's military and police forces as well as some provincial administrations, the unresolved status of opposition parties or any kind of loyal opposition, a lack of debate on issues of public policy, egregious corruption, a tendency toward authoritarianism, and enhanced political partyism leading to increased politically inspired violence.

By end-1997 it was clear that Cambodia desperately required a period of political stability in order that the several achievements of the post-UNTAC period might be consolidated. The last thing the country needed was a further electoral campaign, particularly a negative campaign or one marked by violence. Yet no one, either inside or outside the country, could suggest a postponement of the scheduled election without appearing to be antidemocratic. Thus the 1998 election promised to be as devoid of any real substance—or a vision for the future—as the 1993 UNTAC-sponsored election. The CPP's apparent political dominance, coupled with a badly fractured opposition, augured ill for a free and fair electoral contest, much less the peaceful observance of whatever outcome might result from the ballot box.

Given these gloomy prospects for Cambodia's immediate political future, it became ever more apparent that an electoral process, no matter how regularly or frequently practiced, is neither an adequate measure of Western-style democracy nor a guarantee of democratic practice. The Cambodian experience, as well as experience in many other countries, provided ample evidence that peace cannot be ordained by a simple agreement or proclamation. Nor can democracy be established by the ballot box alone. Rather, peace and democracy can be achieved only as the result of a careful and necessarily lengthy process. Given acceptance of the logic of the rehabilitation-to-development continuum, it is surprising that there is less recognition that "building democracy" or "establishing civil society" also are developmental and time-bound processes. To expect otherwise or to demand too much, too fast, from transitional societies like Cambodia, risks certain disappointment.

From Rehabilitation to Development: Cambodia's Economic Transition

In early 1996, Keat Chhon, minister of finance and senior minister in charge of rehabilitation and development, provided a progress report on Cambodia's post-UNTAC rehabilitation experience:

Two years ago, when the *National Programme to Rehabilitate and Develop Cambodia* was framed, Cambodia was faced with many challenges imposed on it by its past. It had to cope with managing several initiatives all at once in many different directions. . . . I am glad to say that Cambodia has made significant strides in a little more than two years. Our economy is now growing steadily and our GDP, though low, is due to double in seven years. Our revenues have increased. . . . Inflation has come down drastically from over 150 percent a few years ago to less than 1 percent last year. Our national currency has been stable for over a year. Laws are being framed where none existed. Security has been ensured in all populated areas. But, we have to spend a considerable portion of our national resources to combat the incursions of outlawed elements in some parts of our borders. Public Administration reform is on the way. A free press has grown and flourishes. Our efforts to create a conducive environment for private investment are bearing fruit as manifest in over $2 billion worth of such investments which we have approved. At the same time, rural development, health and education have received high priority. Relative to the tragic past, there is now in Cambodia . . . a sense of freedom and choice, which will grow and become part of our lives in a short time.[14]

The Cambodian minister of finance's optimistic summary of very real post-UNTAC achievements, however, needed to be balanced by a more cautionary view of Cambodia's economic future. According to the World Bank, the increase in Cambodia's real GDP per capita averaged 4 percent in 1994 and 7.6 percent in 1995. Although conceding that such growth had resulted in a small but significant improvement in living standards, World Bank economist Michael Ward warned that Cambodia's

recent growth, strengthened and distorted by UNTAC's temporary presence . . . remains superficial and unbalanced. The benefits are not being spread evenly throughout the different aspects of the economy and levels of society. Much of it continues to be concentrated on Phnom Penh and other urban areas which represent only 10 to 15 percent of the total population. In the initial 1991–92 period, the economy grew from a very low base and this reflected activity stimulated by the new liberalization and policies of market reform. Economic expansion was also achieved by exploiting existing real resources and by running down the country's already severely weakened infrastructure. In the years following, growth was driven largely by the massive increase in consumption demand brought about by the presence of UNTAC.[15]

Ward further pointed out that although the Royal Government, with foreign technical assistance, had established overall plans for the difficult task of economic renewal, a coherent overall strategy was lacking and that effective implementation of the government's economic vision would depend on Cambodia's ability to establish more evident aspects of good governance, including improved institutional capacity, an enhanced ability to deliver social and commercial services with a just legal framework, and much strengthened ability to implement public investment projects.[16]

The July 1997 coup de force had a severe negative impact on Cambodia's economic growth prospects. In response to the coup several of Cambodia's largest donors suspended or cut back their aid programs.

As a result, in 1997 alone Cambodia lost as much as $U.S.100 million in aid resources, with no evidence that the previously high levels of aid disbursements might easily or quickly be restored, whatever the country's political circumstances. Regrettably, reductions in external assistance placed key social and poverty reduction projects and programs at risk. The coup also had a negative impact on foreign investment and the country's tourism industry. By late 1997 Cambodia faced a collapse of budget financing with a $U.S.58 million budgetary shortfall.[17]

The *Declaration on the Rehabilitation and Reconstruction of Cambodia* (one component of the Paris Agreements) outlined three key principles for external assistance to Cambodia in the transitional period and beyond: respect for Cambodia's sovereignty, respect for local capacity, and balance in the provision of assistance. Although the framework for Cambodia's rehabilitation as outlined by the *Secretary-General's Consolidated Appeal for Cambodia's Immediate Needs and National Rehabilitation* was never fully accepted by the international donor community, donors nevertheless strongly supported Cambodia's reconstruction and development. As of the July 1997 Consultative Group Meeting, donors had pledged more than $U.S.3 billion in external assistance, a considerable sum, particularly on a per capita basis given Cambodia's relatively small population. At the same time, much of such pledged assistance was directed to expatriate technical assistance as well as for necessary—and necessarily costly—investment in infrastructure or infrastructural rehabilitation.

In a statement prepared for the March 1995 meeting of the International Committee for the Reconstruction of Cambodia (ICORC), the NGO community commented on the considerable progress during the first year of implementation of the Royal Government's *National Programme to Rehabilitate and Develop Cambodia*. The statement noted, however, that the rehabilitation process itself "highlighted the complex nature of development problems—that is, how to build a consistent, cohesive, and efficient administration able to provide basic services, a minimum standard of living and basic human rights to the whole population while also developing mechanisms to govern the country and reconstruct the economy in a democratic, socially equitable, legally acceptable, and environmentally sound framework."[18]

This book has reviewed the salient features of the Cambodian "aid market" and has analyzed trends in external assistance to Cambodia. In assessing the country's post-UNTAC rehabilitation and reconstruction experience, this book has endorsed the commonly held view that Cambodia's limited trained and experienced human resource base and the weakness of all Cambodian institutions will continue to constrain the country's absorptive capacity for many years to come. Indeed, the lack of resources to meet the country's many needs, insufficient human resources, and an inadequate or absent institutional and administrative framework have together limited Cambodia's transition from rehabilitation to reconstruction to development. It also has revealed the ways in which certain patterns and policies of international assistance may, in fact, have exacerbated the problems of institutional and administrative capacity in Cambodia's public sector. This book also has highlighted the country's extreme dependence on external assistance, including various forms of technical assistance, and has provided warning of donor fatigue—particularly in the wake of the July 1997 coup and uncertainty over Cambodia's political future.[19]

Significant work remains to place the country's development path more firmly under the direction of Cambodians. This book has reviewed efforts to better coordinate assistance to Cambodia and has advocated increased donor discipline, including "positive conditionality," as well as sustained, long-term support to Cambodia's further transition toward authentic and sustainable development. Of critical importance is the improvement of basic health and education services and accelerated rural development, which are the key to a better future for the country and its people. The gap between Royal Government and international agency rhetoric on the priority of human development and the reality of aid and resource allocations remains a serious concern. Although a number of major donor-led rural development programs have been implemented in Cambodia, it is far from certain whether the various approaches adopted will contribute in any meaningful way to sustainable development. The Appendix offers an assessment, as of late 1996, of three of the largest donor-funded rural development initiatives.

Cambodia and Social Change

Of all of Cambodia's post-UNTAC transitions, the most difficult to address is the process of social change, particularly as such change influences or affects social behavior (including, not unimportantly, political behavior). No society can undergo the kind of trauma and difficulty as was experienced by Cambodia during the 1970s and 1980s and into the 1990s and emerge unscathed. Although it is possible to discern certain changes in Cambodian social behavior, it is much more difficult to determine the impact of such change, including its effect on the various strands of the country's social fabric.

After years of social turmoil, the UNTAC operation as well as donor-led rehabilitation and reconstruction efforts in the post-UNTAC period entailed considerable social engineering. As noted by Frederick Brown and Robert Muscat, "Cambodia emerges from a generation of conflict as a damaged society in which the social legacy may be more deeply inhospitable to reconciliation and rehabilitation than the economic legacy."[20] Suggesting that donor involvement in the repair and redesign of Cambodia's social fabric represented "a more daunting task than that faced by those countries that made remarkable recoveries from World War II," Brown and Muscat commented:

> Although driven essentially by the need to establish a legitimate government, the international community has perforce plunged into the business of redesigning a society through its superimposition of new forms and norms of governance and of the relations between the state and the individual. Social re-engineering is inherent in much of the donor-financed rehabilitation follow-on now getting under way.[21]

Despite such social engineering, time-honored aspects of Cambodian society, particularly traditional patron-client relationships and a ready deference to authority, prevail. Such traditions and their well-prescribed patterns of behavior will continue to rule Cambodian society and hence condition the country's future development.

Some of the changes wrought on Cambodian society by the country's tumultuous recent past have been discussed, particularly those social changes that most influence the country's political development or Cambodia's continuing transition toward development. Included in the litany of such social changes are a lack of social trust; a generalized propensity to think or plan only for the short term; a lack of social cohesion, including essential social safety nets; many psychosocial problems that are only partially understood; and the declining influence of religion and the Cambodian monarchy.

To this list must be added other changes that are the consequences of the country's several recent transitions. Among such changes, for lack of a better term, is what might be described as "uncaring society," including a decline in social solidarity. Such change has manifested itself through depersonalization of societal relations, increased monetization of social transactions, and a tendency toward self (and immediate family) reflected in a kind of wild civil libertarianism. Although the country has known much violence, post-UNTAC Cambodia also saw the further entrenchment of a "culture of violence" as the result of too many weapons and diminished sanctity accorded to human life. The country's rapid transitions also were accompanied by increased political violence, increased domestic violence, and increased sexual exploitation. Corruption was rampant at all levels and seemed to be institutionalized as an integral part of Khmer society.

Despite this depressing catalogue of social ills, post-UNTAC Cambodia also saw some evidence of social reconstruction, including important efforts addressed to the resurrection of village-based social structures. Four years after the end of the UNTAC operation, however, it remained somewhat too early to predict whether or to what extent Cambodia's "civil society" was being restored, reinvented, or otherwise developed. The proliferation of many indigenous nongovernmental organizations and other local groups as well as an open and sometimes aggressive press was an encouraging sign of the country's social regeneration, though against a still troubled social and political environment. It also remained unclear whether the reestablishment of the organs of civil society and the practice of public participation would necessarily promote or reinforce a new or better Cambodian society including, supposedly, a firmly democratic society.

Beyond Transition: Whither Cambodia?

Cambodia, emerging from the post-UNTAC period, inspired optimism and pessimism. While noting the continued lack of peace and stability, the 1995 SIDA evaluation mission concluded that despite Cambodia's enormous political, economic, and social problems, it was difficult to view Cambodia's "Second Kingdom" without a sense of optimism: "The energies manifest in the bustle of commerce, the constant movement of people and goods in the capital and provincial towns, hold promise for a future in which the people, through enterprise and resourcefulness, will finally shape a peaceful and better destiny."[22]

Indeed, Cambodian society has proved wonderfully resilient. That Cambodia and Cambodian society continued to survive, although not necessarily flourish, after a generation of traumatic social upheaval and dramatic political and economic change, was a testament to the strength of its people and the adaptability of Cambodian culture and traditions. Having weathered the tumult of the past twenty-five years, Cambodia undoubtedly will withstand the vicissitudes of further change, including continued progress on the path of its several transitions.

At the same time, given the opportunities provided by the Paris Agreements, the United Nations Transitional Authority in Cambodia, and considerable international support, as of end-1997 it was difficult not to be saddened by promises unrealized and potential unmet. Four years beyond the end of the UNTAC operation, it was clear that Cambodia would not be spared further problems and difficulties, some of which might have been avoided with enhanced insight, better planning, greater commitment, improved discipline, and real political will. The reassertion or amplification of many of the most negative aspects and influences of Cambodian society also provoked more than a degree of pessimism about Cambodia's future. Much of Cambodia's post-UNTAC political ethos, including zero-sum politics at the expense of consensual decisionmaking, rampant corruption, and the further degradation of the natural resource base, cast a depressing light on the country's further political and economic evolution. Similarly, all but overwhelmed by long-standing problems of poverty and its many consequences, Cambodia faced a new set of problems, including the epidemic spread of HIV/AIDs, a culture of violence and increasing crime, and other negative social influences.

During a visit to Cambodia in early 1996, Winston Lord, American assistant secretary of state, asked NGO representatives whether they were optimistic or pessimistic about Cambodia's future. In a balanced reply, NGOs said that such a simplistic measure did not fit the Cambodian context. Rather, Cambodia's post-UNTAC situation was compared to "the sea which is covered with waves—the level of progress, development, and freedom is constantly bouncing up and down."[23]

Whither Cambodia and what of its several transitions? An Australian aid worker, interviewed on the subject of Cambodia's post-UNTAC future, said:

We always talk about Cambodia being in transition. Transition always suggests that you are moving very smoothly from one set of circumstances to presumably a better set of circumstances. But nothing in Cambodia suggests smoothness to me at all. Cambodia's future is more like rice tossed up from a winnowing basket. Some bits fall to the ground sooner than others, and you never really know what the pattern is going to be until all the pieces are there. For Cambodia, I don't think the pattern will be clear for a long, long time.[24]

Cambodia, with its glorious history, a tragic recent past, and a still-troubled future, provides endless opportunity for analysis as well as speculation. As Cambodia continues its political, economic, and social transitions, the best that can be hoped for is that Cambodians—and particularly Cambodian politicians—will not forget the painful lessons of the past twenty-five years and, with continued international support, will strive ever harder to build a better future for the country and its people.

Appendix

Promoting Rural Development

The Royal Government of Cambodia's presentation to the March 1995 meeting of the International Committee for the Reconstruction of Cambodia (ICORC-3) identified rural development as the government's overriding objective:

> The development of Cambodia's rural economy is central to the Royal Government's plans for raising the living standards of all Cambodians and, in a major sense, represents the Royal Government's ultimate objective. Some 85 percent or more of the country's population lives in rural areas and is directly or indirectly dependent on agriculture for employment and incomes, and agriculture itself contributes almost half of GDP. Given the importance of the rural economy to the national economy, and the potential linkage between poverty and social instability, it is perhaps not surprising that in those factors that foster rural development lie the seeds of a strategy for raising living standards nationally; for eradicating poverty; for reducing disparities in incomes and economic opportunities between rural and urban areas; and, crucially, for strengthening national reconciliation and internal security.[1]

As was revealed by the 1994–95 *Development Cooperation Report*, however, external assistance allocations over the 1992–95 period did not reflect the Royal Government's stated focus on rural development. Fearing the "negative effects that could result from these regional imbalances" (such as a rural exodus to urban areas, reduced productive activity, reduction of trade, increased unemployment, and so on) the

Royal Government in mid-1995 called on donors to "quickly prioritize the reallocation of external assistance to the benefit, notably, of rural development (such as for basic infrastructure for transportation, farm-to-market roads, irrigation systems, basic education and health services)."[2] Such emphasis on rural development was reiterated in a Ministry of Rural Development position paper tabled at a May 1996 Donors meeting. Asserting rural development as the "vision for the 21st century," the position paper stated: "'Returning to the Village' is the theme for the Rural Development Activities to alleviate the poverty in Cambodia for the next five years, as many programs and projects are being implemented to rehabilitate the rural infrastructures and to strengthen and to empower the local grass-roots organizations at the village level in order to achieve sustainable development and self-reliance."[3]

As is examined below, however, the Royal Government allowed donors, as much by design as by default, to plan and implement rural development interventions, including the selection of activities as well as localities. The following pages review the experience to the end of 1996 of three of the largest and most ambitious rural development initiatives launched with donor support.

The Cambodia Area Rehabilitation and Regeneration (CARERE) Project

The Cambodia Area Rehabilitation and Regeneration (CARERE) Project was one of the most ambitious development efforts in the post-UNTAC period. The CARERE project, funded by UNDP and the donor community and executed by the United Nations Office for Project Services (UNOPS), supports the Royal Government of Cambodia's *National Programme to Rehabilitate and Develop Cambodia*, particularly through the Royal Government's *SEILA* program, the government's experiment in decentralized planning and financing of integrated local development. *SEILA* is the Khmer word for "foundation stone"; in Khmer literature, *SEILA* also denotes "clarity of vision" or "inner strength."

The CARERE project was a second-generation project built on what came to be called CARERE1 (Cambodia Resettlement and Reintegration Project). The earlier project, similarly financed by UNDP with international donor support, was launched in 1992 to assist in the resettlement and reintegration of some 370,000 refugees repatriated from camps along the Thai-Cambodian border and an almost equal number of internally displaced persons (IDPs) affected by armed conflict. CARERE1 provided funding and implementation support for emergency, quick-impact rehabilitation projects that contributed to the improvement of basic rural infrastructure and the provision of essential social services. CARERE1 was targeted to the northwestern provinces of Banteay Meanchey, Battambang, Pursat, and Siem Reap, where most of the returnees had indicated their intention to settle and represented an important complement to the UNTAC/UNHCR repatriation operation.

CARERE1 was the first major rural area development project launched in Cambodia. Although designed to address the resettlement and reintegration needs of returnees and the internally displaced, CARERE1 focused on communities as a whole so as to promote effective reintegration and to avoid, as much as possible, any distinction between returnees and others in the northwestern region, since both were in need of the same basic infrastructure and essential services.

CARERE1, modeled to some extent on the UNDP/UNOPS PRODERE program in Central America, typified the kind of donor-driven and donor-funded rehabilitation and reconstruction efforts undertaken in the post-UNTAC period. Its impetus was on rapid implementation of investment activities in different infrastructure sectors, with a subsidiary objective of providing immediate labor-based employment for displaced persons. Although the project pledged to assist in the establishment and strengthening of local management and delivery mechanisms, its emphasis was on the immediate delivery of goods and services, initially directly by UN agencies but gradually undertaken with the more active involvement of Royal Government ministries, provincial technical departments, community groups, local development organizations, and international as well as local nongovernmental organizations. From 1992 to mid-1995, CARERE1 delivered a total of $U.S.25.55 million in assistance, including $U.S.12 million in technical assistance and $U.S.13.55 million in subprojects. A summary of CARERE1's outputs is shown in box A-1.

In 1994 CARERE began a shift away from the direct implementation of rehabilitation projects toward efforts directed to capacity building of government departments and community groups to help them to manage and implement development plans and projects. The internal refocusing of CARERE's implementation strategy was intended to promote

---

BOX A-1

INTERVENTIONS OF THE CAMBODIA RESETTLEMENT AND REINTEGRATION PROJECT, 1991–95

—Construction of 163 kilometers of labor-based roads and rehabilitation and maintenance of 133 kilometers of machine-based secondary roads;

—Demining of access roads and abandoned villages, enabling 12,000 displaced persons and returnees to resettle and take up productive activities;

—Production of more than 1,350 hand-dug wells, 200 drilled wells, and excavation of 127 ponds, providing access to potable water to an estimated 250,000 people;

—Rehabilitation of irrigation schemes, enabling 21,000 hectares of agricultural land to be brought back into production, benefiting 20,000 families; assisting land preparation and provision of agricultural inputs resulting in production of nearly 17,000 tons of rice, benefiting 11,000 returnee families; and provision of vegetable seeds to 55,000 returnee families;

—Construction of 193 new schools with 737 classrooms and rehabilitation of 121 schools with 393 classrooms, with a combined capacity of more than 72,000 students;

—Construction of twenty-eight infirmaries, primarily at com-

---

a more sustainable form of development as well as greater indigenous control or ownership of the development process. Such refocusing also helped to initiate and strengthen support for the processes of decentralization and participation adopted by the Royal Government.

In December 1994 the Royal Government issued a decree establishing provincial rural development committees (PRDCs) in all provinces to act as a forum for discussion of provincial development issues and for coordination of departmental activities. In Banteay Meanchey province, CARERE aided the provincial authorities in the establishment of a "pyramid" of lower level development committees to facilitate dialogue between the PRDC and village communities, and to encourage a bottom-up planning process as a basis for allocating CARERE assistance.

mune level, and ten health centers at district and province level, serving a combined population of 320,000 persons;

—Construction of eight new agricultural stations and training centers and the establishment of eleven tree nurseries, which contribute to the production of improved varieties of rice seed and fruit trees; extension services in crop management; and training, management, and development planning for provincial ministry staff and farmers;

—Formation of provincial water and sanitation committees to assist the Royal Government to define standards and coordinate interventions in the sector;

—In collaboration with UNICEF and WHO, the development of provincial health plans, patient referral services, nurse training, and the establishment of provincial health training facilities and outreach primary health care training programs; and

—Provision of training in income generation, technical, and administrative fields as well as functional literacy programs to more than 1,600 persons (70 percent women), training in community development and agricultural techniques to almost 500 persons, and water use education to more than 30,000 schoolchildren.

Source: United Nations, *Summary of United Nations Programmes in Cambodia*, presentation to the International Committee on the Reconstruction of Cambodia, March 1995.

Through the *SEILA* program, the kind of participatory rural development structure developed in Banteay Meanchey ultimately may be implemented by the Royal Government on a national scale. Such a structure, consisting of a hierarchical network of village development committees (VDCs), commune development committees (CDCs), district development committees (DDCs), and provincial rural development committees was conceived as a means to encourage communities to become actively involved in the decisions that affect their development.

Based on the success of CARERE1, and using the *SEILA* model of decentralization and participation, UNDP/UNOPS over the course of 1995 developed the Cambodia Area Rehabilitation and Regeneration project, or CARERE2 (more commonly referred to as simply "CARERE" given widespread—and positive—recognition of the original acronym). The new project, approved in February 1996, was "designed to facilitate the rapid, sustained shift from direct implementation by project staff to intensive capacity building focused at the Cambodian institutions charged with development, particularly in anticipation of the eventual departure of donors."[4] In particular, CARERE2 was to focus on providing the technical and financial assistance to enable the first fully supported pilot of the *SEILA* participatory rural development structure. According to the CARERE2 project document: "CARERE will be an experiment in decentralized planning and financing of participatory rural development, aimed at alleviating poverty, strengthening civil society, promoting dialogue between the constituents of the Cambodian society, and contributing to the spread and consolidation of social stability and peace throughout the country."[5]

CARERE2 was designed to support the establishment of a fully functioning provincial structure (*SEILA*) able to plan and support the kind of provincial development that responds to the needs and aspirations of its citizenry. Through intensive capacity building, CARERE hoped to actualize a process of bottom-up planning that would shift the development paradigm in the five "CARERE provinces" from a donor (supply) driven external process to a participatory, people-centered (demand) driven internal process of change. Besides generating an increased measure of local participation in decisionmaking and resource allocation, the "new" CARERE also was expected to contribute to the regeneration of the institutions of civil society.

Because institutional interlinkages and issues of governance and popular participation were only nascent in Cambodia, and because notions of decentralization of decisionmaking, planning, and financing of development as of 1996 remained at the level of policy dialogue, the CARERE project afforded the opportunity to test, in an applied environment, a variety of capacity building and participatory development approaches that could inform national policy in the future.[6]

For 1996–99, CARERE2 planned a contribution from UNDP core resources of $U.S.20.5 million for technical assistance and the CARERE2 administrative "machine" and aimed to mobilize an additional $U.S.20 million (at minimum) of donor cost sharing for the implementation of subproject rehabilitation and development activities at the commune and village level. In particular, the United Nations Capital Development Fund (UNCDF) agreed to assist in the establishment of a Local

Development Fund (LDF) for Cambodia and also pledged up to $U.S.3 million toward capitalization of the Fund, with additional donor contributions to be channeled through a Trust Fund established by UNDP and executed by UNOPS. With more than 85 percent of UNDP's contribution to CARERE2 directed to some 1,300 person/months of expatriate technical assistance, the Local Development Fund represented an essential complement to CARERE2's capacity-building and community development activities in the five target provinces.

Besides its scale, CARERE2 was impressive in its scope or vision for promoting sustainable and community-based development in Cambodia. According to a July 1995 "prospective evaluation" of CARERE, "by supporting the Cambodian initiative for local development, CARERE [that is, CARERE2] is in a position to make a contribution of historical proportions to the long-term reconstruction of Cambodia."[7]

Some of the basic premises of the "new" CARERE, however, needed to be further examined. First, it remained an open question whether CARERE conformed to the Royal Government's vision of rural development or whether a particular model of development was being imposed on the country by external actors, however well intentioned. By incorporating methods of participatory rural appraisal, decentralized or bottom-up planning, "social inclusion" and local empowerment, CARERE2 very much reflected the latest in development thinking, which, as worldwide experience has shown, does not necessarily address the real needs of poor societies—at least in the short term. Although the limited experience with the CARERE2 methodology in Banteay Meanchey gave some indication that the approach did, indeed, engender a development process, it remained too early to tell if it was a sustainable process that would allow communities to take greater responsibility for their own development, including the capacity of communities to mobilize and manage their internal resources.

The linkage among CARERE's stated objectives also seemed somewhat unclear: "The long-term objective of CARERE2 is to alleviate poverty, and thereby contribute to the spread of peace in Cambodia, by strengthening the bonds of civil society to the structures of the State and empowering the Cambodian rural population to become fully participating members in the development process."[8] That effective rural development was the only means to secure lasting peace in Cambodia—particularly with respect to the continuing influence of the Khmer Rouge—was accepted as a truism. The absolute connection between rural development and the reemergence of civil society, however, remained largely in the realm of theory, at least in Cambodia. Furthermore, the CARERE2 project document provided little detail on how the project would contribute to poverty alleviation in the five target provinces. It was assumed that improved rural infrastructure and improved delivery of basic services (funded through the complementary Local Development Fund) would necessarily result in enhanced employment and income-generating opportunities, and that such interventions would also have multiplier economic and social effects in other sectors. It also was assumed, probably correctly, but assumed nonetheless, that a process of capacity building through community development would be an essential precondition to sustainable forms of development at a local level.

It was suggested that the implementation of *SEILA* through CARERE2 would contribute to, if not lead, the reestablishment of civil society in rural Cambodia. The linkage between those structures established by *SEILA/CARERE* and "civil society," however, were particularly unclear. Participatory development through the determination by representative committees of development priorities and the allocation of scarce development resources might be considered an important aspect of civil society. But even the effective operation of the *SEILA* model, however, would not encompass all of civil society. The adoption of an inherently inclusive and participatory approach was presented by CARERE as a means to reinforce Cambodian civil society, but without any explication of the way it might be strengthened or the developmental or other effect of such strengthening. Without a full understanding of the contemporary nature of civil society in contemporary rural Cambodia, in either more settled communities or in newly established villages, *SEILA/CARERE* proposed new institutional structures. The relationship between these newly created structures and other forms of civil society—pagoda committees, parent associations, or "single purpose" groups (such as water-user groups, revolving funds, informal savings groups, and so on)—also remained somewhat unclear except in terms of a direct funding relationship. At best, then, it appeared that CARERE hoped to co-opt existing local structures, organizations, and "political" interests in prosecuting a particular approach to rural development in Cambodia.

As of late 1996 there also was no real indication of the Royal Government's commitment to the *SEILA/CARERE* model. For example, several months after the approval and signing of the CARERE2 project, the Royal Government still had not agreed to the establishment of a high-level "task force" under the responsibility of the Council for Agriculture and Rural Development (CARD) as a "dialogue forum on policy issues arising from the *SEILA* experiment and, eventually, as a decision-making body regarding the future of the experiment and its applicability on a national scale."[9] Although it was too early to expect the Royal Government to commit itself to the nationwide adoption of the *SEILA* approach—particularly in the absence of the same level of funding and technical assistance support as had been committed by CARERE to the five target provinces—the Royal Government's somewhat cautious response possibly signaled a lack of commitment to the overall *SEILA*/CARERE2 approach.[10]

Nor was there much indication of how future local elections might affect implementation of the *SEILA* approach, particularly beyond the five provinces targeted by CARERE2. Would such elections merely formalize and extend the institutional and planning frameworks pioneered by CARERE, or would they introduce a new and specifically political focus to governance in rural Cambodia to the detriment of the development process? Might such politicization, along the same disappointing (party) lines that characterized Cambodia's national political scene, preempt, or otherwise preclude CARERE2's "re-emergence of civil society" goals?

The CARERE2 project document outlined several "risks" that might affect the successful implementation of the CARERE "experiment." Such risks, however, were downplayed or otherwise minimized by proposing meaningless, or at least somewhat platitudinous, countermeasures. For example, in response to the "potentially serious risk" that it might prove difficult to find suitable persons (preferably "bright, young university graduates") to serve as the core of proposed province-based planning teams, the project document suggested that "the remedy is to start the search for such people immediately so that training can commence as soon as possible."[11] Similarly, the project document identified a potential risk that government staff trained as community development workers might lack the incentive to spend sufficient time at the village level owing to low government salaries and the difficulty of travel in rural areas. The proposed remedy was incentives like "training and travel and subsistence allowances," as well as the strong involvement of local NGOs to supplement government capacity.[12]

The risk of "a natural tendency of higher level officials to resist decentralization of decision-making powers and an urge to maintain control of funds . . . leading to efforts to 'recentralize' the development process" could, according to the project document, be remedied by "a strong government message to all concerned that the decentralization policy is one that the government is seriously committed to" as well as by the continued "education of key officials in the [unspecified] benefits that will accrue from this approach over time."[13]

The CARERE2 project document did not address risks associated with any politicization of institutional structures and mechanisms at the village, commune, or district levels; nor did it address what by late 1996 had become a ubiquitous problem in Cambodia: corruption and other "rent-seeking" forms of behavior, especially in connection with the approval and utilization of funding resources.

Given the size of the CARERE2 project ($U.S.20.5 million of core UNDP resources plus at least an equal amount in donor funding for rehabilitation and reconstruction subprojects), it was surprising, although honest, that the project was consistently referred to as an "experiment." Although it appeared that CARERE2 might, indeed, make a contribution of historic proportions in its five target provinces, on face value the project's planned outputs—all focusing on capacity building and community development training—were quite modest. CARERE2's main planned outputs for the 1996–99 period included:

—Establishment of a professionally trained planning unit in the Secretariat of each provincial rural development committee (PRDC) in the five *SEILA* provinces;

—Socioeconomic and sector surveys in each of the five provinces that assess the socioeconomic situation of the province, its development constraints and opportunities, and the characteristics of its population;

—Four annual (1997–2000) provincial development plans for each of the five *SEILA* provinces;

—Training of some 100 field staff in each province in established processes of VDC formation and in participatory development planning techniques;

—Establishment of at least 500 village development committees, at least 40 commune development committees, and some 20 district development committees in the five target provinces, together with associated development plans "rolled up" to the next level of responsibility; and

—Outputs associated with the training of selected officials as well as the establishment of guidelines for funding and reporting criteria as well as for project design, appraisal, approval, implementation, monitoring, evaluation, and financial management.

Although such outputs likely represented essential preconditions to sustainable rural development in Cambodia, it was somewhat difficult to see how they might contribute directly, and to what measure, to CARERE2's stated objectives: poverty alleviation, the regeneration of civil society, and the spread and consolidation of social stability and peace throughout the country.

European Rehabilitation Program for Cambodia (PERC)

Beginning with the signing of the Paris Agreements on October 23, 1991, the European Union became one of the largest sources of funding for Cambodia's rehabilitation and reconstruction. For the six-year period 1991–97 the European Union pledged some $U.S.145 million in support of a wide range of rehabilitation, reconstruction, humanitarian assistance, technical assistance, human rights, and other activities.

The EU's Emergency Rehabilitation Program (ERP), initiated in May 1992, provided some 20 million ECU ($U.S.24 million) for rehabilitation activities in Cambodia's northwestern provinces. The program, implemented through European-based NGOs already working in Cambodia, was intended to be a "flexible, action-oriented, highly operational rehabilitation programme yielding both immediate and long-term benefits."[14] Like the UNDP/UNOPS CARERE program, the aim of the EU's Emergency Rehabilitation Program was to develop and reinforce the socioeconomic environment to effectively benefit the local population and to facilitate the resettlement and reintegration of returnees and internally displaced persons. A summary of activities undertaken through the ERP is provided in box A-2.

The European Rehabilitation Program in Cambodia (PERC), launched in May 1995, represented a second phase of European Union support to Cambodia's reconstruction and development. The 67.1 million ECU ($U.S.80.5 million) PERC program, to be implemented over a two-year period, was composed of several separate program components, including a Rehabilitation and Support Program for the Cambodian Agricultural Sector (PRASAC); a nationwide support program for

BOX A-2
EUROPEAN UNION/CAMBODIA
REHABILITATION PROGRAMME (ERP)

Rehabilitation activities undertaken by European-based NGOs with ERP funding included the following: village-based sanitation training; rehabilitation of town markets; water resources rehabilitation and development; water source data collection; rehabilitation of urban water distribution networks; urban solid waste collection systems; rainwater catchment and storage systems; waste water treatment systems; training in hydrology; rehabilitation of irrigation networks; agricultural training; establishment of rice banks, cow banks, and rural credit schemes; forestry training; production of tree seedlings; rehabilitation and construction of rural roads; bridge construction; training of monks in community development; adult literacy; skills training; construction of classrooms; hospital rehabilitation; assistance to para- and tetraplegics; training of health and sanitation personnel; supply of medical equipment and drugs; contribution to the establishment of a blood bank; antituberculosis activities; training of midwives; demining; and mine awareness campaigns.

Source: Kingdom of Cambodia and the Delegation of the European Commission, "Investing in the Future" (Bangkok: Delegation of the European Commission, January 1995), p. 9.

primary education; a technical assistance program in support of institutional development; a six-month extension of the ERP program to "consolidate" rehabilitation efforts in Battambang, Pursat, and other northwestern provinces; promotion of human rights through training and institutional development; community health and social development in two suburban areas of Phnom Penh and a primary health program in Sihanoukville (implemented by European NGOs); institutional support for urban planning in Phnom Penh; funding for "strategic" or "preinvestment" studies, such as an assessment of the country's natural resource base or the development of Siem Reap province and the Angkor Temples area; as well as the establishment of a European Union Technical Coordination Office in Phnom Penh.

Of the total funding provided for the European Rehabilitation Program in Cambodia, more than half (36.8 million ECU or $U.S.44.2 million) was allocated to PRASAC. Whereas earlier EU-funded rehabilitation activities had focused on the country's northwestern provinces, for PRASAC the EU selected six central and southeastern provinces (Kompong Cham, Kompong Chhnang, Kompong Speu, Prey Veng, Svay Rieng, and Takeo). The EU justified its choice of these provinces by the fact that they were among the most densely populated provinces in the country, together accounting for more than 50 percent of Cambodia's total population. In addition, the six provinces had been somewhat neglected by initial donor-funded rehabilitation efforts that had been concentrated in the northwestern provinces. The establishment of a major rural rehabilitation program in these provinces, then, served the interest of the Royal Government through a more equitable national distribution of rehabilitation and reconstruction activities; it also gave the EU considerable profile (and without the need for any major coordination of donor efforts).

The PRASAC program was conceived as a predevelopment program that would "revive and relaunch agricultural activities" in the six target provinces. The thirty-month program also was explicitly designed to "reinforce the role and the credibility of the new government's initiatives" by producing tangible "results immediately or in the very short term."[15] Besides directly benefiting up to 150,000 rural families, the PRASAC program was expected to establish favorable conditions for the further and autonomous development of rural farming communities. Activities to be undertaken through the PRASAC program included small and medium irrigation network improvement, the creation of a system of basic agricultural credit, agricultural skills training, the introduction of efficient technologies, potable water resources development, and the promotion of cottage industries and the creation of small crafts enterprises. Implementation responsibility for the PRASAC program was contracted to three private European firms (bureau d'etudes), each covering two provinces and each providing their own experts or subcontracting project components to NGOs or other agencies.

The $U.S.44.2 million PRASAC initiative generated great controversy, particularly within the NGO community. The program was criticized as being too hastily conceived and too ambitious given its thirty-month time frame: "The very same haste which is seen by the EU as the best way not to waste time is viewed by some NGOs as the best way to waste money."[16] Other analysts questioned whether the "predevelopment" PRASAC program would truly provide a jump-start to a longer process of rehabilitation, reconstruction, and development in the six provinces—particularly in the absence of a longer-term commitment by the European Union to sustained assistance. Such criticism, dismissed by European Union Ambassador J. Gwyn Morgan, in a September 1995 interview with the *Phnom Penh Post*, challenged conventional wisdom about Cambodia's progress along the so-called relief to development continuum.

NGOs who were supporting projects in the PRASAC provinces also complained that "Europe is muscling into provinces where it has never been before. . . . It may walk over initiatives which have been prepared over many years in provinces it does not know at all."[17] The European Union initiative also was criticized for recruiting or otherwise commandeering much of the limited human resources at the provincial level, at the expense of NGO-supported activities and the Royal Government's own programs. As with CARERE, there also was some criticism that too much of PRASAC's funding was directed to expatriate technical assistance and support costs at the expense of field-level rehabilitation activities.

NGOs with experience in rural credit expressed concern that the rural credit component of the EU-funded PRASAC program might supplant or otherwise undermine existing rural credit schemes initiated over a period of years: "Credit schemes require time, time to identify villages, time to train staff, time to assess the needs. Time, then, to set up the system. Thirty months is not enough. It [the PRASAC credit scheme] will collapse, with bad impacts for the NGOs' work afterward."[18]

In view of such concerns, the NGO Forum on Cambodia in March 1996 hired a team of consultants to undertake a study examining different approaches to development and the strategies adopted by the European Union and local and international nongovernmental organizations in Cambodia. The study also was intended to complement the European Union's own internal midterm evaluation of the PERC/PRASAC program. The terms of reference for the NGO-commissioned study directed it to focus on credit and water management projects implemented by the EU and NGOs in two provinces (Svay Rieng and Kompong Chhnang). It was proposed that the study might result in improved dialogue and cooperation among all groups concerned as well as suggestions on ways of improving and extending credit and water projects to ensure sustainability and maximum benefit to rural communities.

The NGO Forum on Cambodia study, *Differing Approaches to Development Assistance in Cambodia: NGOs and the European Commission*, found PRASAC "unduly inward-looking, with very limited transparency" and stated that PRASAC's "initial emphasis on demonstrating political support to the new Cambodian government as rapidly as possible led to shortcuts in professional planning procedures and a degree of incoherence in programme design."[19] The NGO study found that the design of the PRASAC program suffered from limited baseline information, unclear assumptions, limited consultation, and an overambitious and unduly quantitative approach. The report also suggested that as part of the program design process the European Union should have given increased attention to the economic status of beneficiaries and to gender issues. The NGO Forum–contracted study concluded:

> PRASAC displays serious weaknesses in design and planning, primarily because the developmental sectors in which it works are not amenable to a 'rapid impact' approach. The sustainability of its programme is jeopardized both by the uncertainties over PRASAC's future after June 1997, and lack of clarity surrounding the institutions PRASAC is trying to promote. These problems are particularly acute in the credit sector.[20]

The consultants' report noted that "PRASAC targets for credit schemes were highly overambitious even in their revised form, and will take several years to take root even if their institutional framework is clarified."[21] As for the sustainability of PRASAC's rural credit initiatives, the NGO Forum report noted that "the assumption that such schemes will be run effectively by local government is unlikely to be viable" and warned that "non-governmental alternatives on a national scale, or possibly some variety of parastatal option, will also take time to develop."[22]

Given substantial donor assistance to Cambodia, debate over the importance and utility of large donor-funded programs such as the EU's PRASAC was likely to continue. Although European Union officials privately acknowledged that the thirty-month time frame for such a major program was far too short, the EU defended its PRASAC program as an important contribution to Cambodia's rehabilitation as well as something that reinforced the role and credibility of the Royal

Government. Although this may, indeed, have been true, might some alternative use of the EU's $U.S.44.2 million contribution have had the same or even greater development impact, especially given PRASAC's very high (and costly) technical assistance component? For example, a well-chosen program in support of demobilization or civil service reform might have had greater impact while at the same time giving both the Royal Government and the EU the same desired profile. Instead, the European Union chose to invest in a program that, at best, might lay the foundation for a longer-term development process in the six central provinces—while at the same time providing the country's new post-election government with some measure of field-level credibility.

The Social Fund of the Kingdom of Cambodia

The Social Fund of the Kingdom of Cambodia (SFKC), an autonomous public institution, was established by Royal decree in December 1994 for an initial five-year period. It was to provide grant funding for the implementation of small-scale and simple technology community projects and short-term training activities proposed by community groups, local authorities, provincial and district departments of line ministries, or local or international nongovernmental organizations. The Social Fund was capitalized through a $U.S.20 million loan from the World Bank and was modeled on similar World Bank–supported Social Funds in other countries. Projects eligible for funding included education, health, and social affairs facilities; infrastructure (water supply, sewerage/latrines, culverts and bridges, drainage); equipment (for schools, health facilities, or vocational training centers); and "services projects" (small business and public health training).

Like both CARERE and the EU's European Rehabilitation Program in Cambodia (PERC), the Social Fund was designed to "kick start" the rehabilitation and development process at a community level while also supporting the reestablishment of civil society and enhancing the credibility of the Royal Government. Materials prepared by the SFKC Promotions Department bore such slogans as "Small work is a big step in rebuilding the country" and "SFKC–Working for a Brighter Future!" As outlined in an SFKC brochure outlining "sub-projects eligibility criteria," the Social Fund's main objectives included the following:

—To respond to the needs of poor communities within the kingdom and to alleviate their poverty;

—To increase employment opportunities for the poor in both rural and urban areas; and

—To promote social welfare through the implementation of small projects for the rehabilitation of social and economic infrastructure and for supporting socially productive activities.[23]

As a funding agency, the Social Fund was not intended to be directly involved in the identification, initiation, or sponsoring of projects; rather the Social Fund was designed to respond to the community-based demand for projects by sponsoring community agencies. At the same time, the SFKC established a "menu" of eligible project activities with specific criteria and prepared a number of standardized project applications, including estimates of building materials for the construction of capital facilities. Such projects were ranked, with priority given to primary school facilities/equipment and water supply. The Social Fund also established indicative allocations for each kind of project and each province to ensure nationwide coverage.

Under Social Fund guidelines, projects were to employ "least cost designs" and were expected to "deliver benefits in excess of costs." Projects receiving Social Fund support also were expected to provide employment opportunities for the poor through use of labor-intensive techniques or by otherwise generating a significant social impact. In the case of the construction of school or health facilities, sponsoring groups were expected to demonstrate a definite need as well as the availability of public land, staffing, and sufficient budgets to cover operating costs. The Social Fund was not to be used to supplement recurrent budget expenditures of the Royal Government, nor was it intended to replace normal sectoral activities and responsibilities of the Royal Government.

Once projects were screened for eligibility, appraised through site visits by SFKC staff, and approved by the Social Fund's executive board, the project's applicant or sponsor assumed responsibility for subcontracting an implementing agency to perform the work. Although the Social Fund had no direct implementation responsibility, project funds were disbursed directly by the fund to implementing agencies, with SFKC staff also supervising and monitoring project implementation to ensure the technical quality of the project and to check on the financial administration of the funds.

The preparation by the Social Fund of standardized project designs and simple application forms made it very easy for communities and groups to simply pick and choose among a number of possible projects. Indeed, there was little disincentive for communities or other groups to submit an application on speculation although, as with CARERE-funded projects, recipient communities were expected to provide a counterpart contribution of some 5 percent of total project costs either directly in support of the project or in the form of some kind of complementary activity, for example, the rehabilitation or construction of ponds, fences, or gardens or the provision of furniture or other equipment, and so on.

By March 1996, after only a few months of effective operation, the Social Fund of the Kingdom of Cambodia had received more than 1,850 project applications from community groups and local governments, with rehabilitation or construction of school facilities accounting for more than 80 percent of all proposals. As of March 1996, more than seventy projects had been approved, and some fifty projects were under way. The total cost of all project proposals submitted to the Social Fund exceeded the fund's initial $U.S.20 million capitalization, thus demonstrating the demand for such project activities.

That such demand exists, however, is neither surprising nor new. In the post-1979 period, the People's Republic of Kampuchea regime allowed communities to rebuild their wats (pagodas) only after they had first constructed school facilities. In succeeding years, communities organized "flower ceremonies" to raise funds for community projects, including both wats and schools. Many international NGO community development activities were initiated through projects involving the construction of community facilities. Food-for-work and other labor-intensive or employment-generating activities focused on community infrastructure.

What was new to Cambodia was the use of loan funds—though on concessional terms—to support community-sponsored initiatives. As with other major donor-funded rural development programs, the establishment of the World Bank-financed Social Fund raised questions about long-term sustainability, as well as questions concerning the impact—at least in the short term—on poverty alleviation, particularly for the poorest or most vulnerable segments of Cambodian society. As of late 1996 it was too early to calculate the productive return of Social Fund projects, especially for investment in school and health facilities rehabilitation and construction—and particularly when the Royal Government remained unable to provide adequate support in terms of salaries, materials, and equipment.

There also was the question of whether the Social Fund represented a productive use of scarce development resources, particularly given that the government and people of Cambodia would have to repay the World Bank soft loan with nominal interest. Would the projects funded by the Social Fund generate sufficient return—in either a productive or social sense—to amortize the debt obligation? How might it be made sustainable without accruing further debt or allocating other limited (and donor-controlled) resources?

In the case of the Social Fund there also was the question about whether the Social Fund—or rather completed projects at the grassroots level—would indeed lend the Royal Government enhanced credibility. Similarly, there was the attendant risk that the Social Fund might be used in a more narrow sense to win partisan political support. Would it support the reemergence of civil society by promoting enhanced community organization and cooperation? Could the completion of a simple application form by a community group engender a larger and longer process of community development? It was argued that through successful completion of one simple project, community groups might gain the experience and confidence necessary to attempt larger and more complex projects. Although it is too early to tell whether this might be true in post-UNTAC Cambodia, it was at least as likely that the Social Fund of the Kingdom of Cambodia represented a (relatively) cost-free "gravy train" of chief benefit to more organized or more cohesive communities or community groups, without necessarily engendering or reinforcing civil society in Cambodia.[24]

Notes

Preface

1. Other reports already printed under this program include V. Tickner, *Food Security: A Preliminary Assessment*, UNRISD Discussion Paper 80 (Geneva, 1996); Cambodia Development Resource Institute, *Rethinking Food Security: A Report on the Preliminary Findings of the CDRI/UNRISD Study on Food Security and Coping Strategies in Cambodia* (Phnom Penh, 1997); and J. Boyden and S. Gibbs, *Children of War: Responses to Psycho-Social Distress in Cambodia*, (Geneva, UNRISD, 1997). The UNRISD program, Vulnerability and Coping Strategies in Cambodia, is supported by a grant from DANIDA.

2. The War-Torn Societies Project, currently under way in Eritrea, Mozambique, Guatemala, and Somalia, aims to assist the international donor community, international organizations, nongovernmental organizations, and local authorities and organizations to understand and respond better to the complex challenges of postconflict periods.

3. Grant Curtis, "Transition to What? Cambodia, UNTAC and the Peace Process," in Peter Utting, ed., *Between Hope and Insecurity: The Social Consequences of the Cambodian Peace Process* (Geneva: United Nations Research Institute for Social Development, 1994), pp. 41–69.

4. Research studies commissioned by the Swedish International Development Authority included the following: Bernt Bernander and others, *Facing a Complex Emergency: Evaluation of Swedish Support to Emergency Aid to Cambodia* (Stockholm: Swedish International Development Authority, 1995); Jan Ovesen, Ing-Britt Trankell, and Joakim Öjendal, *When Every Household Is*

an Island: Social Organization and Power Structures in Rural Cambodia, preliminary draft report, "Assessment and Analysis of Present Knowledge Regarding Social Organization and Power Structures in Rural Cambodia" (Stockholm: Swedish International Development Authority, November 1995); Per Ronnås, *From Disaster Relief to Development Assistance: How Can Sweden Best Help Cambodia?* (Stockholm: Swedish International Development Authority, 1995); and Michael Vickery and Ramses Amer, *Democracy and Human Rights in Cambodia* (Stockholm: Swedish International Development Authority, 1996).

Chapter 1

1. A 1996 monograph by Jonathan Moore, former American ambassador to the United Nations, addressed the role of the United Nations in responding to the challenges of "rehabilitation in Third World transitions." See Jonathan Moore, *The UN and Complex Emergencies: Rehabilitation in Third World Transitions* (Geneva: United Nations Research Institute for Social Development, 1996). A wide-ranging 1995 SIDA study evaluated Swedish support to Cambodia in the context of the many needs resulting from a "complex emergency." Bernt Bernander and others, *Facing a Complex Emergency: Evaluation of Swedish Support to Emergency Aid to Cambodia* (Stockholm: Swedish International Development Authority, 1995). The War-Torn Societies Project, referred to in the preface, similarly is directed to an enhanced understanding of the many and complex challenges faced by societies emerging from periods of conflict.

UN General Assembly resolution A/50/227, adopted on May 24, 1996, called for "an early exploratory review to be prepared jointly by the United Nations and the Bretton Woods institutions to assess mechanisms, programs, and relationships at the field, headquarters, and intergovernmental levels, with a view to identifying areas in which communication, cooperation, and coordination could be improved." Among other areas of study, the review was to examine "the use of existing resources in the transition from emergency relief to rehabilitation and development."

2. The Paris Agreements comprised *Agreement on a Comprehensive Political Settlement of the Cambodia Conflict, Agreement concerning the Sovereignty, Territorial Integrity and Inviolability, Neutrality and National Unity of Cambodia,* and *Declaration on the Rehabilitation and Reconstruction of Cambodia.* The full texts are published as Document 19, UN Document A/46/608-S/23177, in *The United Nations and Cambodia 1991–1995*, United Nations Blue Book Series, vol. 2 (New York: Department of Public Information, 1995), pp. 132–48.

Chapter 2

1. Frederick Z. Brown, ed., "Introduction," *Rebuilding Cambodia: Human Resources, Human Rights, and Law* (Johns Hopkins University, Paul H. Nitze School of Advanced International Studies, 1993), p. 4.

2. The International Conference on Cambodia was convened jointly by France and Indonesia following several years of diplomatic efforts loosely coordinated by Rafeeudhin Ahmed, the UN undersecretary general for humanitarian affairs. Besides the four Cambodian factions, the conference was attended by the five permanent members of the UN Security Council (China, France, the Soviet Union, the United Kingdom, and the United States), the six members of ASEAN (Brunei Darussalam, Indonesia, Malaysia, Philippines, Singapore, Thailand), Cambodia's other neighbors (the Lao People's Democratic Republic and Viet Nam), Australia, Canada, India, Japan, and Zimbabwe (in its capacity as chairman of the Non-Aligned Movement). When the International Conference on Cambodia reconvened in 1991, the Socialist Federal Republic of Yugoslavia replaced Zimbabwe as the representative of the nonaligned movement.

3. United Nations document A/45/472-S/21689, August 31, 1990, in *The United Nations and Cambodia 1991–1995*, United Nations Blue Book Series, vol. 2 (New York: Department of Public Information, 1995), pp. 89–92.

4. William Shawcross, *Cambodia's New Deal*, Contemporary Issues Paper 1 (Washington: Carnegie Endowment for International Peace, 1994), p. 11.

5. United Nations document A/46/608-S/23177, October 30, 1991, in *The United Nations and Cambodia 1991–1995*, section III, article 3.

6. Some of the social and economic effects of the UNTAC operation were discussed in articles contained in Peter Utting, ed., *Between Hope and Insecurity: The Social Consequences of the Cambodian Peace Process* (Geneva: United Nations Research Institute for Social Development, 1994).

7. Shawcross, *Cambodia's New Deal*, p. 23.

8. Ibid., p. 25.

9. Ibid., p. 29.

10. United Nations document A/46/608-S/23177, annex 3, par. 1.

11. UNICEF, rather than UNTAC, provided pens, paper, and other supplies for the opening session of the Constituent Assembly.

12. Shawcross, *Cambodia's New Deal*, p. 31.

Chapter 3

1. A May 1995 article notes the "ahistorical and naive paradigm" that the U.S. foreign policy community insists on applying to internal ethnic, na-

tionalist, or separatist conflicts: "Guided by faith in the nostrums of the liberal tradition and by the mechanistic notion, learned in civics class, that a community is built by balancing competing interests, American foreign-policy experts urge societies riven by conflict to avoid 'winner takes all' politics and to guarantee that regardless of election results, the weaker groups, too, will have a voice in national political and cultural affairs. To accomplish this, coalition governments, the guaranteed division of key offices, and a system of reciprocal vetoes are recommended. . . . All these measures may seem reasonable enough. But they depend upon a host of faulty assumptions, perhaps the most important being that the strongest group in a divided society will be willing to make major concessions—concessions that in fact jeopardize its preponderant position. The 'solutions' then presuppose agreement and stability as much as they secure them for they can be implemented only when there is already a strong desire for compromise." Benjamin Schwarz, "The Diversity Myth: America's Leading Export," *Atlantic Monthly*, May 1995, pp. 57–67, quotation on p. 60.

2. United Nations document A/45/472-S/21689, August 31, 1990, in *The United Nations and Cambodia 1991–1995*, United Nations Blue Book Series, vol. 2 (New York: Department of Public Information, 1995), p. 89.

3. Raoul Jennar, "Cambodia after the UNTAC Mission," in Mathews George Chunakara, ed., *Indochina Today: A Consultation on Emerging Trends* (Hong Kong: Christian Conference of Asia, 1994), pp. 41–52, p. 44.

4. In discussing the difficulties of the country's coalition government, a Cambodian colleague sadly if ironically recounted the following parable: A scorpion was owed a favor by a crocodile. The crocodile reluctantly agreed to ferry the scorpion across the Mekong River on his back, but only after the scorpion convinced the crocodile that the use of his poisonous sting would result in the death of both. Upon reaching the far bank, however, the scorpion does, indeed, sting the crocodile. As the crocodile dies, he asks the scorpion "Why?" to which the scorpion replies "Because of Cambodia."

5. *Concise Oxford Dictionary*, new ed. (Oxford: Oxford University Press, 1976).

6. Nate Thayer, "New Government: Who's Really in Control," *Phnom Penh Post*, November 19–December 2, 1993, p. 1.

7. Thayer, "New Government," p. 2.

8. Ibid.

9. A March 1995 *Phnom Penh Post* article documented the number of senior Cambodian officials who were citizens of foreign countries, including "the Queen, the First Prime Minister, the Ministers of Foreign Affairs, Interior, Education, Agriculture, Rural Development, Women's Affairs, Tourism, Information, and even Culture. As well, the head of the powerful Cambodian Development Council, at least 30 members of Parliament, numerous provincial

governors, secretaries and under secretaries of state, civil servants, ambassadors, and military generals hold foreign citizenships." Nate Thayer, "Expat Returnees Pose Legal Questions for West," *Phnom Penh Post*, March 10–23, 1995, p. 16.

10. Matthew Grainger and Moeun Chhean Nariddh, "Governor Hits Out against CPP Control," *Phnom Penh Post*, February 24–March 9, 1995, p. 1.

11. Ibid., pp. 1, 3.

12. Shawcross, *Cambodia's New Deal*, p. 45.

13. The failure to establish unified command of the country's military and police structures contributed to the events of July 1997.

14. Interestingly, over time both Chea Sim and Sar Kheng came to be seen as "moderate" counterbalances to Hun Sen's "strong man" tendencies. Sar Kheng, as cominister of interior, was mooted—mostly by non-Cambodian sources—to be Hun Sen's chief CPP rival and logical successor.

15. In March 1997 Prince Sirivudh did indeed attempt to return to Phnom Penh but was prevented from boarding a Cambodia-bound plane because of Hun Sen's assertion that the prince, a convicted criminal, would be arrested upon arrival. The July 1997 ouster and self-imposed exile of Prince Ranariddh further complicated the matter of succession following King Sihanouk's demise—or oft-threatened abdication, given that Prince Ranariddh (Sihanouk's son) and Prince Sirivudh (Sihanouk's half-brother) appeared to be the leading contenders to succeed King Sihanouk as Cambodia's constitutional monarch.

16. Interestingly, elements of all four conditions contributed to the events of July 1997.

17. *Le Mekong* (translation from French), no. 26, June 1995, p. 5.

18. Ibid.

19. Shawcross, *Cambodia's New Deal*, p. 56.

20. John C. Brown, "Khmer Democracy: Where's the Participation," *Phnom Penh Post*, August 27–September 9, 1993, p. 7.

21. Brown, "Democracy Must Be Participatory," *Phnom Penh Post*, August 27–September 9, p. 8.

22. Shawcross, *Cambodia's New Deal*, p. 57.

23. In September 1997 the National Assembly refused to endorse new ministerial appointments to replace members of the Council of Ministers who did not return to Cambodia following the July "coup." The refusal, by secret ballot, was presented by Second Prime Minister Hun Sen as evidence of continued democratic practice in Cambodia. While not, arguably, without some degree of truth, the National Assembly's refusal more likely was based on the fact that the assembly had been presented with a complete slate of candidates, rather than presented with individuals on a case-by-case basis.

24. The "protected" cable was first published on October 5, 1994, in the *Sydney Morning Herald*. An edited text subsequently was published in the

Phnom Penh Post. "Australian Diplomat's Cambodia Analysis," *Phnom Penh Post,* November 4–17, 1994, pp. 12–13.

25. *Globe and Mail* (Toronto), April 18, 1995, p.1.

26. Robert J. Muscat, "Rebuilding Cambodia: Problems of Governance and Human Resources," in Frederick Z. Brown, ed., *Rebuilding Cambodia: Human Resources, Human Rights, and Law,* (Washington: Johns Hopkins Foreign Policy Institute, Paul H. Nitze School of Advanced International Studies, 1993), p.18.

27. Steven Heder, "Shawcross Book Highlights post-UNTAC Blues," *Phnom Penh Post,* February 24–March 9, 1995, p. 19.

28. Ibid.

29. See, for example, "The Debate to Etch History in Stone," *Phnom Penh Post,* June 16–29, 1995, pp. 18–19, in which Steven Heder, professor, School of Oriental and African Studies (and former director of UNTAC's Information and Education component) rejects the arguments of fellow academic Ben Kiernan (serving as the director of the U.S. government-funded Cambodian Genocide Program).

30. Nate Thayer, "Faded Red: The Death Throes of the KR," *Phnom Penh Post,* April 21–May 4, 1995, p. 7.

31. Ibid.

32. By late 1996 King Sihanouk voiced a new wariness of the Khmer Rouge, warning that short-term political concessions might help to keep the movement alive. Such warnings did not deter the CPP or FUNCINPEC from separately trying to encourage further defection of Khmer Rouge elements. The conclusion on July 3, 1997, of a secret agreement by which the Khmer Rouge's Anlong Veng faction would join the FUNCINPEC-led National Unity Party (NUP) sparked the coup that ousted Prince Ranariddh.

33. Nate Thayer, "New Government: Who's Really in Control," *Phnom Penh Post,* November 19–December 2, 1993, p. 2.

34. Thayer, "Faded Red," p. 7.

35. Ibid.

36. "Cambodia's Wood-Fired War," *Economist,* June 17, 1995, pp. 27–28, p. 27.

37. Ibid., p. 27.

38. Craig Etcheson, "Pol Pot and the Art of War," *Phnom Penh Post,* August 13–26, 1993, p. 3.

39. Ieng Sary and Saloth Sar—later known as Pol Pot—were fellow students and friends in France (and ultimately became brothers-in-law by marrying two sisters). When Pol Pot returned to Cambodia to wage guerrilla war, Ieng Sary spent years in Beijing and Hanoi as head of the resistance movement's external relations. During the 1975–78 Democratic Kampuchea regime, Ieng Sary served as deputy premier and foreign minister. In 1979 the "Pol Pot/Ieng Sary clique" was tried in absentia for genocide by the Vietnamese-installed government in Phnom Penh. Ieng Sary and other members of the Khmer Rouge leadership

were found guilty and sentenced to death. Ieng Sary continued to serve as the Khmer Rouge's liaison with Beijing, although his influence in the movement was reported to have waned following the Paris Agreements and the cessation of Chinese military support." Nayan Chanda, "Fall of the High Flyer," *Far Eastern Economic Review*, August 22, 1996, p. 16.

40. "Making Peace with Cambodia's Devils," *Economist*, August 17, 1996, p. 21.

41. "Cambodia Makes a Hard Decision," *Bangkok Post*, September 12, 1996, p. 12.

42. Nayan Chanda, "The Enemy Within," *Far Eastern Economic Review*, August 22, 1996, pp. 14–16, p. 16.

43. "King Warns of 'Explosive' Situation as Tension Rises," *Bangkok Post*, December 2, 1996, p. 5.

44. "Peace Poker," *Economist*, August 31, 1996, p. 23.

45. Nate Thayer, "Brother Number Zero," *Far Eastern Economic Review*, August 7, 1997, pp. 14–24.

46. Nate Thayer, "Day of Reckoning," *Far Eastern Economic Review*, October 30, 1997, pp. 14–20.

47. John McAuliff, "Welcome to Cambodia—Where Nothing Is Ever as It Seems" (New York: U.S.-Indochina Reconciliation Project, July 1997), p. 3.

48. According to the Royal Government's July 1997 *White Paper*, FUNCINPEC's leadership was aggrieved that the party had been unable to award patronage positions to lower levels of bureaucracy. The *White Paper* noted, however, that "in the spirit of reconciliation, the CPP had already agreed to integrate more than 11,000 persons from FUNCINPEC and more than 7,000 from the BLDP into the government ranks. Furthermore, among the police cadre, more than 15,000 FUNCINPEC and more than 4,000 BLDP personnel were taken in. In the framework at that time, the CPP, as a coalition partner, was prepared to accept FUNCINPEC personnel at the district level. However, Prince Ranariddh was never able to provide a list of people who were to assume positions at the local level." Kingdom of Cambodia, *White Paper Background to the July 1997 Crisis: Prince Ranariddh's Strategy of Provocation* (Phnom Penh, Ministry of Foreign Affairs and International Cooperation, July 1997), p. 6.

49. As noted by McAuliff, "FUNCINPEC's underlying weakness was suggested by the fact that of the 1,100 members of its National Council, 75 percent came from the refugee camps on the border, 5 percent were returnees from overseas, and only 20 percent had been resident inside the country, principally in Phnom Penh." McAuliff, "Welcome to Cambodia," p. 3.

50. For reasons that remain unclear, Pen Sovan was replaced as prime minister in 1985 by Hun Sen, who retained the key portfolio of minister of foreign affairs. Pen Sovan was subject to years of virtual house arrest in Takeo province before he reemerged as a political figure.

51. Marisa Chimprabha, "Cambodia's Ung Huot Works to Assuage Fears," *Nation* (Bangkok), September 14, 1997, p. A7.

52. In March 1955, King Norodom Sihanouk abdicated the throne in favor of his father in order to take command of Cambodian politics. He subsequently announced the foundation of a national political movement, the *Sangkum Reastr Niyum*. The *Sangkum* won an overwhelming victory in an election later that year, allowing Sihanouk to consolidate his power and influence, as well as to introduce constitutional reforms. Despite often violent suppression of any opposition, under Sihanouk's leadership, the country enjoyed some measure of stability. When compared with what followed, the *Sangkum Reastr Niyum* era is remembered by many Cambodians as Cambodia's Golden Age. See David Chandler, *The Tragedy of Cambodian History: Politics, War, and Revolution* (Yale University Press, 1991), pp. 77–84.

53. In an echo of Hun Sen's 1985 selection as prime minister of the People's Republic of Kampuchea (PRK), Ung Huot retained his responsibilities as minister of foreign affairs.

54. "The Coup in Cambodia," *International Herald Tribune*, July 10, 1997, p. 8 (reprinted from the *Washington Post*).

55. Kingdom of Cambodia, *White Paper*. This official government document was written or at least edited by a foreign adviser to the Ministry of Foreign Affairs. The concluding paragraphs of the *White Paper*, however, suggested that Hun Sen may also have been involved directly in the preparation of the document, which by carefully outlining Prince Ranariddh's "strategy of provocation" provides a justification for the CPP's use of military force: "Now, over five years later [after the Paris Agreements], one faction in the government wants to make a deal with the Khmer Rouge outlaws. Prince Ranariddh wants to ally itself [*sic*] with the Pol Potists. It could not be for the sake of national reconciliation because the hard-liners at Anlong Veng have never accepted the principle of national reconciliation. The military or political arrival of the Khmer Rouge in Phnom Penh would not enhance the stability of the government: the daily calls for violence against the CPP and *me* on DK radio means that the Khmer Rouge is not interested in strengthening the government but further dividing it and the nation." *White Paper*, p. 12. Emphasis added.

Although the *White Paper* presented a convincing, if somewhat convenient justification for CPP military action, it is to be noted that neither Prince Ranariddh nor FUNCINPEC refuted either the succession of events outlined in the *White Paper* or the specific charges relating to the importation of weapons, the nonauthorized redeployment of troops, or secret negotiations with the Anlong Veng-based Khmer Rouge. Ranariddh's subsequent refusal to return to Phnom Penh to face court proceedings also lent some credibility to the *White Paper's* rationale for the CPP's resort to military force. Not surprisingly, the somewhat biased Western media rarely noted the various charges against

Prince Ranariddh, focusing instead on the bloody coup d'etat which deposed him.

56. *White Paper*, p. 9. Although the introduction of Khmer Rouge troops probably did not pose a real threat to the Royal Cambodian Armed Forces, from a CPP perspective it certainly signaled an end to the power-sharing arrangement with Ranariddh's FUNCINPEC. Highlighting the specter of Khmer Rouge infiltration of Phnom Penh also was consistent with the CPP's skillful use of the Khmer Rouge/Pol Pot "bogey-man" as a key element of its electoral strategy.

57. *White Paper*, p. 3. Although in the post-UNTAC period both FUNCINPEC and the CPP actively courted Khmer Rouge defectors, including elements loyal to Ieng Sary, such negotiations had included both coalition partners, even if most Khmer Rouge defectors in the end were absorbed into the CPP-dominated Royal Cambodian Armed Forces. The *White Paper* noted that in the case of Royal Government negotiations with Ieng Sary, "There was a unified government policy at the time to encourage those defections in the northwest." The *White Paper* also emphasized that "the Khmer Rouge elements at Pailin, Samlot, and elsewhere unconditionally left the hard-liners, pledged their allegiance to the central government, and actually engaged in armed clashes with their former colleagues" and stressed "This is no mere side issue. The secret negotiations between the Khmer Rouge and elements of FUNCINPEC struck at the heart of the coalition government." *White Paper*, p. 12.

FUNCINPEC's negotiations with the hard-line Khmer Rouge provoked little reaction from the international community, including little comment on the apparent resurrection of a CGDK-type coalition and the prospect of renewed civil war. Had Hun Sen and the CPP attempted such "secret" negotiations, it is certain that the international press would have seized on such dealings as proof of the Khmer Rouge origins of Hun Sen and other senior CPP officials.

58. Indeed, the fact that Hun Sen was taking a well-publicized family holiday in Viet Nam at the outbreak of fighting gave some evidence that the use of military force against FUNCINPEC was unplanned. Alternatively, conspiracy theorists would point to the fact that the holiday gave Hun Sen a perfect alibi—although popular anti-Vietnamese sentiment and questions about Hun Sen's connections with Hanoi made a Vietnamese beach resort a somewhat dubious choice as his holiday destination.

The fact that Cambodia was poised to become a full member of the Association of South-East Asian Nations (ASEAN) later in July, as well as the CPP's clear political and military superiority, also pointed to the strong likelihood that the July "coup" was less a planned attack by the CPP against FUNCINPEC than an escalating series of events precipitated by FUNCINPEC which then spun out of control.

59. Since 1975 Phnom Penh had experienced only very limited military action and no heavy artillery. The July 1997 weekend of gunfire, shelling, and looting

thus frightened most Phnom Penh residents. The subsequent evacuation of some foreign nationals also alarmed many Cambodians, who feared that the withdrawal of foreigners signaled a return to all-out civil war. Surprisingly, telephone and electricity service remained mostly intact throughout the weekend of fighting, allowing many residents to follow local and international television coverage of the coup, including on CNN. One foreign technical assistance adviser somewhat ironically quipped, "Yes, we had to take cover under our dining room table, but the greatest hardship was running out of gin!" (Personal communication).

60. In a well-publicized report on human rights abuses in the wake of the July fighting, the United Nations Center for Human Rights (UNCHR) detailed forty-one cases of extrajudicial killings of senior FUNCINPEC military leaders and soldiers loyal to them and more than fifty instances of "cremations of individuals in suspicious circumstances." Nick Lenaghan, "Report to Gov't as PM Rounds on Rights Staff," *Phnom Penh Post*, August 29–September 11, 1997, p. 3. The UNCHR report noted, "It is difficult to know in each case whether these killings resulted from orders or were committed by local officials who took the opportunity to settle old disputes. It is, however, significant that no one has been arrested or prosecuted for any of the killings described in this report." Although far from exonerating the CPP's leadership, the report noted that "the number of executions has significantly decreased since the end of July" and also conceded, "There is so far no evidence of an organized nationwide campaign to arrest political party officials and members."

61. Ambassador Tony Kevin interviewed by Huw Watkin, "Tony Kevin: Captives, Cables and Non-Coups," *Phnom Penh Post*, September 26–October 9, 1997, p. 8.

62. Ibid. Political analyst Raoul Marc Jennar, meanwhile, stated that the July events represented nothing less than a coup d'etat given that the CPP, by use of force, imposed a radical change on the international agreements that led to the establishment of the post-UNTAC coalition government. Jennar also maintained that the destruction of FUNCINPEC and Khmer Nation Party offices, intimidation of FUNCINPEC and BLDP officials and their families, and the detention of FUNCINPEC party officials, as well as a number of extrajudicial killings all violated the Cambodian Constitution, thus qualifying the July events as a coup d'etat. Raoul Marc Jennar, "La situation politique au Cambodge, au 9 juillet 1997," p. 3.

63. Chea Sim in a statement "translated from Khmer by the Cabinet of the Acting Head of State."

64. Ibid.

65. Kyra Dupont and Eric Pape, "King Withdraws, Mourning a 'Broken' Nation," *Phnom Penh Post*, October 24–November 6, 1997, p. 3.

66. Message from His Majesty King Norodom Sihanouk, King of Cambodia,

to the *Phnom Penh Post*, October 1997. Commemorative Supplement to the *Phnom Penh Post* on the Auspicious Occasion of the 75th Birthday Anniversary of His Majesty Preah Bat Samdech Preah Norodom Sihanouk, King of Cambodia, *Phnom Penh Post*, October 24–November 6, 1997.

67. In his exit interview, the outgoing Australian ambassador noted that many of the postcoup improvements "could not have been achieved under the former coalition government. . . . Development projects [were] stalled because of disagreement between the parties, government departments were greatly handicapped by the constant jockeying for position between the two sides. There's a lot more being done [now] in terms of internal government. The paradox is that externally [as] things are getting worse and worse, Cambodia seems to be moving towards the status of a pariah state." "Tony Kevin: Captives, Cables, and Non-Coups," p. 9.

68. Events elsewhere in the world in September and October 1997 brought Cambodia's significant progress toward democracy into sharp relief. Laurent Kabila's military take-over in Zaire (renamed the *Democratic* Republic of Congo) was followed by a coup d'etat in Congo Brazzaville. In the case of the latter, the democratically elected president, Pascal Lissouba, was overthrown by Denis Sassou-Nguesso—the country's former ruler who lost power in a 1992 election—who proclaimed himself president and promised to restore the country to democratic rule. Four months of fighting left as many as 10,000 dead, with the capital, Brazzaville, all but destroyed by fighting and looting. In the case of the Congo, there was no international demand for the return of the ousted president. No other country was deprived of its seat in the UN General Assembly. Donor assistance, including humanitarian aid, was not suspended.

In Colombia, local elections saw the murder of thirty candidates and the kidnapping of hundreds of others, including two international election monitors. In Algeria, the lead-up to local elections saw massacres of entire villages; over a three-month period more than 1,500 civilians were massacred. Yet when UN Secretary General Kofi Annan said, "The killing has gone on far too long," he was "roundly told off by the Algerian government for interfering in its domestic affairs" (*Economist*, September 6, 1997, p. 15). The *Economist* also reported, "Algeria's press is weakened by fear as well as censorship. More than 50 journalists have been killed in the six years of violence. . . . There have been no independent investigations of the massacres." More tellingly, particularly in contrast to international condemnation of the July 1997 coup de force in Cambodia, the *Economist* noted that in Algeria "Led by France, but not seriously contested by anybody else, the West has cast a tolerant eye on the Algerian regime since Liamine Zeroual legitimized his presidency with a convincing election in November 1995. The general election last June was plainly rigged to favour the president's party, but the world chose to give it the benefit of multi-party doubt."

69. As noted by Tony Kevin, the outgoing Australian ambassador, "Part of the problem with this continuing activity by FUNCINPEC outside the country is that it tends to de-legitimize the work of FUNCINPEC politicians inside Cambodia. It's paradoxical, because if we want multi-party democracy developed in Cambodia, surely it's in our interest to encourage the FUNCINPEC people working here." "Tony Kevin: Captives, Cables and Non-Coups," *Phnom Penh Post*, p. 8. Apart from allowing Ranariddh to lead FUNCINPEC in the next election, it was unclear what the United States or other countries opposing Hun Sen expected would be gained from Ranariddh's return to Phnom Penh and his restoration as first prime minister. At best, it would result in the kind of renewed coalition government already achieved with Ranariddh's replacement by Ung Huot. At worst, Ranariddh's return would renew the same kind of political animosity—as well as political, legislative, and administrative stalemate—that led to the July 1997 fighting in Phnom Penh and further armed resistance in border areas controlled by FUNCINPEC military forces and the remaining hard-line Khmer Rouge. Whatever Hun Sen's deficiencies, in the post-UNTAC period Prince Ranariddh proved himself a less than able politician as well as something less than a paragon of democratic virtue.

70. At the Consultative Group Meeting held in Paris only days before the July coup, donors made it clear that they were unhappy with the pace of reform in Cambodia. The International Monetary Fund, in particular, threatened to further suspend any financial assistance until the Royal Government improved its handling of national receipts, particularly revenue derived from the forestry sector.

It should be noted, however, that some of the lack of transparency criticized by the IMF and other donors was a direct consequence of post-UNTAC power sharing, including through bifurcated control of key economic ministries, party-based corruption, and lack of effective decisionmaking. As noted by an IMF official, "The Cambodian government has lost close to $U.S.100 million in the past year because of its inability to collect logging revenue and the *ad hoc* granting of tax breaks in return for kickbacks to politicians and political parties." Nick Lenaghan and Huw Watkin, "Little Light at End of Economic Tunnel," *Phnom Penh Post*, October 10–23, 1997, p. 8.

71. Nick Lenaghan and Huw Watkin, "Budget Blowout Looms," *Phnom Penh Post*, October 10–23 1997, p. 1.

72. Lenaghan and Watkin, "Little Light at End of Economic Tunnel," p. 8.

73. As noted by the Economist Intelligence Unit: "The loss of a large proportion of Cambodia's international aid would have a huge impact. Cambodia funds much of its budgetary capital expenditure through foreign assistance. The World Bank estimates that the current-account deficit has reached around 16 percent of GDP, without official transfers. In the worst case scenario, if the U.S.A. cuts nonhumanitarian assistance and uses its veto to block multilateral

lending to Cambodia, the Hun Sen government will be faced with a collapse of budget financing. This would be likely to result in monetization of the deficit, causing a surge in inflation. The loss of aid would also cause a sharp drop in Cambodia's external reserves, and heavy downward pressure on the riel." Economist Intelligence Unit, *Country Report Cambodia, Laos,* 3d Quarter, 1997, p. 9. Cambodia's postcoup economic difficulties were exacerbated by financial crises in other countries in the region, notably Indonesia, Malaysia, South Korea, and Thailand.

74. Lenaghan and Watkin, "Little Light at End of Economic Tunnel," p. 8.

75. Nick Lenaghan, "Projects Close Down as USAID Cuts Bite," *Phnom Penh Post,* November 7–20, 1997, p. 12.

76. Lenaghan, "Projects Close Down," p. 12.

77. NGO Forum on Cambodia, *NGO Forum Statement to the International Donor Community,* July 15, 1997. According to a covering letter to the statement, "The NGO Forum on Cambodia represents international and local non-government organizations committed to people-centred sustainable development for Cambodians. The Forum's mandate is to speak out on issues of concern to the people of Cambodia and to local and international NGOs working there."

Chapter 4

1. Kingdom of Cambodia, *National Programme to Rehabilitate and Develop Cambodia* (Phnom Penh: Kingdom of Cambodia, February 1994), p. 1.

2. Ibid. p. i.

3. Ibid., p. i.

4. Ibid., p. i.

5. Ibid., p. iii.

6. Cambodia Development Resource Institute, *From SAP to CAP: A Report Based on the Deliberations of the International Round Table on Structural Adjustment Programme in Cambodia, January 24–26, 1996,* CDRI Conference Report (Phnom Penh: Cambodia Development Resource Institute, 1996).

7. K. P. Kannan, *Economic Reform, Structural Adjustment and Development in Cambodia,* Working Paper 3 (Phnom Penh: Cambodia Development Resource Institute, 1997).

8. The *National Programme* listed seventeen priority areas seen as critical to rural development, including water supply, rural roads, primary health care, rural credit, training and capacity building, and so on. To address these "interconnected priorities" the *National Programme* indicated that the Royal Government would pursue two "parallel strategies": "First, it is seeking to improve the management of rural development programmes, primarily by supporting

greater consultation and better coordination among the development partners. The principal objective is to strengthen the planning and delivery capacities, and mechanisms of various agencies and organizations working in rural Cambodia, which should be made effective in the short term. Second, it is seeking to improve and to increase the linkages between the design and implementation of development programmes, mainly by promoting participatory methodologies and an integrated approach to rural development." *National Programme to Rehabilitate and Develop Cambodia*, p. 21. However sound the methodology, such "parallel strategies" promised little in effective rural development over the initial, foundation-laying rehabilitation period.

9. Ibid., p. 1.

10. Ibid., annex II, "Sectoral Programme Highlight."

11. The distinction between "pledges" versus "commitments" is fraught with uncertainty owing to differences in donors' budget years, the use of different categories of assistance, and a tendency for donors to carry pledges or unallocated commitments forward into different time periods. In the case of Cambodia, various donor meetings have resulted in the following pledges of financial support: $U.S.880 million at the Ministerial Conference on the Rehabilitation and Reconstruction of Cambodia (Tokyo, June 1992); a further $U.S.119 million for a total of $U.S.1 billion in rehabilitation assistance at the first meeting of the International Committee on the Reconstruction of Cambodia (ICORC-1) held in Paris in September 1993; $U.S.643 million for 1994–95 at ICORC-2 (Tokyo, March 1994) and an additional $U.S.15.8 million for demining activities; and $U.S.473 million at ICORC-3 (Paris, March 1995). At the July 1996 Consultative Group Meeting in Tokyo, the Royal Government requested $U.S.940 million in additional funding for the 1996–98 period to cover the capital investment, capital investment-related technical assistance, and free-standing technical assistance needs outlined in the country's first Public Investment Program (PIP). The Consultative Group Meeting resulted in a further $U.S.500 million in donor pledges to "consolidate Cambodia's reconstruction." When combined with earlier donor commitments, the July 1996 Tokyo pledges brought total external development assistance pledged to Cambodia since the October 1991 signing of the *Agreements on a Comprehensive Political Settlement of the Cambodia Conflict* to more than $U.S.2.5 billion—exclusive of the $U.S.2.2 billion cost of the UNTAC operation.

At the July 1–2, 1997, Consultative Group Meeting in Paris, donors pledged to provide a minimum of $U.S.450 million for 1997. In addition, NGOs pledged some $U.S.35–40 million of their core resources. The July 5–6 ouster of Prince Norodom Ranariddh and the subsequent suspension of some donor-funded programs—including IMF and World Bank financial support—resulted in a sharp decline in disbursements for donor-supported activities and cast serious doubt on continued high levels of donor support to Cambodia.

12. Kingdom of Cambodia, *Implementing the National Programme to Rehabilitate and Develop Cambodia* (Phnom Penh: Kingdom of Cambodia, February 1995).

13. Indeed, in his statement to the Third Meeting of the International Conference on the Reconstruction of Cambodia (ICORC-3), Keat Chhon referred to ICORC-1 as the "Renaissance Conference" which "saw Cambodia rise again." ICORC-2, according to the senior minister in charge of rehabilitation and development, was the "Recovery Conference" marked by the "setting up of essential institutions and, also, by the reforming of the financial and monetary situation of the country, aimed at favouring a balanced and sustainable development process." The minister deemed ICORC-3 to be the "Responsibility Conference," which reflected the necessity of the Royal Government to better fulfill its commitments to the Cambodian people and the international donor community. At the time, Keat Chhon optimistically suggested that the next international donor conference—the July 1996 Tokyo Consultative Group Meeting—might serve as the "Taking Off Conference," as Cambodia was launched further along on the path toward sustainable development.

14. *Implementing the National Programme to Rehabilitate and Develop Cambodia,* p. v. See the Appendix for an examination of three major donor-funded rural development efforts.

15. *Implementing the National Programme to Rehabilitate and Develop Cambodia,* p. 74.

16. Ibid.

17. Statement of Keat Chhon at the May 10, 1996, Consultation Meeting between the Royal Government and External Partners. The Socioeconomic Development Plan detailed the need for $U.S.2.2 billion in investment of all kinds, capital and technical assistance, in the public sector over the 1996–2000 period. The plan indicated that 65 percent of such investment would be of direct benefit to rural areas, although also noting that urban-based investment would provide indirect benefit to rural Cambodia. In his statement at the Donor Consultation Meeting Keat Chhon promised, "Good governance and enhanced capacity within government will be pursued. The government's role will be *pro-democracy, pro-growth, pro-private sector (including agriculture), pro-poor,* and *pro-environment.*" This "all things for all people" litany of good intentions led one foreign commentator to question the Royal Government's commitment to anything other than fine but empty words.

18. Statement of Chea Chanto, minister of planning, at the May 10, 1996, Consultation Meeting between the Royal Government and external partners.

19. Ibid.

20. Cambodia's progress toward reconstruction and development was further reviewed at the July 1997 Consultative Group Meeting in Paris. According to the meeting's proceedings, "Generally, donors were impressed with the achievements of the Royal Government in the last few years. As a whole, the Govern-

ment maintained macro-economic stability. The inflation rate was kept under a single digit level as a result of tight budgetary discipline. The Riel/U.S. Dollar exchange is in good condition and stable. Foreign exchange reserves were kept relatively high and the balance of payments deficit was financed through foreign direct investment and external assistance. In this favourable macro-economic environment, GDP grew by nearly 7 per cent per annum. Donors acknowledged that with all these achievements, Cambodia has fared better than other countries which have undergone similar civil wars, conflicts, and unrest." Kingdom of Cambodia, *Proceedings of the Consultative Group Meeting*, Paris, France, July 1–2, 1997 (Phnom Penh: Council for the Development of Cambodia, July 1997), p. i. Given heightened tension among the Royal Government's coalition partners, several donors noted that continued political instability could jeopardize the effective delivery of donor-funded aid programs. This warning turned out to be more than prescient, with several donors suspending or scaling down their aid programs in Cambodia in the wake of the July 1997 coup de force.

21. John P. McAndrew, *Aid Infusions, Aid Illusions: Bilateral and Multilateral Emergency and Development Assistance in Cambodia, 1992–95*, Working Paper 2 (Phnom Penh: Cambodia Development Resource Institute, January 1996), pp. xii–xiii.

22. A donor-driven approach to the provision of external assistance was not unique to Cambodia. The unusual degree of donor influence on the direction and pace of Cambodia's development path was to some extent a legacy of the UNTAC period. Although UNTAC's Rehabilitation and Economic Affairs Component attempted to coordinate or otherwise impose order on the rehabilitation process, it actually presided over a very laissez-faire approach to external assistance that continued into the post-UNTAC period.

23. *Aid Infusions, Aid Illusions*, p. xiii.

Chapter 5

1. A 1995 Swedish International Development Authority (SIDA) evaluation report, *Facing a Complex Emergency*, suggested that donor efforts to assist in the rebuilding of war-torn countries such as Cambodia has involved "an intricate mixture of a planned process with strong emphasis on aid coordination, macro-economic and sectorial analysis, planning for development—and what must be described as an 'aid market' with strong elements of competition, conflicting interests, and lack of coordination." Although noting donor as well as Royal Government efforts to coordinate, plan, and direct the reconstruction process, the SIDA report says that in the case of Cambodia, it is difficult to avoid the conclusion that the aid process in fact also is quite unplanned, uncoordinated

and more resembling a 'free and quite competitive market'." Bernt Bernander and others, *Facing a Complex Emergency: Evaluation of Swedish Support to Emergency Aid to Cambodia* (Stockholm: Swedish International Development Authority, 1995), p. 157.

2. United Nations Transitional Authority in Cambodia, *United Nations Secretary-General's Consolidated Appeal for Cambodia's Immediate Needs and National Rehabilitation*, Phnom Penh, April 1992.

3. Ibid., p. 70.

4. Ibid., p. 74.

5. An assessment of UNTAC's rehabilitation efforts is found in the author's "Transition to What? Cambodia, UNTAC, and the Peace Process," in Peter Utting, ed., *Between Hope and Insecurity: The Social Consequences of the Cambodian Peace Process* (Geneva: United Nations Research Institute for Social Development, 1994), pp. 41–69.

6. Bernander and others, *Facing a Complex Emergency*, p. 74.

7. Ibid., p. 75.

8. The Coordinating Committee (CoCom) of the Ministry of Health has, quite exceptionally, served as a highly effective coordinating body involving all parties supporting activities in the health sector. Nevertheless, such a mechanism has not necessarily resolved differences of opinion over the most appropriate rural health structure for the country or concern about the Asian Development Bank's plans to experiment with the contracting out of health services at the district level.

9. A notable exception was the International Monetary Fund's decision to withhold a second $U.S.20 million loan installment as a consequence of the Royal Government's failure to centralize through the Ministry of Finance all revenues accruing from the forestry and other sectors. Matthew Grainger, "IMF Freezes Funding," *Phnom Penh Post*, May 31–June 13, 1996, p. 1.

10. At the July 1997 Consultative Group Meeting in Paris, several donors emphasized the need for improved governance, including in the area of national revenue collection. Several donors also noted that continued political instability might jeopardize the implementation of donor-funded aid programs. The July 1997 coup de force provided a pretext for some donors to curtail or scale back their assistance to Cambodia. Although it is to be recognized that donors wanted to express their dissatisfaction with Cambodia's transition to effective multiparty democracy, the use of aid funding as a political tool inflicted most damage on the country's people. Notably, during much of the post-UNTAC period many of the matters of particular interest to the donor community—such as lack of transparency in revenue collection, increasing military expenditures, and legal and public administration reform—were hostage to ongoing tension among the Royal Government's coalition partners. In the months following Prince Ranariddh's ouster and his replacement as first

prime minister by Ung Huot, diplomatic and aid personnel reported that the
renewed coalition allowed progress in terms of both effective administration
and improved governance.

11. Kingdom of Cambodia, *Development Cooperation Report 1994–1995* (Phnom
Penh: Cambodian Rehabilitation and Development Board, Council for the Development of Cambodia, June 1995).

12. Kingdom of Cambodia, *Development Cooperation Report 1995/1996*, "Summary Tables" (Phnom Penh: Cambodian Rehabilitation and Development
Board, Council for the Development of Cambodia, May 1996). Arithmetic errors
contained in "Summary Tables" have been corrected.

13. Such pledges and disbursements were exclusive of the $U.S.2.2 billion
provided by the international community for the various aspects of the UNTAC
operation, including peacekeeping, repatriation, and resettlement of 370,000
"refugees," as well as organization of the May 1993 national election.

14. According to the "Summary Tables," 32.22 percent of total disbursements
were directed to Phnom Penh. The smaller percentage figure, however, does
not correspond to the total disbursement figure for the capital city given that
most donor agencies were based in Phnom Penh and thus spent a portion of
their assistance budgets in the capital, even if their actual project activities
might take place elsewhere.

15. As noted by the *Development Cooperation Report*, assistance provided by
nongovernmental organizations (NGOs) was not included in the breakdown of
disbursements by province. Although inclusion of the $U.S.18.7 million in NGO
assistance in 1994 and a projected $U.S.10.9 million for 1995 would slightly alter
the province-by-province allocation of assistance owing to the wide geographic
spread of NGO-supported activities, it would not significantly affect the overall
pattern of distribution of external assistance, particularly the overwhelming
concentration of assistance in the country's capital.

16. World Bank, *Cambodia Rehabilitation Program: Implementation and Outlook:
A World Bank Report for the 1995 ICORC Conference* (Washington: World Bank,
1995), p. 75.

17. Electricity projects in the capital under construction as of mid-1996 in-
cluded two 5-megawatt thermal plants funded by Japan; an 18.6-megawatt
Finnish-built plant funded by the Asian Development Bank; a 10-megawatt
plant funded by the World Bank; and seven 5-megawatt plants constructed by
Independent Power Producers, a private company. By the end of 1996 Phnom
Penh was expected to have up to 80 megawatts of installed capacity. Matthew
Grainger, "Neighbourly Power Deal Struck by PMs," *Phnom Penh Post*, March
22–April 4, 1996, p. 15.

18. Kingdom of Cambodia, *Report on the Socio-Economic Survey of Cambodia
1993/94* (Phnom Penh: National Institute of Statistics, Ministry of Planning,
September 1995).

19. Jan Ovesen, Ing-Britt Trankell, and Joakim Öjendal, *When Every Household Is an Island, Social Organization and Power Structures in Rural Cambodia, Assessment and Analysis of Present Knowledge Regarding Social Organization and Power Structures in Rural Cambodia*, Preliminary Draft Report (Stockholm: Swedish International Development Authority, November 1995), p. 24.

20. Bernander and others, *Facing a Complex Emergency*, p. 38.

21. Ibid.

22. *Development Cooperation Report 1994–1995*, p. 14.

23. McAndrew, *Aid Infusions, Aid Illusions*, p. xi.

24. Cambodia Development Resource Institute, *From SAP to CAP: A Report Based on the Deliberations of the International Round Table on the Structural Adjustment Programme in Cambodia, January 24–26, 1996* (Phnom Penh: Cambodia Development Resource Institute, 1996).

25. K. P. Kannan, *Economic Reforms, Structural Adjustment and Development in Cambodia* (Phnom Penh: Cambodia Development Resource Institute, 1997).

26. M. S. Shivakumar, *Development Aid through Technical Assistance: Some Lessons from the Cambodian Experience*, final draft paper for OECD 1996 annual general meeting of the Organization for Economic Cooperation and Development, p. 1.

27. World Bank, *Cambodia Rehabilitation Programme: Implementation and Outlook, A World Bank Report for the 1995 ICORC Conference* (Washington: World Bank, 1995), p. 51.

28. *Development Cooperation Report 1994–1995*, p. 17.

29. *Rehabilitation Program: Implementation and Outlook*, p. 50.

30. Ibid.

31. Ibid., p. 49.

32. Ibid., pp. 49–50.

33. As quoted by Shivakumar, *Development Aid through Technical Assistance*, p. 13.

34. McAndrew, *Aid Infusions, Aid Illusions*, p. 6.

35. *Development Aid through Technical Assistance*, p. 14. As an example, Shivakumar noted that the Royal Government would require at least $U.S.100 million in external assistance to provide technical support for the 1998 national election. UNTAC, of course, had no mandate to assist in the establishment of a permanent, indigenous electoral institution, even though the practice of regular elections is popularly equated with the kind of democratic process that UNTAC was expected to introduce to Cambodia.

36. *Development Cooperation Report 1994–1995*, p. 5. The Royal Government sought a total of some 4,500 working months of technical assistance over the 1994–95 period.

37. Ibid.

38. Ibid., p. 15.

39. Ibid., p. 24.

40. Ibid., p. 8.

41. The Asian Development Bank nevertheless committed itself to the provision—on a grant basis—of some $U.S.8.7 million in technical assistance for 1996. Shivakumar, *Development Aid through Technical Assistance,* p. 13.

42. "Opening Statement," International Committee on the Reconstruction of Cambodia (ICORC-2), Tokyo, March 1994.

43. Royal Government of Cambodia, "Issues in Implementing the National Programme to Rehabilitate and Develop Cambodia," position paper submitted to ICORC-3, Paris, March 14–15, 1995, p. 1.

44. "Issues in Implementing the NPRD," p. 2.

45. Robert J. Muscat, "Rebuilding Cambodia: Problems of Governance and Human Resources," pp. 13–42, in Frederick Z. Brown, ed., *Rebuilding Cambodia: Human Resources, Human Rights, and Law* (Johns Hopkins Foreign Policy Institute, Paul H. Nitze School of Advanced International Studies, 1993), p. 27.

46. Bernander and others, *Facing a Complex Emergency,* p. 75.

47. Ibid., p. 91.

48. Ibid.

49. Ibid., p. 77.

50. United Nations Research Institute for Social Development, "The Challenge of Rebuilding Wartorn Societies: Problems of International Assistance in Conflict and Post-Conflict Situations, A Project Proposal" (Geneva: UNRISD, October 1993), pp. 6–7.

51. Bernander and others, *Facing a Complex Emergency,* p. 76.

52. Personal communication (with a World Health Organization-recruited adviser).

53. Personal communication (with a UNICEF staff member).

54. Bernander and others, *Facing a Complex Emergency,* p. 75.

55. Kingdom of Cambodia, *National Programme to Rehabilitate and Develop Cambodia* (Phnom Penh: Kingdom of Cambodia, February 1994), p. 1.

56. Keat Chhon, "Statement on Socio-Economic Development Status, Programmes and Proposals," Consultation Meeting, May 10, 1996.

57. Kingdom of Cambodia, Cambodia Investment Board, "Private Investment Projects Approved by Sector to 31 December 1994." It is to be noted, however, that proposed investment in the tourism and services sector was dominated by the controversial $U.S.1.3 billion Naga Island Casino Resort project planned by the Malaysian company Ariston Sdn Bhd.

58. Michael Hayes, "The Malaysian Business Connection," *Phnom Penh Post,* January 27– February 9, 1995, p. 13.

59. *Phnom Penh Post,* June 14–27, 1996, including Ker Munthit and Matthew Grainger, "South Korea Joins the Mekong Goldrush," p. 1; Ker Munthit, "An

Expanding South Korean Presence," p. 4; Chris Fontaine and Imran Vittachi, "Bluechip Investors Mull over Cambodia," p. 12; and Chris Fontaine, "Caltex Heralded as 'Sign of Political Change'," p. 15. The same issue of the *Phnom Penh Post* carried articles on competition and corruption in the construction sector (Robert Lang, "Heavy Competition in the Building Game," p. 14) and labor abuses in the garment industry (Imran Vittachi, "Cambodian Dilemma: Labor Rights or Investors?" p. 15).

60. Ker Munthit, "An Expanding South Korean Presence," *Phnom Penh Post*, June 14–27, 1996, p. 4.

61. Kingdom of Cambodia, Ministry of Industry, Mines and Energy, "Policy Position Paper for Sectorial Investment in the Industrial, Energy, and Mineral Sectors," March 1996, p. 2.

Chapter 6

1. Royal Government of Cambodia, *Implementing the National Programme to Rehabilitate and Develop Cambodia* (Phnom Penh: Kingdom of Cambodia, February 1994), p. 5.

2. Michael Ward, "Constraints on Re-Building Cambodia's Economy," paper delivered to Conference on Cambodia's Economy, University of Washington, Seattle, November 3–5, 1994, p. 1.

3. Such studies include May Ebihara, Carol A. Mortland, and Judy Ledgerwood, *Cambodian Culture since 1975* (Cornell University Press, 1994); Meas Nee (with Joan Healy), *Towards Restoring Life: Cambodian Villages* (Phnom Penh: Jesuit Refugee Service, 1995); and Jan Ovesen, Ing-Britt Trankell, and Joakim Öjendal, *When Every Household Is an Island: Social Organization and Power Structures in Rural Cambodia*, preliminary draft report, "Assessment and Analysis of Present Knowledge Regarding Social Organization and Power Structures in Rural Cambodia" (Stockholm: Swedish International Development Authority, November 1995).

4. Serge Thion, "The Cambodian Idea of Revolution," pp. 11–33, in David Chandler and Ben Kiernan, *Revolution and Its Aftermath in Kampuchea: Eight Essays*, Asian Studies Monograph Series 25 (Yale University, 1983), p. 11.

5. Lindsay Cole French, "Enduring Holocaust, Surviving History: Displaced Cambodians on the Thai-Cambodian Border, 1989–1991," Ph.D. dissertation, Harvard University, August 1994, pp. 161–62.

6. James C. Scott and Benedict J. Kerkvliet, "How Traditional Patrons Lose Legitimacy: A Theory with Special Reference to Southeast Asia," in S. Schmidt, L. Guasti, and C. Lande, eds., *Friends, Followers and Factions* (University of California Press), p. 443, as cited by French, "Enduring Holocaust," p. 163.

7. Ovesen, Trankell, and Öjendal, *When Every Household Is an Island*, p. 54, note 37.

8. French, "Enduring Holocaust," p. 187.

9. Michael Ward has suggested that Cambodia's present administrative structure "is a legacy of a vast, thinly disguised and widely spread system of patronage," with public employment in the country's bloated administration continuing to be "the main means through which ordinary Cambodians tap into the state apparatus to guarantee a personal social security net." Michael Ward, "Constraints on Re-Building Cambodia's Economy," Conference on Cambodia's Economy, University of Washington, Seattle, 1994, p. 3.

The Cambodian People's Party skillfully used the patron-client system to gain the support and loyalty of underpaid civil servants. A former colleague of the author, working in a middle-level position in a ministry, was given a used but serviceable car, worth some $U.S.3,000, so that he "wouldn't have to drive to work in the rain." In accepting the car, however, he had to surrender his motorbike, which then presumably was passed on by the CPP to a lower-level worker/supporter.

10. Frederick Brown, ed., *Rebuilding Cambodia: Human Resources, Human Rights, and Law* (Johns Hopkins Foreign Policy Institute, Paul H. Nitze School of Advanced International Studies, 1993), p. 31.

11. Psychiatrists Mollica and Jalbert quoted by Eva Arnvig, "Women, Children and Returnees," in Peter Utting, ed., *Between Hope and Insecurity: The Social Consequences of the Cambodian Peace Process* (Geneva: United Nations Research Institute for Social Development, 1994), p. 154.

12. Psychiatrists Mollica and Jalbert quoted in Arnvig, "Women, Children, and Returnees," p. 154.

13. Paul Davenport, Sr. Joan Healy, and Kevin Malone, *Vulnerable in the Village: A Study of Returnees in Battambang Province, Cambodia, with a Focus on Strategies for the Landless* (Phnom Penh: Overseas Service Bureau/World Vision Australia, 1995).

14. A preliminary consideration of these issues is contained in Jo Boyden and Sara Gibbs, *Children of War: Responses to Psycho-Social Distress in Cambodia* (Geneva, UNRISD/INTRAC, 1997). Ongoing work on these issues is being carried out by UNICEF-Cambodia and the International Development Research Center (IDRC).

15. Writing of Khmer communities in the United States, Lindsay French similarly found "the events of 'Pol Pot time' had both exacerbated existing community divisions and devastated the most basic structures of sociability; that people were struggling not only with personal loss and pain but also with the decimation of those social structures and cultural institutions that had provided a framework for social interaction in the past, and some measure of cultural stability and continuity over time." "Enduring Holocaust," p. 32.

16. Bernt Bernander and others, *Facing a Complex Emergency: Evaluation of Swedish Support to Emergency Aid to Cambodia* (Stockholm: Swedish International Development Authority, 1995), p. 18.

17. The lack of a planning mentality is connected with a reluctance to make decisions. Both tendencies may be rooted in experience from the Khmer Rouge period, where "responsibility" too often meant "culpability"—and death. As a result, few Khmer are prepared to make decisions or take decisive action without explicit instruction or approval from higher authority. This tendency is manifested in many senior government officials devoting considerable time to what essentially are routine administrative matters (although a proclivity to "micro-management" also seems to be a Cambodian administrative trait).

18. Bernander and others, *Facing a Complex Emergency*, p. 73.

19. Robert Putnam, quoted by Nicholas Lemann, "Kicking in Groups," *Atlantic Monthly*, April 1996, pp. 22–26, quotation on p. 22.

20. Putnam as quoted in Lemann, "Kicking in Groups," p. 22.

21. Ibid.

22. Unrealistic time frames also were applied to Cambodia. William Shawcross, *Cambodia's New Deal*, Contemporary Issues Paper 1 (Washington: Carnegie Endowment for International Peace, 1994), was written one year after the May 1993 elections. It served as a report card on the country's progress toward democracy and development. Shawcross gave Cambodia a barely passing grade. An April 1996 report of the U.S. General Accounting Office (GAO) stated that the conditions of civil war and genocide that existed before 1991 were not the benchmarks by which the Royal Government should be judged: "We believe that the standards of behaviour set out in the Paris Peace Accords, the various international conventions that Cambodia has signed, and the Cambodian Constitution are appropriate standards against which to measure the current government's progress." The 1996 GAO report stood at variance to statements by the U.S. State Department, which gave qualified support to the Royal Government's achievements. See Matthew Grainger, "Democracy or Diplomacy? U.S. Departments Clash over Cambodia," *Phnom Penh Post*, April 19–May 2, 1996, p. 6.

23. Michael Vickery and Ramses Amer, *Democracy and Human Rights in Cambodia, Final Draft Report* (Stockholm: Swedish International Development Authority, 1996), p. 12.

24. Hun Sen, Cambodia's second prime minister, in April 1996, warned the public about the negative effects of such politicization: "Don't be cheated and hope that by joining a political party, you will get a government job." Jason Barber, "Rumors Cause PMs to Count Guns," *Phnom Penh Post*, May 19–June 2, 1996, p. 3. While criticizing FUNCINPEC's promises of government service, Hun Sen also was promoting the CPP's superior use of political patronage.

25. Interestingly, much of USAID's "democracy" funding (such as its support

to the Asia Foundation) was directed through nongovernmental channels. Although such support can be seen as supportive of the reemergence of "civil society" in Cambodia as one aspect of democracy, it also can be interpreted as having a decided antigovernment stance. That such a large percentage of U.S. aid funding to Cambodia was programmed outside of government structures stood in contrast to American statements in support of the Royal Government.

26. Aun Porn Moniroth, *Democracy in Cambodia: Theories and Realities* (Phnom Penh: Cambodian Institute for Cooperation and Peace, 1995), p. 48.

27. Moniroth, *Democracy in Cambodia*, p. 3.

28. Bernander and others, *Facing a Complex Emergency*, p. 18.

29. In 1996 the budget of the Royal Palace reportedly was greater than some ministries as the result of accelerated distribution of public welfare goods.

30. For example, in 1995 the Ministry of Education, Youth, and Sports was due a substantial sum of money as part of a World Bank loan. The funding, however, was diverted to the Ministry of Defense in support of the annual dry season offensive against the Khmer Rouge. Although the (FUNCINPEC) minister was opposed to the reallocation of World Bank funding, he could do nothing since the diversion of the loan funding had been approved by the first prime minister. The minister reportedly asked expatriate advisers assigned to the ministry why they "had let it happen." Personal communication.

31. The April 1996 international conference on corruption organized by the Center for Social Development and another NGO, the Parliamentary Organization for Social Development and Democracy, with funding provided by the Asia Foundation, was a notable exception to necessary caution on the part of nongovernmental organizations or other civil society groups.

32. UNRISD/PSIS, *Rebuilding War-Torn Societies: An Action-Research Project on Problems of International Assistance in Post-Conflict Situations* (Geneva: UNRISD, March 1995).

33. Putnam as quoted in Lemann, "Kicking in Groups," p. 25.

34. Ibid.

35. "Towards Restoring Life" is the title of a meditation on community development by Meas Nee of *Krom Akphiwat Phum* ("the group to develop the village"), a Battambang-based NGO. Meas Nee (with Joan Healy), *Towards Restoring Life: Cambodian Villages* (Phnom Penh: Jesuit Service Cambodia, 1995).

36. Nee, "Towards Restoring Life," p. 47.

37. Ibid., pp. 54–55.

38. Ovesen, Trankell, and Öjendal, *When Every Household Is an Island*, p. 53.

39. Following the ouster of the Khmer Rouge in 1979, the newly installed government of the People's Republic of Kampuchea attempted to increase food production through "Solidarity Groups" or *krom samaki*. Such groups consisted of ten to fifteen families working either their own or communally held land but pooling labor, farm tools, and draught animals and sharing the yield. Solidarity

Groups also were established in other productive sectors. The policy—conceived of necessity for reasons of food security and economic survival as much as a step toward socialism—gradually was abandoned.

40. Davenport and others, *Vulnerable in the Village*.

41. Robert J. Muscat, "Rebuilding Cambodia: Problems of Governance and Human Resources," in Frederick Z. Brown, ed., *Rebuilding Cambodia: Human Resources, Human Rights, and Law* (Johns Hopkins Foreign Policy Institute, Paul H. Nitze School of Advanced International Studies, 1993), p. 34.

42. Ovesen, Trankell, and Öjendal, *When Every Household Is an Island*, p. 48.

43. Ibid.

44. Ibid.

45. Ibid.

46. This view is refuted by a study, "Community Contribution to Education," which found that education enjoyed greater community support in Cambodia than in other countries in the region. And, indeed, an enormous amount of "public works" is undertaken at the village level in Cambodia, including support for village-level institutions and services as defined and determined by the local level. Mark Bray, "Counting the Full Cost: Parental and Community Financing of Education in East Asia," Directions in Development Series (Washington: World Bank, 1996).

47. Muscat, "Rebuilding Cambodia," p. 32.

48. Davenport and others, *Vulnerable in the Village*, p. 52.

49. Nee, *Towards Restoring Life*, p. 58.

50. Ibid., p. 79.

51. These same generational differences were apparent in attitudes toward both the monarchy and King Sihanouk, with older Cambodians having greater respect for the monarchy based on nostalgia for the Golden Age of Sihanouk's postindependence Cambodia.

52. It earlier was noted that no religious representative was included as part of the Supreme National Council. One can only speculate how differently the UNTAC-led peace process might have played out had the country's supreme patriarch or some other religious (or civil society) leader been designated as the neutral chairman of the Supreme National Council.

53. In a message on the occasion of his seventy-fifth birthday, the king said: "As Constitutional Monarch, I cannot enter the political arena to try to solve the very difficult problems dividing our Nation. But as Father of all Cambodians, I can suggest ideas and propose possible solutions to our problems. It is a matter of profound sadness to me that my recent proposals to put an end to the current military confrontation have been rejected by our leaders. My role as Father of the Cambodian Nation has thus been diminished and I can only observe with deep anguish and desperation the conflict engulfing our homeland and our international isolation." "Message from His Majesty King Norodom Sihanouk,

King of Cambodia to the *Phnom Penh Post*," commemorative supplement to the *Phnom Penh Post* on the seventy-fifth birthday of His Majesty King Norodom Sihanouk on October 31, 1997, *Phnom Penh Post*, October 24–November 6, 1997.

54. Ovesen, Trankell, and Öjendall, *When Every Household Is an Island*, p. 30.

55. Seanglim Bit, *The Warrior Heritage*, p. 68, as cited by Shari Prasso, "Violence, Ethnicity and Ethnic Cleansing: Cambodia and the Khmer Rouge," University of Cambridge, Department of Social Anthropology, May 1995, p. 25.

56. "A nation prey to drugs, guns, and violence, increasingly stratified by social class, torn by racial tension, and riven by insecurity, will be a weak player on the world stage. It may also be a threatened democracy." Ronald Steel, "The Domestic Core of Foreign Policy," *Atlantic Monthly*, June 1995, pp. 85–92, quotation on p. 86. Although describing contemporary American society, Steel's statement equally could have applied to post-UNTAC Cambodia.

57. Domestic violence is explored in Cathy Zimmerman, *Plates in a Basket Will Rattle: Domestic Violence in Cambodia* (Phnom Penh, December 1994).

58. The report of an October 1990 UNDP "fact-finding" mission examined the various roles played by NGOs in Cambodia over the course of the 1980s. United Nations Development Program, *NGO Assistance to Cambodia 1979–1990: Lessons for the United Nations Development System* (New York: UNDP, October 1990). A July 1992 report commissioned by the NGO community for presentation to the Ministerial Planning Conference on the Rehabilitation and Reconstruction of Cambodia similarly reviewed the NGO experience in Cambodia and the changes and challenges likely to face NGOs as a result of increased bilateral and multilateral assistance to Cambodia. Joel Charny, *NGOs and the Rehabilitation and Reconstruction of Cambodia* (Phnom Penh: Cooperation Committee for Cambodia, Advocacy Task Force of the NGO Development Workshop, NGO Forum on Cambodia, and Japanese NGO Committee on Cambodia, July 1992).

59. Eva Mysliwiec, *Punishing the Poor: The International Isolation of Kampuchea* (Oxford: Oxfam, 1988).

60. Interestingly, NGO-led advocacy efforts seemed to have no impact on the Royal Government's policies toward the Khmer Rouge. Indeed, by end-1996 both FUNCINPEC and the CPP were actively courting dissident elements of the Khmer Rouge to consolidate their own power bases. Although few external actors agreed with the government's approach to "national reconciliation," the principle of noninterference in Cambodian political affairs was (latterly) observed.

61. Charny, *NGOs and the Rehabilitation and Reconstruction of Cambodia*, p. i.

62. NGO statement to the Third Meeting of the International Committee on the Reconstruction of Cambodia (ICORC), Paris, March 14–15, 1995, pp. 4–5.

63. As noted by the Coordination Committee for Cambodia's 1995 *Annual Report*: "In the past three years the issue of partnership has also become more

critical. Large infusions of aid by bilateral and multilateral donors often seek immediate results at the expense of nurturing Cambodian participation. At times NGOs have unwittingly exacerbated this situation by providing services for bilateral and multilateral donors that bypass local institutions. More critically, NGO meetings are normally conducted in English, without Khmer translation, cultivating a dominance of Western voices and points of view. The task of strengthening civil society in Cambodia demands that local and foreign NGOs devote greater attention to the task of developing genuine partnerships and coordinated advocacy strategies." Cooperation Committee for Cambodia, *Annual Report 1995* (Phnom Penh: CCC, 1995), p. 3.

64. Royal Government of Cambodia, "Analysis of NGO Activity in Cambodia" (Phnom Penh: NGO Coordination Unit, Council for the Development of Cambodia, 1996), p. 4. According to the draft report, "These figures are estimates only as comprehensive and accurate data on the number of NGOs in Cambodia and the financial value of NGO assistance are not available, and such data that do exist are frequently understated due to incomplete or less-than-accurate reporting."

65. Thun Saray, "The Way Ahead to Civil Society," *Phnom Penh Post*, January 26–February 8, 1996, p. 7.

66. NGO statement to the Third Meeting of the International Committee on the Reconstruction of Cambodia (ICORC), p. 1. The financial contribution of NGOs to Cambodia's reconstruction and development was excluded from official disbursement figures in the Royal Government's *Development Cooperation Report 1994–1995* "due to incomplete data." The "Summary Tables" of the 1995–96 *Report* indicates $U.S.33.598 million in NGO disbursements over the 1992–95 period. The wide discrepancy in yearly disbursements ($U.S.1.068 million in 1992, $U.S.5.322 million in 1993, $U.S.17.949 million in 1994, but only $U.S.9.259 million in 1995) suggest continued difficulty in recording total NGO financial contributions to the country's reconstruction and development.

67. The CDC analysis, for example, claimed that "Human Rights NGOs play an important function in the development of a civil society in Cambodia by, for example, encouraging informed political discussion, providing information about the Constitution and the Law and supporting the judicial system. In addition, they frequently serve a quasi-political function. Plurality of opinion is to be encouraged and these fledgling NGOs need to be managed with care." At the same time, the analysis acknowledged that while (local) NGOs "are generally accepted for their non-political activities . . . there is tension when they voice criticisms in the political arena." "Analysis of NGO Activity in Cambodia," p. 14.

68. "Analysis of NGO Activity in Cambodia," p. 9.

69. *Five Year Socio-Economic Development Plan for Cambodia 1995–2000*, cited in "Analysis of NGO Activity in Cambodia," p. 18.

70. "Analysis of NGO Activity in Cambodia," p. 6.

71. Ibid., p. 8.

72. Ibid.

73. Thun Saray, "The Way Ahead to Civil Society," *Phnom Penh Post*, January 26–February 8, 1996, p. 7.

74. "Analysis of NGO Activity in Cambodia," p. 8.

75. Saray, "The Way Ahead to Civil Society," p. 7.

76. Jason Barber, "Courts Respond to Defenders," *Phnom Penh Post*, May 17–30, 1996, p. 4.

77. Holloway's "protected" cable, dated June 9, 1994, subsequently was leaked to the *Sydney Morning Herald* and published on October 5. An edited text of the diplomatic cable was later printed in the *Phnom Penh Post*. "Australian Diplomat's Cambodia Analysis," *Phnom Penh Post*, November 4–17, 1994, pp. 12–13. Written during his final days as ambassador to Cambodia, the cable, which among other things was critical of King Norodom Sihanouk, proved highly embarrassing to the government of Australia and to John Holloway, who was serving as an adviser to the Cambodian minister of foreign affairs at the time of the leak. The *Post* chose not to print Holloway's criticism of the king "out of a concern that officials in Phnom Penh might use the accusation of *lèse majesté* to close down the *Post*."

78. Economist Intelligence Unit, *Country Report Indochina: Vietnam, Laos, China*, 3rd Quarter 1994, p. 41.

79. The SIDA evaluation report defined "rent seeking" as "various official and unofficial forms of capturing benefits from external (and other) public sources for non-productive purposes." Bernander and others, *Facing a Complex Emergency*, p. 160. Another SIDA report, *Developing Rural Cambodia*, outlined some of the many types of corruption affecting post-UNTAC Cambodia: leakage of financial resources (for example, from timber resources), patronage (including political patronage and traditional patron-client relationships), bribery in connection with the provision of public services (for example, payments for licenses and permits, unofficial checkpoints), official neglect of financial control, and nonoptimal choice of projects and project sites. Swedish International Development Cooperation Agency, *Developing Rural Cambodia: A Background Study for Proposed Swedish Development Co-operation with Cambodia* (Stockholm: Department for Asia, Swedish International Development Cooperation Agency, 1995).

80. Keat Chhon as quoted by Nate Thayer, "Expat Returnees Pose Legal Questions for West," *Phnom Penh Post*, March 10–23, 1995, p. 16.

81. In the same article previously cited, *Phnom Penh Post* reporter Nate Thayer quoted two senior government officials as saying they had "proof" that another senior government official—holding an American passport—had received a $U.S.10 million kickback for awarding the Sihanoukville gambling concession to a Malaysian company and that the corrupt process had done "immeasurable

damage to [Cambodia's] reputation among investors." *Phnom Penh Post*, March 10–23, 1995, p. 16.

82. The *Phnom Penh Post* gave extensive coverage to the Royal Government's sale of logging concessions, despite an April 1995 logging ban. In December 1995 the environmental NGO Global Witness made public a Ministry of Agriculture list of thirty companies—eleven with approved concessions and nineteen awaiting government approval—whose combined concession area totaled some 6.5 million hectares, virtually all of the country's entire forest reserves. The *Post* report alleged widespread corruption, including payoffs to the Khmer Rouge, the Royal government, the country's two prime ministers, lower-level Cambodian military personnel, and the Thai ministers of Interior and Agriculture. Mang Channo, Michael Hayes, and Matthew Grainger, "Government Set for Massive Logging Re-Think," *Phnom Penh Post*, December 15–28, 1995, p. 1.

In April 1996 the *Post* ran a front page story indicating that the country's two prime ministers had personally signed over a million cubic meters of timber to seventeen Thai companies, in three separate deals marked "confidential." The report quoted a Global Witness spokesman as saying, "The question must be asked where all this money's going." Matthew Grainger, "PMs Sign 'Million Meter' Timber Deals with Thais," *Phnom Penh Post*, April 5–18, 1996, p. 1.

In a related story in the same issue, the *Post* cited a joint World Bank-UNDP-FAO report on the forestry sector that "takes a shot at foreign logging companies—though none are mentioned by name—as taking five times more timber than Cambodian forests can stand, and getting it at a fifth of world prices." Citing the World Bank-UNDP-FAO report, the *Post* article said that whereas Cambodia currently was getting about $U.S.20 million a year in forestry revenue, "By auctioning concession rights, pumping up royalties in line with world prices, and enforcing environmental rules, the Kingdom could earn $100 million a year—and the logging could be sustainable." Matthew Grainger, "Government Rapped over Logging Practices," *Phnom Penh Post*, April 5–18, 1996, p. 5.

83. Royal Government of Cambodia, "The Rule of Law," position paper presented to ICORC-3, Paris, March 14–15, 1995, p. 1.

84. Royal Government of Cambodia, "The Rule of Law," p. 1.

85. Bernander and others, *Facing a Complex Emergency*, p. 160.

86. Ibid., p. 93.

87. Bernander and others, *Facing a Complex Emergency*, p. 160. However, "rent seeking" was not limited to the Cambodian side alone. The overheated Cambodian "aid market" prompted practices and behaviors hardly to the credit of donors, businesses, technical assistance personnel, development consultants, and others.

88. In mid-1996, for example, a mid-level Council of Ministers official demanded payment to set up meetings for a bilateral donor mission (personal communication). Although hardly corrupt when compared with other reports

involving the payment of millions of dollars to senior government officials, the endemic use of influence for private gain—to the detriment of the country and its people—was a defining characteristic of post-UNTAC Cambodia.

89. At the July Consultative Group Meeting, donors were somewhat more outspoken on corruption, particularly about diversion of revenues from the national budget. The International Monetary Fund, for example, in its statement said: "As true friends of Cambodia, we should, however, insist that Cambodia's well known problems of governance not be allowed progressively to mount to an extent that seriously threatens the economic future of the country. This, unfortunately, is now a reality in Cambodia. The rapid depletion of the natural resource base and the massive diversion of revenues from the national budget are clear writings on the wall. Uncontrolled and illegal logging activities in recent years have resulted in rapid depletion of the country's valuable resources with little benefit to the government. While there are of course no precise data, our rough estimates suggest that losses to budget arising from illegal activities in forestry were well over $U.S.100 million in 1996, more than one-third of total budgetary revenue collected in that year. Forestry is not the only area of illegal activity. Corruption is spread over a wide area, which includes: (i) concessions, such as monopoly rights and land leases, given to foreign investors without payments to the budget; (ii) tax and tariff exemptions granted to domestic and foreign companies, including those that arise from improper exemptions granted under the overly generous Investment Law; (iii) noncollection of taxes by tax officials; and (iv) nonpayment of taxes on commercial activities by the military, including leases of government land. This list is, by no means, exhaustive. The amount of resources diverted from the budget by these activities could be even larger than the losses from activities in forestry. . . . Overall, the diversion of public resources has probably reached the same amount as actual budget revenue collection, or nearly 10 percent of GDP." Kingdom of Cambodia, Proceedings, Consultative Group Meeting, Paris, July 1–2, 1997, statement of the International Monetary Fund (Phnom Penh: Council for the Development of Cambodia, July 1997).

Chapter 7

1. William Shawcross, *Cambodia's New Deal*, Contemporary Issues Paper 1 (Washington: Carnegie Endowment for International Peace, 1994).

2. In the wake of the July 1997 coup de force and as the result of competing claims for legitimacy by Prince Ranariddh (the country's duly elected first prime minister) and the renewed Royal Government Coalition of Hun Sen and Ung Huot, the United Nations Credentials Committee in September 1997 de-

cided to leave vacant Cambodia's seat at the UN General Assembly. Thus the Phnom Penh government again found itself ostracized by the international community, and Cambodia—and the Cambodian people—again were denied representation by the very body that through the UNTAC operation had overseen the "comprehensive" political settlement of the Cambodian conflict.

3. Jonathan Moore, *The UN and Complex Emergencies: Rehabilitation in Third World Transitions* (Geneva: United Nations Research Institute for Social Development, 1996), p. 33.

4. Steven Heder, "Shawcross Book Highlights Post-UNTAC Blues," *Phnom Penh Post*, February 24–March 9, 1995, p. 19.

5. Keat Chhon, "A Brief Review of Our Socio-Economic Vision, Programs, and Achievements," Lecture Series Report 5 (Cambodian Institute for Cooperation and Peace (CIPC), February 1996). The CIPC, supported by the Friedrich Ebert Stiftung Foundation, was "established with a view to provide a neutral, non-governmental forum for discussion and dissemination of knowledge, ideas and views on various subjects relating to cooperation and peace." Besides his government responsibilities, Keat Chhon also served as the CIPC's co-vice chairman.

6. Ronald Bruce St. John, "The Political Economy of the Royal Government of Cambodia," *Contemporary Southeast Asia*, vol. 17 (December 1995), pp. 265–81, p. 274.

7. St. John, "The Political Economy of the Royal Government of Cambodia," p. 274.

8. In a February 1996 statement to the Cambodian Institute for Peace and Cooperation, Keat Chhon gave a paean to Cambodian democracy that stood in marked contrast to the country's post-UNTAC experience: "Pursuit of democracy is a cardinal principle in the Constitution of our Kingdom. The Royal Government and our leaders are fully committed to democratic norms and methods. We want to ensure that our people are able and empowered to exercise their choice of representatives at the national and local levels in periodic elections in a free manner and in a multi-party setup. That is crucial for peace, stability and sustainability of our efforts to re-build and ensure progress in Cambodia. We know we owe this legacy to our generations to come. We also know and believe that democracy is not something you merely put on paper and mention in speeches. It is indeed a matter of actual practice. It has to be nurtured and allowed to evolve stage by stage, get enriched and refined and progress through continuous and active practice and observance. It is the art of dialogue and persuasion as opposed to conflict and confrontation. In its practice, we have to listen to each other, understand each other, tolerate others' views and yield to the majority's wishes. For democracy to take root, develop and flourish, the essential elements are knowledge through dissemination, debate, analysis and discussion and open choice." Keat Chhon, "A Brief Review."

9. Heder, "Shawcross Book," p. 19.

10. St. John, "The Political Economy of the Royal Government of Cambodia," p. 274.

11. Heder, "Shawcross Book," p. 19.

12. Ibid.

13. See chapter 3, note 52.

14. Keat Chhon, "A Brief Review."

15. Michael Ward, "Constraints on Re-Building Cambodia's Economy," paper delivered to conference on Cambodia's economy, University of Washington, Seattle, 1994, p. 6.

16. Ibid., p. 9.

17. Nick Lenaghan and Huw Watkin, "Budget Blowout Looms," *Phnom Penh Post*, October 10–23, 1997, p. 1.

18. NGO statement to the International Committee for the Reconstruction of Cambodia, Paris, March 1995, p. 1.

19. As noted by William Shawcross, "In the world beyond Cambodia donor fatigue is a very real condition. Many of those most enthusiastic about helping Cambodia have finite resources—of both patience and money—and there are many other areas of the world that command greater attention, for obvious and often good reasons." Shawcross, *Cambodia's New Deal*, p. 102.

20. Frederick Z. Brown and Robert J. Muscat, "The Transition from War to Peace: The Case of Cambodia," unpublished manuscript, Washington, Overseas Development Council, 1995, p. 71.

21. Brown and Muscat, "The Transition from War to Peace," p. 71.

22. Bernt Bernander and others, *Facing a Complex Emergency: Evaluation of Swedish Support to Emergency Aid to Cambodia* (Stockholm: Swedish International Development Authority, 1995), p. 3.

23. NGO Forum, *Forum News*, February-March 1996, p. 1.

24. Margaret Slocombe, a long-time Cambodia resident, in a *Sunday Morning* radio interview, Canadian Broadcasting Corporation, March 1994.

Appendix

1. Royal Government of Cambodia, *Implementing the National Programme to Rehabilitate and Develop Cambodia* (Phnom Penh: February 1994), p. 26.

2. Kingdom of Cambodia, *Development Cooperation Report 1994–1995* (Phnom Penh, February 1994), p. 14.

3. Kingdom of Cambodia, Ministry of Rural Development, "Rural Development in Cambodia," Phnom Penh, May 1996.

4. Royal Government of Cambodia, United Nations Development Program,

United Nations Office for Project Services, *Putting the SEILA Programme in Place, 1996 Workplan of the Cambodia Area Rehabilitation and Regeneration (CARERE) Project* (Phnom Penh: Royal Government of Cambodia/UNDP/UNOPS, January 1996), p. 3.

5. Royal Government of Cambodia and United Nations Development Program, *Project Document of the Cambodia Area Rehabilitation and Regeneration Project*, CMB/95/011, Phnom Penh, January 1996, p. 1.

6. *CARERE2 Project Document*, CMB/95/011, p. 20.

7. Christophe Bouvier, Leonardo Romeo, and Nora Gibson, *Prospective Evaluation of the CARERE Project*, final draft report (Phnom Penh: UNDP/ UNOPS/UNCDF and the Netherlands Government, July 1995), p. 11.

8. *CARERE2 Project Document*, CMB/95/011, p. 33.

9. Ibid., p. 27.

10. At the same time, in its presentation to the May 1996 Donors Meeting, the Ministry of Rural Development indicated a target of 2,500 VDCs by March 1998 (or 20 percent of total villages) and 7,500 VDCs by 2000 (60 percent of total villages), up from only 500 village development committees established by the end of 1995. The presentation also forecast a PIP budget allocation of $U.S.161 million for rural development activities, representing some 14 percent of the country's total projected PIP requirements. The ministry intended to allocate more than half ($U.S.78 million) of such resources to the construction of provincial rural development offices. A further $U.S.9 million was targeted to health education and primary health care training, although the ministry was without any direct delivery capacity.

11. *CARERE2 Project Document*, CMB/95/011, p. 51.

12. Ibid.

13. Ibid.

14. The Kingdom of Cambodia and the European Commission, *Investing in the Future* (Bangkok: Delegation of the European Commission, January 1995), p. 9.

15. The European Commission, "European Rehabilitation Programme for Cambodia (PERC)," providing "general information on PERC" (Phnom Penh, 1994), p. 2.

16. Benjamin Quenelle, "Funding Giant Faces Its Critics," *Phnom Penh Post*, September 8–21, 1995, p. 8.

17. Quenelle, "Funding Giant," p. 8.

18. Ibid.

19. Chris Dammers and others, *Differing Approaches to Development Assistance in Cambodia: NGOs and the European Commission* (Phnom Penh: NGO Forum on Cambodia, August 1996), p. 1; also published by International NGO Training Center (INTRAC), Occasional Paper 13, Oxford, United Kingdom, 1996, p. 1.

20. Dammers and others, *Differing Approaches to Development Assistance in Cambodia*, p. 1.

21. Ibid., p. 3.

22. Ibid.

23. Social Fund of the Kingdom of Cambodia, "Sub-Projects Eligibility Criteria," Phnom Penh, Social Fund of the Kingdom of Cambodia, 1995, p. 2.

24. As of the end of May 1997, the Social Fund of the Kingdom of Cambodia had received more than 5,000 eligible applications valued at $U.S.52 million and had approved 1,216 subprojects valued at 13.6 million. Of the approved subprojects, 1,080 had been contracted ($U.S.12.2 million) and 364 handed over ($U.S.3.9 million). As of May 1997 the Social Fund had certified a total of $U.S.7.0 million of works as complete. The subprojects approved included 570 school rehabilitation projects benefiting 320,000 students; 549 water supply projects providing improved access to water for 350,000 people; 62 health projects providing improved health facilities for a population of 743,000; 18 rural road projects for a population of 205,000 people; 10 irrigation systems benefiting 25,855 farmers; and 6 vocational training centers benefiting 500 students. Kingdom of Cambodia, Proceedings of the Consultative Group Meeting, Paris (Phnom Penh: Council for the Development of Cambodia, July 1997). The Social Fund's report to the Consultative Group Meeting estimated that by the end of 1997, the Social Fund would receive eligible applications of $U.S.50 million in excess of the initial World Bank IDA credit (of $U.S.20 million). If nothing else, the volume of applications to the Social Fund provided convincing proof of widespread demand for community-based rehabilitation and development activities.

Index